Vector Models for
Data-Parallel Computing

Vector Models for Data-Parallel Computing

Guy E. Blelloch

The MIT Press
Cambridge, Massachusetts
London, England

This book was printed and bound in the United States of America.

Library of Congress Cataloging-in-Publication Data

Blelloch, Guy E.
    Vector models for data-parallel computing / Guy E. Blelloch.
      p. cm.—(Artificial intelligence)
    Includes bibliographical references and index.
    ISBN 0-262-02313-X
    1. Vector processing (Computer science) 2. Parallel processing (Electronic computers) I. Title. II. Series: Artificial intelligence (Cambridge, Mass.)
QA76.5.B5456   1990
004'.35—dc20   90-39401
                                                        CIP

Contents

Series Foreword

Artificial intelligence is the study of intelligence using the ideas and methods of computation. Unfortunately, a definition of intelligence seems impossible at the moment because intelligence appears to be an amalgam of so many information-processing and information-representation abilities.

Of course psychology, philosophy, linguistics, and related disciplines offer various perspectives and methodologies for studying intelligence. For the most part, however, the theories proposed in these fields are too incomplete and too vaguely stated to be realized in computational terms. Something more is needed, even though valuable ideas, relationships, and constraints can be gleaned from traditional studies of what are, after all, impressive existence proofs that intelligence is in fact possible.

Artificial intelligence offers a new perspective and a new methodology. Its central goal is to make computers intelligent, both to make them more useful and to understand the principles that make intelligence possible. That intelligent computers will be extremely useful is obvious. The more profound point is that artificial intelligence aims to understand intelligence using the ideas and methods of computation, thus offering a radically new and different basis for theory formation. Most of the people doing work in artificial intelligence believe that these theories will apply to any intelligent information processor, whether biological or solid state.

There are side effects that deserve attention, too. Any program that will successfully model even a small part of intelligence will be inherently massive and complex. Consequently, artificial intelligence continually confronts the limits of computer-science technology. The problems encountered have been hard enough and interesting enough to seduce artificial intelligence people into working on them with enthusiasm. It is natural, then, that there has been a steady flow of ideas from artificial intelligence to computer science, and the flow shows no sign of abating. The purpose of The MIT Press series

Artificial Intelligence is to provide people in many areas, both professionals and students, with timely, detailed information about what is happening on the frontiers in research centers all over the world.

J. Michael Brady
Daniel G. Bobrow
Randall Davis

Preface

This book is a revised version of my Doctoral Dissertation, which was completed at the Massachusetts Institute of Technology in November, 1988. The main purpose of the work was to explore the power of data-parallel programming; this exploration lead to the following conclusions:

1. The advantages gained in terms of simple and clean specifications of applications, algorithms, and languages makes a data-parallel programming model desirable for any kind of tightly coupled parallel or vector machine, including multiple-instruction multiple-data (MIMD) machines.

2. The range of applications and algorithms that can be described using data-parallel programming is extremely broad, much broader than is often expected. Furthermore, in most applications there is significantly more data-parallelism available than control parallelism.

3. The power of data-parallel programming models is only fully realized in models that permit nested parallelism: the ability to call a parallel routine multiple times in parallel—for example, calling a parallel matrix-inversion routine over many different matrices, each possibly of a different size, in parallel. Furthermore, to be useful, it must be possible to map this nested parallelism onto a flat parallel machine.

4. A set of scan primitives are extremely useful for describing data-parallel algorithms, and lead to efficient runtime code. The scan primitives can be found in every algorithm in this book with uses ranging from load-balancing to a line-of-sight algorithm.

The work does not claim that data-parallel programming models are applicable to all problems, but it demonstrates that for a very wide class of problems, data-parallel programming models are not only applicable, but preferable, for programming tightly coupled machines.

Outline

This book is organized into four parts, *models*, *algorithms*, *languages* and *architecture*, which are summarized as follows:

1. **Models:** formally defines a class of strictly data-parallel models, the *parallel vector models*. The definition is based on a machine that can store a vector in each memory location and whose instructions operate on these vectors as a whole—for example, elementwise adding two equal length vectors. In the model, each vector instruction requires one "program step". The model also supplies a complexity measure based on the lengths of the vectors.

2. **Algorithms:** shows how data structures including graphs, grids and trees can be represented with vectors so that many useful operations, such as summing neighbors in a graph, can be executed in a constant number of program steps. It then describes algorithms for a wide variety of problems, ranging from sorting to linear-programming, and from finding the minimum-spanning-tree of a graph to finding the closest-pair in a plane.

3. **Languages:** describes how a class of very-high-level languages, the *collection-oriented languages* can be mapped onto the parallel vector models. This class of languages includes SETL, PARALATION LISP, and APL. This part also describes a working compiler for PARALATION LISP. The compiler is the first compiler for a data-parallel programming language that compiles nested-parallel constructs into completely parallel code.

4. **Architectures:** describes the implementation of parallel vector models on the Connection Machine. The techniques used are applicable to most tightly coupled computers, both SIMD and MIMD. This part also shows how various scan instructions can be implemented efficiently in hardware.

The book tries as much as possible to be complete, in the sense that it tries to show all sides of the story. To show that a parallel quicksort can be written in three lines of impeccable code, but that it then runs twice as slow on 10 processors of an Encore Multimax than a C version of quicksort on a single processor, would be incomplete.

Acknowledgments

I would mostly like to thank Charles Leiserson, my advisor, for convincing me to take these ideas and turn them into a thesis. He helped me recognize what was important and made many contributions to this work. I would also like to thank the rest of my thesis committee, Tom Knight, Jim Little, and Guy Steele, for their invaluable help. Tom Knight introduced me to parallel computing and first got me interested in the Connection Machine. Jim Little helped flesh out many of my ideas and was a great person to talk to about anything. Guy Steele helped me understand the importance of clean and simple definitions.

I would like to thank Danny Hillis and David Waltz for their guidance. As with Charles, Danny helped convince me that the material in this book would make a good thesis. Dave gave me a lot of advice on general approaches to research. I spent many hours talking with Gary Sabot and Cliff Lasser about parallel languages. Without Gary's PARALATION LISP, I would have never implemented the compiler I discuss in Chapter 9. Without Cliff's work on *Lisp, Connection Machine programming would have been set back a year.

The work on grid operations and the algorithms based on them is joint work with Ajit Agrawal, Cynthia Phillips and Robert Krawitz. Some of the work on computational geometry algorithms is joint work with James Little. Some of the work on the PARALATION LISP compiler is joint work with Gary Sabot. Some of the work on graph algorithms is joint work with Andrew Goldberg and Charles Leiserson. Some of the work on tree manipulations is joint work with Charles Leiserson. The split-pack sort was thought up by John Rose, Abhiram Ranade and me. The radix-sort described in Section 4.5.4 was thought of independently by Craig Stanfill, Abhiram Ranade and me. The quicksort using segmented scans was thought of by Guy Steele and me. These sorting algorithms are simple enough that I am sure many people have thought of them before. Charles Leiserson suggested the proof that a floating-point `+-reduce` would never lose more than one bit.

In addition to my thesis committee, I would like to thank Paul Resnick and Gary Sabot for making detailed comments on a draft of the book. These comments greatly improved the presentation of the book.

I had many helpful conversations with, and suggestions from, Philip Agre, Alan Bawden, Todd Cass, Michael Drumheller, Carl Feynman, Donna Fritzsche, Lennart Johnsson, Brewster Kahle, John Mallery, Stephen Omohundro, Alan Ruttenberg, James Salem, Karl Sims, and Lewis Tucker. I am grateful to the people I met during my interviews for many useful comments. Especially to John Canny, Thomas Cheatham, Allan Fisher, Thomas Gross, John Hennesey, Paul Hudack, Richard Karp, H.T. Kung, Dragutin Petkovic, Jorge Sanz, Mark Snir, Jeff Vitter, and Daniel Weise.

I would like to thank Esther Peres for proofreading the book, Cheah Schlueter for helping me with the index, and Jerry Roylance and Chris Lindblad for implementing the tools used to automatically insert the figures into this thesis with absolutely no cutting or pasting. I would also like to thank the School of Computer Science at Carnegie Mellon University for giving me the time to convert my dissertation into this book.

This work was motivated and supported by the excellent environments at Thinking Machines and at the M.I.T. Artificial Intelligence Laboratory. If there were a handful of people I had to name whose ideas most affected this thesis, I would name Kenneth Batcher, W. Daniel Hillis, Kenneth Iverson, Charles Leiserson, Jacob Schwartz, Guy Steele and Uzi Vishkin.

Chapter 1

Introduction

In the past decade there has been a titanic quantity of research and development on parallel computing. This work has spanned the three core areas of computer science: *theory*, *languages* and *architecture*. Unfortunately, the work in these three areas has evolved almost independently: the most attractive algorithmic models and the most general languages have not been implemented on the most successful machines, and the algorithms have not been described using the languages.

This book defines a class of data-parallel machine models called *parallel vector models* and demonstrates that these models are an excellent framework on which to unify these three areas of parallel computing. Parallel vector models can be mapped onto a broad variety of architectures and can serve both as algorithmic models to analyze the complexity of algorithms, and as instruction sets for a virtual machine to which higher level programming languages can be compiled. The goal of this unification is to make it possible to program parallel algorithms in high-level languages, to have the algorithms execute efficiently on a diverse set of real machines, to be able to derive theoretical complexity measures of the algorithms, and to have these complexities be an accurate predictor of actual running times (see Figure 1.1).

This introduction outlines the general architecture of the parallel vector models; introduces two important classes of primitive instructions, the *scan* and *segmented* instructions; shows how the model and the instructions can be used to compile part of a parallel quicksort algorithm; and motivates the book.

Quicksort in a Very-High-Level Language (SETL)

---

proc quicksort(s);

if #$s < 2$ then return s; end;

x := random s;
lesser-elts := $\{y$ in $s | y < x\}$;
greater-elts := $\{y$ in $s | y \geq x\}$;

return quicksort(*lesser-elts*) + $[x]$ + quicksort(*greater-elts*);

end proc quicksort;

↓

Parallel Vector Models

↓   ↓

Parallel Computers	**Algorithmic Models**
	(Expected Time)
Vector:	P-RAM:
CRAY Y-MP, Convex C240, Hitachi S-820	$O(n \lg n / p + \lg^2 n)$
Shared Memory:	Circuit Models:
Encore Multimax, Sequent Balance	$s = O(n \lg^2 n) \quad d = O(\lg^2 n)$
Distributed Memory, MIMD:	Hypercube Model:
Intel iPSC/2, Intel/CMU iWARP	$O(n \lg^2 n / p + \lg^2 n)$
Distributed Memory, SIMD:	Grid Model:
NASA MPP, Thinking Machines CM2	$O(n \lg n / \sqrt{p} + \sqrt{p} \lg n)$

Figure 1.1: A high-level, inherently parallel description of quicksort in the language SETL
[100]. The parameter s is a set of input keys. The form #s returns the size of s, *random s*
returns a randomly selected element of s, and $+$ appends two sequences. Ideally we would
like to translate this description into efficient code for a broad variety of architectures and
also to determine the complexity of the algorithm on various theoretical models. This book
suggest that the parallel vector models are a good basis on which to merge these goals.

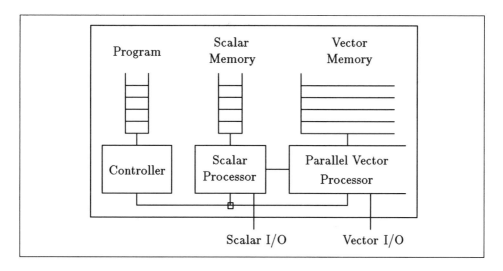

Figure 1.2: The architecture of a V-RAM. The machine is a random access machine (RAM) with the addition of a vector memory, a parallel vector processor, and a vector input/output port. Each location of the vector memory can contain a vector of different length. The parallel vector processor executes operations on whole vectors.

1.1 Parallel Vector Models

As with a random access machine (RAM) model [40] or the Turing machine model [116], the parallel vector models are conveniently defined in terms of a machine architecture, the vector RAM (V-RAM). The V-RAM is a standard serial RAM with the addition of a *vector memory* and a *vector processor* (see Figure 1.2). Each memory location in the vector memory can contain an arbitrarily long vector of atomic values; the vector length is associated with the vector not the memory location. Each instruction of the vector processor operates on a fixed number of vectors from the vector memory and possibly scalars from the scalar memory. A vector instruction might, for example, sum the elements of a vector, rearrange the order of the elements of a vector, or merge the elements of two sorted vectors (see Figure 1.3). A program for a V-RAM is no different from a program for a serial RAM except that it can include these additional vector instructions. A dot-product of two vectors, for example, could be executed with an instruction which elementwise multiplies the elements of two vectors followed by an instruction that sums the elements of a vector. The set of instructions that a V-RAM supplies can have a strong effect on the power of the machine—this is discussed in the next section.

Two time complexity measures are associated with the execution of a program on a

Mv[0]		=	[3	17	7	13	5	1	11	2]
Ms[0] ← sum Mv[0]		=	59							

Mv[0] (data vector)		=	[c	o	g	n	i	t	i	o	n]
Mv[1] (index vector)		=	[2	8	4	1	0	7	6	3	2]
Mv[2] ← permute Mv[0],Mv[1]	=	[i	n	c	o	g	n	i	t	o]

Mv[0]		=	[4	7	11]				
Mv[1]		=	[2	9	12	21]			
Mv[2] ← merge Mv[0],Mv[1]	=	[2	4	7	9	11	12	21]

Mv[0]		=	[5	1	3	4	3	9	2	6]
Mv[1]		=	[2	5	3	8	1	3	6	2]
Mv[2] ← p+ Mv[0],Mv[1]	=	[7	6	6	12	4	12	8	8]

Figure 1.3: Some vector instructions. The sum instruction sums the elements of a vector, the permute instruction rearranges the elements of a vector according to a second vector of indices, the merge instruction merges the elements of two sorted vectors, and the elementwise add instruction (p+) adds corresponding elements of two vectors. $Mv[i]$ is the ith location of the vector memory, and $Ms[i]$ is the ith location of the scalar memory.

V-RAM: the *step complexity* and the *element complexity*. The step complexity is the number of steps executed by a program, and the element complexity is the sum, over the steps, of the lengths of the vectors manipulated in each step. The two complexities can be thought of as the parallel and serial complexities, respectively, and are analogous to the depth and size complexities in the boolean circuit models [117, 26, 37, 38]. To guarantee that the primitives run in reasonable times, and to put useful bounds on simulating them on other models, we place two restrictions on the vector primitives. First, we require that all vector instruction can be simulated on a serial RAM in $O(n)$ time on vectors of length n. With this requirement, the element complexity is an asymptotic upper bound on the time complexity of simulating a V-RAM program on a RAM. Second, we require that all primitives can be executed on a boolean circuit of depth $O(\lg n)$ (are in NC^1 [37]). This guarantees a reasonable bound on the parallel complexity of the algorithms.

We consider the salient features of this machine model, especially as compared to models based on a set of communicating serial processors (multiprocessors), such as the

P-RAM models[1], the message passing models or the hypercube models. First, the total work performed on each "program step" of a V-RAM is not constant since each vector can have a different length, while on a multiprocessor, the total work performed on a step is equal to the number of processors. It is for this reason that the element complexity is important in the V-RAM. Second, the model has very strict serial control; it does not even allow certain elements to be turned off such as allowed in the SIMD P-RAM models, or in the data-parallel model of Hillis and Steele [54]. This book is therefore a interesting demonstration of the power of strict serial control. Third, the V-RAM permits a broader set of primitives—the primitives are no longer limited to local processor computations and various forms of memory references or messages.

Models, such as the parallel vector models, that center around collections of values and operate on these collections as a whole, are henceforth called *collection-oriented* models. Similarly, models based on a set of communicating serial processors, are henceforth called *processor-oriented* models. The key difference is that the collection-oriented models execute a set of parallel primitives, whereas the processor-oriented models execute a set of serial primitives in parallel—one per processor. For example, a vector model *scan* primitive is a parallel primitive executed in serial, while a P-RAM shared-memory-read is a serial primitive executed in parallel, once per processor.

1.2 Vector Instructions

The term "vector model" invokes in the minds of many computer scientists thoughts of highly-regular numerical algorithms, perhaps written in FORTRAN and executed on serial vector machines, such as a CRAY computer [95]. Given a sufficiently weak set of vector instructions, the usefulness of the vector models is indeed restricted to a handful of highly-regular algorithms. This book will demonstrate, however, that given a sufficiently powerful set of instructions, the parallel vector models are useful for a surprisingly wide variety of algorithms.

This section introduces two classes of vector instructions: the *scan*[2] instructions and the *segmented* instructions. The combination of these instructions can be found in almost all the algorithms described in this book. The section also shows how the instructions can be used to execute parts of the quicksort algorithm shown in Figure 1.1.

---

[1] Appendix A contains a brief description of the P-RAM models.

[2] The term *scan* is taken from APL [61]. In the computer theory community the operation is usually referred to as the *all prefix sums* operation. A brief history of the operation can be found in Appendix A.

The Scan Instruction

A scan instruction for a binary associative operator $\oplus$, takes a vector of values A and returns to each position of a new equal-length vector, the operator sum of all previous positions in A. For example:

A	=	[1	3	5	7	9	11	13	15]
+-scan(A)	=	[0	1	4	9	16	25	36	49]

B	=	[3	2	1	6	5	4	9]
max-scan(B)	=	[0	3	3	3	6	6	6]

In the quicksort algorithm (see Figure 1.1), the scan instructions can be used to select the *lesser-elts* and *greater-elts*. Assuming the keys s are stored in a vector, the statement $\{y \text{ in } s | y < x\}$ can be implemented as shown in Figure 1.4. The implementation first distributes the pivot x across a new vector x'; this distribution is itself a type of scan. Then, to select the lesser elements, the implementation elementwise compares the pivot vector with the s vector returning a vector of 1s and 0s. A +-scan on this result returns a unique index to each element less than the pivot. A version of the permute primitive is then used to move the lesser elements into a new smaller vector based on these indices. The *greater-elts* can be selected similarly.

The Segmented Instructions

A segmented vector is a vector partitioned into a set of contiguous segments. The segmented vector can be represented with two vectors, one containing the values and the second containing the length of each segment. For example, the two vectors:

$$A = [\text{s} \quad \text{y} \quad \text{l} \quad \text{l} \quad \text{a} \quad \text{b} \quad \text{l} \quad \text{e} \quad \text{s}]$$

$$L = [3 \quad 2 \quad 4]$$

would represent the vector:

$$A' = [\text{s} \quad \text{y} \quad \text{l}] \quad [\text{l} \quad \text{a}] \quad [\text{b} \quad \text{l} \quad \text{e} \quad \text{s}].$$

The segmented instructions are versions of the vector instructions that execute independently over each segment of a segmented vector. For example, consider the following operations:

A	=	[6]				[1	3	7	9]		
B	=	[2	4	7]		[4	8]				
seg-+-scan(A)	=	[0]				[0	1	4	11]		
seg-merge(A, B)	=	[2	4	6	7]	[1	3	4	7	8	9].

```
                    $ x is the pivot
                    $ s is the set of values
```
lesser-elts := {y in s|y < x}

↓

```
        l ← length(s);
        x'← distribute(x,l);
        f ← s p< x';
        i ← +-scan(f);

        $ select-permute permutes elements s
        $ to index i if flag f is set.
```
lesser-elts ← select-permute(s,i,f);

SETL to Vector Model Translation

s	=	[7	18	6	3	14	9	0	16	11]
x	=	9								
l	=	8								
x'	=	[9	9	9	9	9	9	9	9	9]
f	=	[1	0	1	1	0	0	1	0	0]
i	=	[0	1	1	2	3	3	3	4	4]
lesser-elts	=	[7	6	3	0]					

Example

step complexity	=	1 + 1 + 1 + 1 + 1	=	$O(1)$
element complexity	=	$1 + n + n + n + n$	=	$O(n)$

Complexity

Figure 1.4: The program transformation needed to convert the SETL code, which selects elements of s less than the pivot x, into instructions for a parallel vector machine ($ is the comment character in SETL). Also, an example of the execution of the vector instructions, and the complexity of the vector model code.

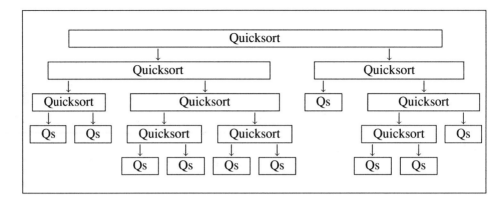

Figure 1.5: The quicksort algorithm. Just using parallelism within each block yields a step complexity proportional to the number of blocks ($O(n)$). Just using parallelism from running the blocks in parallel yields a step complexity at least proportional to the largest block ($O(n)$). By using both forms of parallelism the step complexity is proportional to the depth of the tree (expected $O(\lg n)$).

To illustrate the importance of segments and segmented instructions, consider the quicksort example again. When applied to a set s, quicksort splits the set into two subsets (the elements lesser and greater than the pivot) and calls itself recursively on each set. This recursive invocation generates a tree of calls which would look something like the tree shown in Figure 1.5. If we were to only take advantage of the parallelism within each quicksort to subselect the two sets (the parallelism within each block), we would do well near the root and badly near the leaves. Inversely, if we were to only take advantage of the parallelism available by running the invocations of quicksort in parallel (the parallelism between blocks but not within a block), we would do well at the leaves and badly at the root. In both cases the parallel time complexity is $O(n)$ rather than the ideal $O(\lg n)$ (the expected depth of the tree).

Segments and segmented instructions allow a simple technique for using both kinds of parallelism. Each invocation of quicksort at a single level of the recursion tree is placed in a separate segment of a segmented vector and the segmented instructions are used to split the values independently within each segment. This allows the implementation to execute a whole level of the tree at a time (with a constant number of vector instructions); near the root of the recursion tree the segmented vector contains a few large segments while at the leaves it contains many small segments. The expected step complexity of the algorithm is $O(\lg n)$ (if somewhat careful about picking pivots) and the expected element complexity is $O(n \lg n)$.

Chapter 10 derives a general theorem about how segments can be used to execute nested parallel code, and the compiler discussed in Chapter 11 uses the derived techniques.

1.3 Implementation

This section outlines how a V-RAM can be implemented on two architectures: a shared memory SIMD multiprocessor and a distributed memory MIMD multiprocessor. As examples, it considers two vector instructions: an elementwise add (p+) and a `permute`. Details on how to implement the scan instructions and the segmented instructions are discussed in Chapters 3 and 13. Details of how to implement a V-RAM on the Connection Machine, a distributed memory SIMD multiprocessor, are discussed in Chapter 12.

Shared Memory SIMD Multiprocessor

The vector memory is simulated by placing each vector in a contiguous region of the shared memory and assigning each processor to an independent block of each vector. When executing a vector instruction on a vector a, each processor loops over the elements of a it is responsible for. The processor only needs to know the offset address of the vector, the number of elements per processor, and its processor number, to determine the memory addresses to access. For example, in a p+ instruction, each processor loops over its elements in the two source vectors, adds them together, and stores the result in the destination vector. For a `permute` instruction, each processor reads a value and index for its elements, and writes the value in the destination vector at the position specified by the index (it needs only know the offset of the destination vector). For a vector of length n, and for p processors, each primitive will run in $O(n/p + 1)$ time.

Distributed Memory MIMD Multiprocessor

Each vector is evenly divided among the processor memories. The processors run in single program multiple data (SPMD) mode and each processor is responsible for the elements in its own memory. The p+ only requires local operations. The `permute` instruction requires sending data to other processors—based on the index each source processor determines the destination processor for each of its elements and sends the elements to those processor (this assumes the machine has some kind of routing facility). Synchronization is not required after the elementwise operations, but a barrier synchronization is required after the permute. If the vectors are large compared to the number of processors, the synchronization overhead becomes relatively small, and the latency of the router becomes less significant (just the throughput matters).

1.4   Summary and Roadmap

With a basic understanding of the vector models and how they compare to other parallel
models, we now return to and expand on the central claim of this book, the claim that
parallel vector models can be mapped onto a broad variety of architectures and are good
both as algorithmic models to analyze the complexity of algorithms, and as instruction sets
for a virtual machine to which higher level programming languages can be compiled. We
mention each of the core areas—*algorithms, languages* and *architectures*—separately and
then consider how they fit together.

Algorithms

The parallel vector models can be used to implement a broad variety of algorithms, much
broader than might be expected. This book describes algorithms ranging from graph
algorithms, to numerical algorithms. Table 1.1 lists the algorithms described in this book
along with the section in which they appear and their complexities. The parallel vector
models allow quite concise description of these parallel algorithms since they hide many
low level issues from the algorithm designer, such as synchronization, processor allocation,
and simulation of multiple elements on each processor.

The parallel vector models have a theoretical foundation that is no weaker than other
parallel algorithmic models, such as the P-RAM or boolean-circuit models. The complexity
measures in the parallel vector models can both be mapped onto the complexity measures
of other models (see Section 12.2), and are powerful on their own.

Languages

The parallel vector models form an natural virtual machine on which to compile many very
high-level languages such as APL [59, 60], APL2 [58], CM-LISP [107], NIAL [77, 99],
PARALATION LISP [96], SETL [100]. These languages are all based on manipulating
collections of values as a whole. Chapter 11 describes a compiler that translates a subset of
PARALATION LISP onto the instructions of the scan vector model. Appendix C shows many
algorithms—including a convex-hull, a quicksort and a learning algorithm—implemented
in PARALATION LISP.

By compiling high-level languages onto the vector models, much of a compiler becomes
machine independent—the machine dependent parts are implemented below the level of
the vector models.

Algorithm	Section	Complexity	
		Step	Element
Sorting and Merging n Keys			
Split-Radix Sort	3.4.1	$O(\lg n)$	$O(n \lg n)$
Quicksort	3.5.1	$O(\lg n)$	$O(n \lg n)$
Halving Merge	3.7.2	$O(\lg n)$	$O(n)$
Computational-Geometry n Points			
Closest Pair	6.3	$O(\lg n)$	$O(n \lg n)$
Quickhull (m Hull Points)	6.4	$O(\lg m)$	$O(n \lg m)$
$\sqrt{n}$ Merge Hull	6.5	$O(\lg n)$	$O(n \lg n)$
Line of Sight	6.6	$O(1)$	$O(n)$
Line Drawing	3.6.1	$O(1)$	$O(n)$
Graph n Vertices, m Edges			
Minimum Spanning Tree	7.1	$O(\lg n)$	$O(m \lg n)$
Maximum Flow	7.2	$O(n^2)$	$O(n^2 m)$
Maximal Independent Set	7.3	$O(\lg n)$	$O(m \lg n)$
Biconnected Components	7.3	$O(\lg n)$	$O(m \lg n)$
Numerical $n \times m$ Dense Matrices			
Matrix-Vector Multiply	8.1	$O(1)$	$O(nm)$
Linear-Systems Solver ($n = m$)	8.2	$O(n)$	$O(n^2)$
Step of Simplex	8.3	$O(1)$	$O(nm)$

Table 1.1: A list of the algorithm described in this book along with the section they appear in and their asymptotic complexities. The complexities for the quicksort and quickhull are expected complexities. Some of the algorithms are probabilistic. The split-radix sort complexities assumes that the keys are $O(\lg n)$ bits long.

Architectures

The parallel vector models can be implemented efficiently on a broad variety of tightly coupled architectures including serial machines, vector machines, and parallel machines, with both serial and parallel control. The flexibility of the models arises because the models make no assumptions about how data elements are allocated to processors, and because the models have strict serial control. Chapter 12 describes an implementation on the Connection Machine, a highly parallel SIMD computer [53, 113]. The general technique described can be straightforwardly extended to any synchronous parallel machine with a sufficiently powerful communication network. Chapter 13 describes how the scan instructions can be implemented efficiently in hardware.

In Combination

If an algorithm is defined in a high-level language and compiled through the vector models onto a real machine, how efficient is the final code? To test this, a quicksort routine written in PARALATION LISP (Section C.5), was compiled by a compiler (Chapter 11) into the scan vector model (Chapter 4), and then executed on both a Connection Machine (Chapter 12) and a Symbolics 3600, a serial machine. The compiled code on both machines was within a factor of two as fast as the sorting routine supplied by the machine vendor as part of the system.[3]

Although compiling very high-level languages into code that is within a factor of two of highly optimized code is not unusual for serial machines, it is quite unusual for parallel machines. Of course, these results are not enough to "prove" the usefulness of the vector models, but they show the models have promise.

Roadmap

Figure 1.6 shows a roadmap for the book. Part I, *models*, forms the foundation of the book. It defines the parallel vector models in more detail, describes the implications of including a set of scan operations as primitives of the P-RAM models, and introduces a particular parallel vector model, the scan vector model.

The next three parts correspond to the three core areas: algorithms, languages and architectures. These parts are independent and can be read in any order. Part II, *algorithms*, describes how several important data structures, including trees, graphs and arrays, can be mapped onto the scan vector model so that they can be efficiently manipulated. It then

---

[3]The supplied sorting routine on the Connection Machine is a carefully optimized radix sort and executes about equally fast as a microcoded bitonic sort [11]. The supplied sorting routine on the Symbolics 3600 is a carefully optimized quicksort.

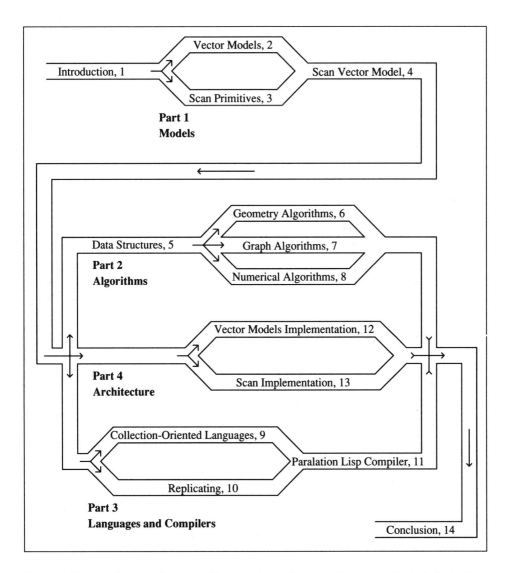

Figure 1.6: A roadmap to the book. Each road is a chapter of the book. Each fork signifies that the branches are independent and can be read in any order. Each join signifies that the following chapter relies to some extent on all the incoming branches.

describes many algorithms for the model. Part III, *languages*, compares a set of high-level languages called the collection-oriented languages. It then describes a technique called replicating and describes a compiler for PARALATION LISP. Part IV, *architecture*, describes how the parallel vector models are implemented on the Connection Machine and how they can be simulated on a P-RAM. It also describes how the various scan operations can be implemented directly in hardware.

Part I

Models

Introduction: Models

This part defines the models on which the rest of this book in founded. It contains three chapters. Chapter 2, *parallel vector models*, defines the parallel vector models, and compares them to other parallel algorithmic models, such as the P-RAM and boolean-circuit models. Chapter 3, *scan primitives*, introduces a set of scan operations, argues that these operations should be considered primitive instructions, and illustrates many examples of how they are used in algorithm design. These two chapters are completely independent: the parallel vector models are introduced without commitment to a particular set of primitives, and the scan primitives are introduced in the framework of the P-RAM models.

Although the parallel vector models and scan primitives are introduced independently, the scan primitives fit naturally into and enhance the parallel vector models. Chapter 4, *scan vector model*, defines a specific parallel vector model that includes the scan primitives in its instruction set, as well as instructions that elementwise operate on vectors and that permute the elements of a vector. Chapter 4 also describes a set of vector operations that can be implemented with the instructions of the scan vector model, a set of segmented versions of the primitive instructions, and a set of other primitive instructions which are not included in the scan vector model, but might be included in other parallel vector models.

All the algorithms described in the book are based on the scan vector model, and the compiler described in Chapter 11 compiles into the instructions of the scan vector model.

Chapter 2

Parallel Vector Models

This chapter defines the *parallel vector models* based on an abstract machine, the V-RAM, compares the models to other parallel algorithmic models including the P-RAM models and the boolean circuit models, and discusses why and when the parallel vector models might be more appropriate than these other models. Some of the definitions outlined in the introduction of this book are repeated in this chapter for the sake of completeness.

2.1   The Vector Random Access Machine

As with a random access machine (RAM) model [40] and the Turing machine model [116], the parallel vector models are conveniently defined in terms of a machine architecture. Figure 2.1 illustrates the general architecture of such a machine, the V-RAM. The V-RAM is a serial random access machine (RAM) with the addition of a vector memory, a parallel vector processor, and vector input and output ports.

The *vector memory* is a sequence of locations each containing a *simple vector*. A simple vector is a linear-ordered collection of scalar values. The number of values in the collection is called the length. We place no limit on the length, and each vector can be a different length. Allowing each vector to have a different length is an important feature of the vector models and is intricately tied in with the complexity measures. Allowing each vector to be arbitrarily long makes it impossible to implement a vector memory directly; it must somehow be simulated on a real machine. One technique to simulate the vector memory is for each vector memory location to contain a pointer into a chunk of locations in a real memory where the values of the vector are actually stored. Chapter 12 describes such an implementation.

The *parallel vector processor* executes primitive instructions on a fixed number of

19

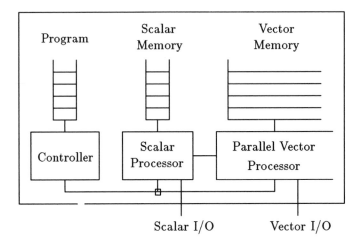

Figure 2.1: The architecture of a V-RAM. The machine is a random access machine (RAM) with the addition of a vector memory, a parallel vector processor, and a vector input/output port. Each location of the vector memory can contain a vector of different length. The parallel vector processor executes operations on whole vectors, such as permuting the elements of a vector or executing a scan operation on a vector.

$$
\begin{array}{lll}
\text{Mv}[0] & : & [4 \quad 7 \quad 11] \\
\text{Mv}[1] & : & [2 \quad 9 \quad 12 \quad 21]
\end{array}
$$

$$\text{Ms}[0] \leftarrow \text{sum Mv}[0]$$

$$\text{Mv}[2] \leftarrow \text{merge Mv}[0], \text{Mv}[1]$$

$$
\begin{array}{lll}
\text{Ms}[0] & : & 22 \\
\text{Mv}[2] & : & [2 \quad 4 \quad 7 \quad 9 \quad 11 \quad 12 \quad 21]
\end{array}
$$

Figure 2.2: Example of a *sum* and a *merge* primitive for a vector model. $\text{Mv}[i]$ is the ith location of the vector memory, and $\text{Ms}[i]$ is the ith location of the scalar memory.

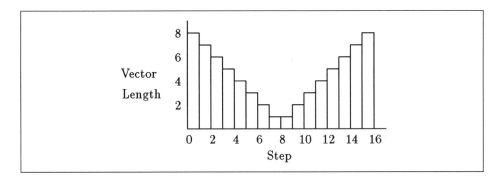

Figure 2.3: Time complexity measures. The *step complexity* is the total number of steps (16 in the example). The *element complexity* is the sum, over the steps, of the length of the vectors manipulated during each step (72 in the example).

vectors and scalars from the vector and scalar memories. A primitive might, for example, read a vector from the vector memory, sum the elements, and write the result in the scalar memory, or it might read two sorted vectors from the vector memory, merge the elements, and write the result back in the vector memory (see Figure 2.2). Particular vector models can differ in the primitive instructions they supply, and these different sets of primitives can lead to different complexities of algorithms. Chapter 4 defines a set of primitive instructions for the *scan vector model*. Section 2.5 discusses principles for selecting a good set of primitives for a vector model, and Section 4.5 discusses other possible primitives.

The *time complexity* of an algorithm in the vector models is specified using two measures: the *step complexity* and the *element complexity*. The step complexity is the number of calls to the primitive instructions and the element complexity is the vector length per primitive instruction call, summed over the number of calls. Since a primitive might take more than one argument, we say that the vector length of a primitive call is the sum of the lengths of the arguments (including the destination). The step complexity can be thought of as the parallel complexity of the algorithm assuming an infinitely wide parallel vector processor, whereas, the element complexity can be thought of as the serial complexity assuming we simulate the parallel vector processor on a serial RAM. The relationship between the step and element complexities is analogous to the relationship between the *depth* and *size* complexities in the boolean circuit models. The depth of a boolean circuit is the number of layers, and the size is the sum over the layers of the number of elements in each layer. Section 12.2 shows how the step complexity and element complexity are related to time complexity in the P-RAM model. Section 2.6 introduces analogous space complexity measures and discusses assumptions on which the step and element complexities are based.

P-RAM models	Vector Models
(1) Fixed number of element operations on each step.	(1) Variable number of element operations on each step.
(2) Complexity is based on one function of two variables: n (the size of the input) and p (the number of processors).	(2) Complexity is based on two functions, the step and element complexities, of one variable: n.
(3) Atomic values are the only primitive data.	(3) Supplies a primitive data structure: the vector.
(4) Parallel or serial control.	(4) Strictly serial control.
(5) Parallelism comes from serial primitives running in parallel.	(5) Parallelism comes from parallel primitives.

Table 2.1: Summary of the differences between the P-RAM models and the parallel vector models.

2.2   Comparison to P-RAM Models

This section compares parallel vector models to parallel random access machine (P-RAM) models [42, 101, 104, 48, 49], Section 2.3 compares them to the boolean-circuit models and the fixed-network models such as hypercube or grid models, and Section 2.4 compares them to the bit-vector models. Vector models are compared to these other parallel algorithmic models for two reasons: first, many important algorithms and techniques found in the literature are set in the context of these other models and we would like to transfer these results to the vector models; and second, we would like to explore possible advantages, or disadvantages, of the vector models. Although this section specifically compares the vector models to the P-RAM models, many of the comparisons are valid when comparing any collection-oriented model to any processor-oriented model. This section assumes a basic understanding of P-RAM models.[1]

The parallel vector and P-RAM models are both natural extensions of the serial RAM model. In the vector models we add to the RAM a set of parallel primitives and an enhanced memory, whereas in the P-RAM models we include multiple copies of the processor part of a RAM, attach it to a shared memory, and execute the same serial primitives in parallel. The two different extensions of the RAM give rise to important differences in the two

---

[1]Appendix A contains a brief description of the P-RAM models.

	Vector Models		P-RAM Models
Algorithm	Step	Element	Time
Split Radix Sort	$O(\lg n)$	$O(n \lg n)$	$O((n \lg n)/p + \lg n)$
Halving Merge	$O(\lg n)$	$O(n)$	$O(n/p + \lg n)$
In General	s	e	$O(e/p + s)$

Table 2.2: Comparison of the description of time complexity measures in the vector models and the P-RAM models. The time complexity in the vector models is specified with two functions of one variable while in the P-RAM models it is specified with one function of two variables. The two algorithms will be discussed in Chapter 3. In both models we assume the primitives include the scan operations.

classes of models. These differences are summarized in Table 2.1. The remainder of this section discusses the four primary differences: the *complexity*, the *control*, the *primitive data*, and the *primitive operations*. To illustrate some of the differences we also discuss the merging problem.

Complexity

A P-RAM executes an equal number of element operations[2] on each step—exactly p—whereas a V-RAM can execute a varying number of element operations on each step—the number depends on the length of the vectors used on the step. As an example of why this difference is important, consider an algorithm that starts with n elements and halves the number of elements on each iteration. In a vector model, the algorithm only needs to halve the vector length on each iteration, therefore, halving the number of element operations. In a P-RAM model, since the number of element operations on each step is constant, the algorithm would either start by simulating multiple elements per processor and halve the number of steps on each iteration, or it would always use n processors and waste most of the processors after the first iteration.

Since the number of element operations in a vector model varies between steps, the number of steps (the step complexity) by itself is inadequate as a measure of time complexity—it does not tell us how many element operations have been executed. The vector models, therefore, include a second measure of time complexity—the sum of the vector lengths over the steps (the element complexity). In the P-RAM models, the element complexity

---

[2]We define the number of element operations of a step as the time complexity of simulating the step on a serial RAM.

is not necessary—the element complexity is simply p times the step complexity. The step complexity in the P-RAM models, however, must contain the extra variable p, which is not necessary in the vector models. Table 2.2 compares the complexity measures for the two classes of models.

What is the relationship between the P-RAM complexity and the vector model complexities? In the two limits $p = \infty$ and $p = 1$ the P-RAM complexity reduces to the step complexity and element complexity, respectively (see Table 2.2). Since the step and element complexities are just the limits of the P-RAM complexity, it might appear that the P-RAM complexity holds more information than the other two complexities. As we illustrate in Section 12.2, this is not the case—we show that in general the P-RAM time complexity can be generated from the two limits with the simple relation

$$O(e/p + s) , \tag{2.1}$$

e is the element complexity and s is the step complexity. I contend that the two limits are a cleaner notation for specifying time complexity even when using a P-RAM model.

Primitive Data

The P-RAM models only supply atomic values as primitive data—the memory is completely flat—and data structures are built out of these atomic values. The vector models, in contrast, supply a primitive data structure: the vector. To take advantages of the parallel vector primitives, other data structures, such as trees or graphs, should be mapped onto the primitive vectors. As an example of how this difference is important, consider representing a tree. In a P-RAM model, we might represent a tree using a linked list in the Euler tour order [112]. This linked list might be scattered over an arbitrarily large area of memory with large portions of unused memory interspersed among the elements. This linked list representation is inappropriate for a vector model. Instead, the tree must be mapped onto vectors, and the vectors should be kept as short (dense) as possible: there should be no unused elements interspersed in the vector. Chapter 5 describe such a mapping.

Having a primitive data structure allows simpler and more precise descriptions of algorithms and allows a more straightforward translation into programs that implement the algorithm. The algorithm designer need not worry about allocating data elements to processors, about keeping track of which processors or memory banks contain data, nor about simulating multiple elements on each processor. Vectors make vector models more abstract than P-RAM models and further removed from an implementation on a real machine. In spite of raising the level of abstraction, algorithms written in the models are likely to be more practical on real machines than P-RAM algorithms since the vector models can supply a broader set of primitives (as discussed below), and because the memory references are more predictable.

Control

Control in the vector models is strictly serial whereas control in the P-RAM models can either be serial (single instruction) or parallel (multiple instruction). The notion of serial control in the P-RAM model is not precise, however, and presents some problems. For example, consider a conditional-jump instruction in a serial control P-RAM. Can some processors take the jump and others not? If so, won't the two sets of processors need to execute different instructions? If we force all processors to take the same branch, from which processor do we look at a flag to decide on whether to take a branch or not? These problems can be worked out but with extra explanation and room for confusion.[3] In contrast, conditional branches are straightforward in the vector models. As in the standard RAM model, conditional branches are scalar primitives and jump based on a single flag in the scalar memory.

Serial control has important advantages over parallel control. First, it simplifies algorithm design: the designer only needs to worry about a single program. Second, it simplifies the debugging of programs: if a programmer stops a program to check the state, she only needs to worry about the single-instruction stream. Third, it allows an implementation on a broader variety of machines: algorithms with serial control can be implemented on SIMD computers, such as the Connection Machine, and possibly on serial pipelined vector processors such as supplied on the Cray computers and other supercomputers.

On the other hand, serial control is more restrictive than parallel control. How many algorithms really need parallel control? This book hopes to demonstrate that even the strict serial control of the vector models can be applied naturally to a very wide variety of problems—certainly every application and algorithm in this book. Not all problems can be conveniently solved with serial control, but because of its advantages, one should stretch its use as broadly as possible.

Primitive Operations

As mentioned earlier, the primitives of a vector model are parallel—they operate on a collection of values. In contrast, the primitives of a P-RAM model are serial—as with the RAM model, they operate on a fixed number of scalar values—and the parallelism comes from applying the serial primitives in parallel. Supplying parallel primitives has two effects. First, it permits a broader set of primitives. For example, we might include in a vector

---

[3]Issues involving conditional jumps appear again in Chapter 10.

P-RAM Models Primitives	Vector Models Primitives
Arithmetic and Logical	Elementwise (Section 4.1.2)
Memory Reference	
Exclusive Write	Permutation (Section 4.1.3)
Exclusive Read	Inverse-Permutation (Section 4.2)
Concurrent Write	Combine (Section 4.5.2)
Concurrent Read	Multi-Extract (Section 4.5.3)
Fetch-and-Op (Multiprefix)	Keyed-Scan (Section 4.5.4)
Global Primitives	
—	Scan (Section 4.1.4)
—	Merge (Section 4.5.1)
—	Reduce (Section 4.2)
—	Pack (Section 4.2)

Table 2.3: A comparison of the primitive operations supplied by the P-RAM models and the vector models. The correspondence is by no means exact. The elementwise primitives, for example, if simulated on a P-RAM require both memory references and arithmetic operations. The vector models can include a much broader variety of primitives.

model a primitive that merges the elements of two vectors. To add a merge primitive to a P-RAM model, we would need to stretch and warp the model—the P-RAM would become more than just a set of RAM processors sharing a common memory. Second, nonprimitive parallel operations, such as sorting, are operations on whole collections. These operations, therefore, have the same interface as the primitive of a vector model, but a different interface than the primitives of a P-RAM model. Having the same interface allows a more uniform description terminology.

By allowing a broader set of primitives, we can more accurately model the running time of algorithms on real machines, while maintaining the high-level description. To more accurately model real machines, we can either add other primitives that are as fast as general permutations[4]—such as the scan primitives—or we can restrict the permutations to a certain class—such as permutations on a grid, or permutations that can be executed deterministically on a single pass of a butterfly network.

---

[4]As discussed in Section 3.2, a permutation of a vector is at least as easy as a memory reference in a P-RAM model.

An Example

As an example of how the P-RAM models and vector models can lead to different algorithms, we consider the merging problem. Shiloach and Vishkin [44, 104] describe a P-RAM algorithm for merging two sorted sets of values of length n and m $(n > m)$. On p processors this algorithm has a complexity of $O(n/p + \lg n)$. The basic idea of the algorithm is to extract p evenly spaced elements from each set, we call these *fenceposts*, to merge the fenceposts using a logarithmic merge such as the bitonic merge [11], and then to use each processor to serially merge the elements between two fenceposts. The logarithmic merge has complexity $O(\lg p)$. Since the fenceposts are n/p apart, the serial merging has complexity $O(n/p)$.

Does this algorithm make any sense in a vector model? Why would we pick p evenly spaced elements when we do not even have the concept of p? In a vector model, we might instead think about somehow reducing the size of the vectors by a constant factor. This is the motivation for the *halving merge* algorithm which will be described in Section 3.7.2. The basic idea of the halving merge algorithm is to extract odd-indexed elements from each vector, to recursively merge the extracted elements, and then to use the result of the merge to merge the even-indexed elements. Unlike the P-RAM algorithm, the halving merge algorithm is recursive. With the primitives of the scan vector model (defined in Chapter 4), the algorithm has an element complexity of $O(n + n/2 + n/4 + \cdots) = O(n)$ and a step complexity of $O(\lg n)$. In an EREW P-RAM model with scan primitives, the algorithm has a step complexity of $O(n/p + \lg n)$—this complexity is based on equation 2.1.

The halving merge algorithm has some advantages over the P-RAM algorithm. First, the halving merge algorithm only needs a single recursive version, whereas the P-RAM algorithm needs a parallel merge to merge the fenceposts and a serial merge to merge between fenceposts. Second, in the halving merge algorithm, the length of the vectors continue to decrease even when the number of elements is less than the number of processors. This has a practical consequence in that it reduces the load on a communication network after we have less elements than processors, and probably speeds up each step.

Translating from P-RAM Algorithms

Many very impressive algorithms and techniques found in the literature are set in the context of the P-RAM model, and it would be a serious drawback if these contributions could not be applied in the vector models. Fortunately, much of this research can be translated to the vector models, and, in fact, many of the algorithms described in this book are modifications of P-RAM algorithms. This translation is possible because the algorithms described in the literature typically only need a single stream of control. The work on nested parallelism described in Chapter 10 greatly simplifies the translation.

2.3   Comparison to Circuit and Network Models

In this section we compare the parallel vector models to the boolean-circuit models [117, 26, 37, 38] and to the fixed-network models. Fixed-network models are processor-oriented models in which the processors are restricted to communicate to a fixed set of neighbors. These models include sets of processors connected by butterfly networks [32, 84, 11], shuffle-exchange networks [109], cube-connected-cycles [89], multidimensional grids [115], or pyramids [110].

As mentioned earlier, the complexity measures of the vector models are analogous to the complexity measures of the boolean-circuit models. In this analogy, each step in a vector algorithm corresponds to a level in a boolean circuit. The step complexity therefore corresponds to the depth (number of levels), and the element complexity to the size (sum over the number of elements in each level). This analogy between step in a vector algorithm and level in a boolean circuit can be made slightly deeper. It turns out that vector algorithms without conditionals and without indirect addressing[5] can be converted into circuits by replacing each primitive with a circuit that implements the primitive (see Figure 2.4).

In spite of this analogy, the two classes of models differ in important ways. First, although circuit models allow arbitrary logic, the vector models restrict the logic to a fixed set of modules. We can think of algorithm design in a vector model as building a circuit out of a fixed sequence of building blocks. This greatly simplifies programming and description at the cost of being less flexible. Second, each step in a vector algorithm might require many levels in a boolean circuit. For example, a merge primitive that merges n elements requires a circuit module of depth $O(\lg n)$.

Third, in vector models the element complexity of a step can depend not only on the input size but also on the particular data. For example, in the line-drawing routine discussed in Section 3.6.1, the number of pixels generated depends on the length of the lines—this depends not only on the size of the input but on the particular input data. To use boolean circuits to solve this problem, a family of circuits must be defined, and each member must solve the problem for a particular line length. The problem is that we do not know which particular member of the family can be used to solve the problem until we have executed part of the computation (determining the lengths of the line). This is a conceptually awkward aspect of the boolean-circuit models. A similar problem arises with programs, such as quicksort, whose step complexity can vary depending on the input data. In quicksort, the worst case step complexity is $O(n)$ and the expected complexity is only $O(\lg n)$.

---

[5]Problems with indirect addressing and conditionals are considered again in Chapter 10.

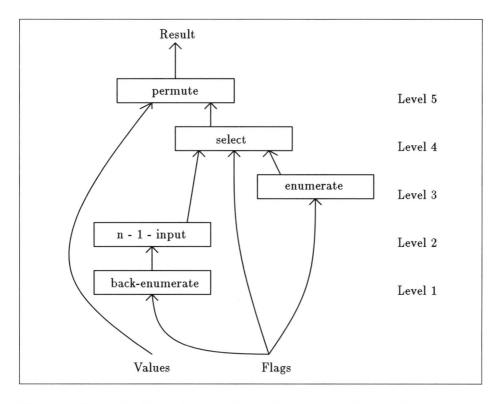

Figure 2.4: Vector algorithms without conditional branches and without indirect addressing can be converted into a circuit by replacing each primitive with a circuit that implements the primitive, and by converting the vector memory locations into bundles of wires. In the above example, we illustrate how the `split` operation, which will be defined in Section 3.4.1, is mapped onto a circuit. The number of independent bundles of wires crossing between two levels in the circuit is equal to the number of vector memory locations required between two steps in the vector algorithm.

We now briefly compare the vector models to the fixed-network models. Since the fixed-network models are processor oriented, many of the comparisons made in Section 2.2 for the P-RAM models also apply here. The fixed-network models, however, are lower-level models than either the vector models or P-RAM models: they can be implemented more directly on a real machine.

Algorithms for low-level models can have two disadvantages over algorithms for high-level models: they must be described at a more detailed level, and they are more machine dependent. The first disadvantage can be remedied by building high-level operations on top of the low-level models and then basing the algorithms on these operations. The operations only need to be defined once, and many algorithms might make use of them. If algorithms are being defined using these high-level operations, however, why not just use a model based on these operations? Using such a model can simultaneously solve the second problem (machine dependence) since we are no longer committed to implementing the operations on a particular machine. This is perhaps the principal motivation for the parallel vector models: a model based on a set of primitive parallel operations without commitment to a particular architecture.

Low-level might still be useful for describing algorithms when the algorithm cannot be described at a higher level and then mapped into an efficient algorithm at the lower level. From a programmer's point of view, I hope that this does not happen very often.

2.4   Comparison to Bit-Vector Models

Perhaps the closest theoretical model to the V-RAM is the bit-vector machine introduced by Pratt and Stockmeyer [87]. In this model, each register (memory location) can contain an arbitrary long vector of bits. The vector instructions included (1) elementwise bit operations over the vectors, such as `logical-or` or `logical-not`, and (2) logical shifts of the vectors right or left by an arbitrary amount. Pratt and Stockmeyer showed how the model can implement arbitrary precision integer arithmetic, and how to transpose and multiply boolean matrices in $O(\lg n)$ program steps. The bit-vector model, however, had only a single complexity measure, the step complexity. Since they did not consider an element complexity, they were able to show that $P = NP$ within the model (just based on the number of program steps). This is because they could simulate the nondeterminism on each step by spreading the branches across the length of a vector, in effect executing each branch in "parallel". This, of course leads to vectors which are exponentially large, and would lead to an exponential element complexity.

If we did introduce an element complexity to the bit-vector machine, we could simulated the V-RAM on a bit-vector machine in the following way with at most polylogarithmic differences in complexities. Since an integer can itself be represented as a sequence of bits, each vector of integers can be represented with a vector of bits broken into word sized blocks. To represent pointers in an n element vector, each block would require $O(\lg n)$ bits. The total bit length would therefore be $O(n \lg n)$. Chapter 4, introduces a particular set of vector instructions for the parallel vector models. We briefly mention here how they can be simulated on the bit-vector machine. The elementwise operations, such as addition, can be simulated by using segmented instructions and all require at most $O(\lg \lg n)$ steps. The permute can be executed by simulating an Omega network using the shifts, and could execute in determenistic $O(\lg^2 n)$ steps. The scan operations could be implemented in $O(\lg n \lg \lg n)$ steps using the tree implementation discussed in Chapter 13.

2.5   Selecting Primitives

Parallel vector models, as with P-RAM models, allow some flexibility in selecting a set of primitives. We, therefore, need principled criteria by which to make this selection. This section briefly considers several such criteria. First, the primitives should be easy to implement and efficient both when implemented in parallel and in serial, both in theory and in practice. Second, the primitives should be implementable on a broad range of architectures—including existing architectures. Third, the primitives should be useful. Fourth, there should be a small set of primitives so that it is easy to describe them and to port the primitives to different machines.

   To restrict ourselves to primitives which are efficient, we only consider primitives which obey the following two criteria:

1. Each primitive when applied to argument vectors of total length n, must require $O(n)$ time on a serial RAM. We call such a primitive, a *serially linear* primitive.

2. Each primitive must be in NC[1]: for vectors of length n, the primitive can be calculated on a boolean circuit of $O(\lg n)$ depth and of polynomial size. See [37] for more details on the class NC[1].

Although these criteria guarantee that the primitives are efficient in theory in both the serial and parallel limits, the constants might be large. To decide on whether a primitive is practically efficient, we must look at the constants on various architectures. When we introduce the scan vector model in Chapter 4, we consider the various criteria and justify our selection of primitives based on these criteria. We also consider these criteria when introducing other primitives in Section 4.5.

2.6 Other Issues

2.6.1 Serially Optimal Algorithms

What is the relationship between the element complexity of an algorithm on a vector model and the complexity of the algorithm on a serial RAM model? We say that a vector primitive is *serially linear* if when applied to argument vectors of total length n, it can be simulated in $O(n)$ time on a serial RAM. We call a model in which all the primitives are serially linear, *serially linear*. If a model is serially linear, then the element complexity gives an upper bound on the time complexity of the algorithm on the serial RAM model. As mentioned in Section 2.5, in this book we only consider serially linear primitives.

   We say that algorithms with an element complexity asymptotically equal to the optimal serial algorithm is serially time optimal. This definition of optimality is similar to the definitions of optimal parallel algorithms suggested by Schwartz [101] and Shiloach and Vishkin [104].

2.6.2 Space Complexity

We define two space complexities: the *vector-space complexity* and the *element-space complexity*. The vector-space complexity specifies the number of locations used in the vector memory, and the element-space complexity specifies the sum of the vector lengths over the locations used in the vector memory. These space complexities are analogous to the two time complexities.

2.6.3 Equal Time Assumption

The step and element complexities rest on the assumption that all the vector primitives require approximately equal time on equal-length vectors. We call this assumption the *equal-time* assumption. This assumption is analogous to the equal-time assumption in the P-RAM models (all primitives require equal time). These equal-time assumptions greatly simplify the complexity analysis of algorithms, but on real machines only approximate the truth.

2.6.4 Do We Need the Scalar Memory?

When we introduced the V-RAM in Section 2.1, the machines had two memories and two processors, one for scalars and one for vectors. It turns out that the scalar memory and processor are not necessary: a vector model can be defined with just a vector memory and vector processor.

We can remove the scalar memory and processor as follows. To implement all the arithmetical and logical scalar operations, we can just use vectors of length one and use the vector arithmetic and logical operations. To implement a conditional-jump operation, instead of jumping on the value of a flag in the scalar memory, the machine might jump based on whether a vector is empty (of length 0) or not. Implementing indirect addressing is awkward without a scalar memory. In indirect addressing, the address argument must be a single integer value. We can use a vector argument and claim it is an error if the vector is not of length 1, but this restriction is awkward. As discussed in Section 10.2, indirect addressing is also a problem for other reasons and is not necessary if the model supplies stacks. We might, therefore, consider not including indirect addressing.

By not having a separate scalar memory and scalar processor, we only need one set of arithmetic and logical operations, thereby reducing the number of instructions necessary by almost a factor of two. An original version of this chapter actually defined the vector model with only the vector memory and processor. Adding scalar memory and processor, however, made the vector models easier to describe and understand.

2.7 Conclusion

In this chapter we introduced a class of models for the design, analysis and implementation of parallel applications and algorithms. I contend that these models, the parallel vector models, better separate the algorithmic issues from the architectural issues of parallel computing than do the other parallel models, including the P-RAM models, the boolean-circuit models, the hypercube models, and the grid models. The parallel vector models conceal from the algorithm designer architecture-dependent issues such as synchronization, processor allocation, and simulation of multiple elements on each processor.

This separation has some important benefits. First, it makes the models more durable. As architectures change, models that rely the least on the specifics of the architectures will best endure these changes. Second, it makes the models very good pedagogical tools. A student learning about parallel computing can concentrate on the algorithmic issues and the architectural issues separately. Third, it simplifies the description of algorithms. The algorithms do not require any machine specific description. Finally, it more cleanly separates the architectural and algorithmic research issues. The architectural issues, such as simulating multiple elements on each processor, can be solved independently from the algorithmic issues.

Chapter 3

The Scan Primitives

This chapter suggests that certain scan operations be included as "unit time" primitives in the parallel random access machine (P-RAM) models. The *scan operations* take a binary operator $\oplus$ with identity i, and an ordered set $[a_0, a_1, ..., a_{n-1}]$ of n elements, and returns the ordered set $[i, a_0, (a_0 \oplus a_1), ..., (a_0 \oplus a_1 \oplus ... \oplus a_{n-2})].$[1] In the P-RAM model, each element is placed in a processor, and the scan executes over a fixed order of the processors.[2] This chapter argues that certain scan operations can be implemented to execute as fast as memory references to a shared memory, can improve the asymptotic performance of many P-RAM algorithms by an $O(\lg n)$ factor, and can simplify the description of many P-RAM algorithms. Table 3.1 summarizes the uses of the scan operations and the example algorithms discussed in this chapter.

As well as introducing the scan operation, this chapter serves as motivation for the parallel vector models. In its course, this chapter will build a parallel vector model on top of the P-RAM model. It first presents a notation based on vectors. These vectors must be of fixed length, since one element is placed on each processor. It later argues that the programming environment should allow vectors of different lengths, including vectors with more elements than processors, since many elements can be placed on each processor, and a simulator can automatically loop over these elements without the programmer having to worry about it. This will leave us with the *scan-vector model*, which is formally defined in Chapter 4.

---

[1] Appendix A gives a short history of the scan operation.

[2] The prefix operation on a linked list (sometimes called the data dependent prefix operation [64]), and the fetch-and-op type instructions [50, 49] are not included.

Uses of Scan Primitives	Example Algorithms
Previous Maximum (3.3)	Line-of-Sight
Enumerating (3.4)	Splitting, Load Balancing
Copying (3.4)	Quicksort, Line Drawing
Distributing Sums (3.4)	Quicksort
Splitting (3.4.1)	Split Radix Sort, Quicksort
Segmented Primitives (3.5)	Quicksort, Line Drawing
Allocating (3.6)	Line Drawing, Halving Merge
Load-Balancing (3.7.1)	Halving Merge

Example Algorithms	Uses of Scan Primitives
Line-of-Sight (3.3)	Previous Maximum
Split Radix Sort (3.4.1)	Splitting
Quicksort (3.5.1)	Splitting, Distributing Sums, Copying, Segmented Primitives
Line Drawing (3.6.1)	Allocating, Copying, Segmented Primitives
Halving Merge (3.7.2)	Allocating, Load Balancing

Table 3.1: A cross reference of the various uses of scans introduced in this chapter with the example algorithms discussed in this chapter. All the uses can be executed in a constant number of steps.

3.1 Why Scan Primitives?

Algorithmic models typically supply a simple abstraction of a computing device and a set of primitive operations assumed to execute in a fixed "unit time". The assumption that primitives operate in unit time allows researchers to greatly simplify the analysis of algorithms, but is never strictly valid on real machines: primitives often execute in time dependent on machine and algorithm parameters. For example, in the serial random access machine (RAM) model [40], we assume that memory references take unit time, even though they must fan in and therefore take time that increases with the memory size. In spite of this inaccuracy in the model, the unit time assumption has taken us a long way in understanding serial algorithms.

In the parallel random access machine (P-RAM) models[3] [42, 101, 104, 48, 49], memory references are again assumed to take unit time. In these parallel models, this "unit time" is large since there is no practical hardware known that does better than deterministic $O(\lg^2 n)$, or probabilistic $O(\lg n)$, bit times for an arbitrary memory reference from n processors.[4] Since unit time is based on the time taken by a memory reference, one should ask if there are other useful primitives that could execute as fast.

We argue that certain scan operations are such primitives and that they should be included as a "unit time" operation in the P-RAM models. We call the exclusive-read exclusive-write (EREW) P-RAM model with the scan operations included as primitives, the scan model. The justifications for the scan model can be summarized as follows:

Architectural Justification: Both in theory and in practice, certain scan operations can execute in less time than references to a shared memory, and can be implemented with less hardware. Our arguments are summarized in Table 3.3 and are discussed in detail in Chapter 13.

Algorithmic Justification: The scan primitives improve the asymptotic running time of many algorithms by an $O(\lg n)$ factor over the EREW model and some by an $O(\lg n)$ factor over the CRCW model. Table 3.2 compares the asymptotic running times of many algorithms. Most of these scan algorithms are described in this chapter and in Chapters 6, 7 and 8.

Linguistic Justification: The scan primitives simplify the description of many algorithms. Since there are no concrete measures of simplicity, we unfortunately cannot illustrate a concise table to prove this point. Much of the remainder of this chapter supports this point through a series of illustrative examples.

---

[3]Appendix A contains a brief description of the P-RAM models.
[4]The AKS sorting network [5] takes $O(\lg n)$ time deterministically, but is not practical.

	Model		
Algorithm	EREW	CRCW	Scan
Graph Algorithms (n vertices, m edges, m processors)			
Minimum Spanning Tree	$\lg^2 n$	$\lg n$	$\lg n$
Connected Components	$\lg^2 n$	$\lg n$	$\lg n$
Maximum Flow	$n^2 \lg n$	$n^2 \lg n$	n^2
Maximal Independent Set	$\lg^2 n$	$\lg^2 n$	$\lg n$
Biconnected Components	$\lg^2 n$	$\lg n$	$\lg n$
Sorting and Merging (n keys, n processors)			
Sorting	$\lg n$	$\lg n$	$\lg n$
Merging	$\lg n$	$\lg \lg n$	$\lg \lg n$
Computational Geometry (n points, n processors)			
Convex Hull	$\lg^2 n$	$\lg n$	$\lg n$
Building a K-D Tree	$\lg^2 n$	$\lg^2 n$	$\lg n$
Closest Pair in the Plane	$\lg^2 n$	$\lg n \lg \lg n$	$\lg n$
Line of Sight	$\lg n$	$\lg n$	1
Matrix Manipulation ($n \times n$ matrix, n^2 processors)			
Matrix $\times$ Matrix	n	n	n
Vector $\times$ Matrix	$\lg n$	$\lg n$	1
Matrix Inversion	$n \lg n$	$n \lg n$	n

Table 3.2: Algorithmic Justification. The scan primitives improves the asymptotic running time of many algorithms by an $O(\lg n)$ factor over a EREW model and some by an $O(\lg n)$ factor over the CRCW model.

	Memory Reference	Scan Operation
Theoretical (VLSI models)		
Time	$O(\lg n)$ [67]	$O(\lg n)$ [68]
Area	$O(n^2/\lg n)$	$O(n)$
(Circuit models)		
Depth	$O(\lg n)$ [5]	$O(\lg n)$ [41]
Size	$O(n \lg n)$	$O(n)$
Actual (64K processor CM-2)		
Bit Cycles (Time)	600	550
Percent of Hardware Dedicated to Operation	30	0

Table 3.3: Architectural Justification. Both in theory and in practice certain scan operations can execute in less time than references to a shared memory, and can be implemented with less hardware.

Since the term *unit time* is misleading—both memory references and scan operations take many clock cycles on a real machine—this book henceforth uses the term *program step* or *step* instead. A step is a call to one of the primitive instructions of the model. The number of program steps taken by an algorithm is the *step complexity*.

3.2 Notation

Before discussing the uses of the scan primitives, we introduce some conventions that will simplify the descriptions of algorithms.

We will assume that the data used by the algorithms in this chapter is stored in vectors (one dimensional arrays) in the shared memory and that each processor is assigned to one element of the vector. When executing an operation, the ith processor operates on the ith element of a vector. For example, in the operation:

$$
\begin{array}{llllllllll}
\text{A} & = & [5 & 1 & 3 & 4 & 3 & 9 & 2 & 6] \\
\text{B} & = & [2 & 5 & 3 & 8 & 1 & 3 & 6 & 2] \\
\text{C} \leftarrow \text{A} + \text{B} & = & [7 & 6 & 6 & 12 & 4 & 12 & 8 & 8]
\end{array}
$$

each processor reads its respective value from the vectors A and B, sums the values, and writes the result into the destination vector C. For now, we assume that the P-RAM always has as many processors as vector elements.

The *scan* primitives can be used to scan the elements of a vector. For example:

$$A \qquad\qquad\qquad = \quad [2 \quad 1 \quad 2 \quad 3 \quad 5 \quad 8 \quad 13 \quad 21]$$
$$C \leftarrow \texttt{+-scan}(A) \quad = \quad [0 \quad 2 \quad 3 \quad 5 \quad 8 \quad 13 \quad 21 \quad 34]$$

In this book we only use five primitive scan operations: `or-scan`, `and-scan`, `max-scan`, `min-scan` and `+-scan`. We also use *backward* versions of each of these scans operations—versions that scan from the last element to the first.

To reorder the elements of a vector, we use the `permute` operation. The `permute` operation, in the form `permute`(A, I), permutes the elements of A to the positions specified by the indices of I. All indices of I must be unique. For example:

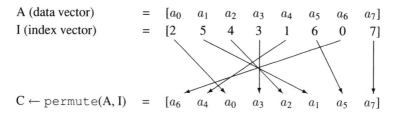

$$\begin{aligned}
&\text{A (data vector)} &&= \quad [a_0 \quad a_1 \quad a_2 \quad a_3 \quad a_4 \quad a_5 \quad a_6 \quad a_7] \\
&\text{I (index vector)} &&= \quad [2 \quad 5 \quad 4 \quad 3 \quad 1 \quad 6 \quad 0 \quad 7] \\
&C \leftarrow \texttt{permute}(A, I) &&= \quad [a_6 \quad a_4 \quad a_0 \quad a_3 \quad a_2 \quad a_1 \quad a_5 \quad a_7]
\end{aligned}$$

To implement the `permute` operation on a EREW P-RAM, each processor reads its respective *value* and *index*, and writes the *value* into the *index* position of the destination vector.

3.3   Example: Line-of-Sight

As an example of the direct use of a scan operation, we consider a simple line-of-sight problem. In the line-of-sight problem, we are given a terrain map in the form of a grid of altitudes and an observation point X on the grid (see Figure 3.1). We want to find which points are visible along a ray originating at the observation point.

A point on a ray is only visible if no other point between it and the observation point has a greater vertical angle. To find if any previous point has a greater angle, the altitude of each point along the ray is placed in a vector (the *altitude vector*). These altitudes are then converted to angles and placed in the *angle vector* (see Figure 3.1). A `max-scan` is then executed on the *angle vector*, which returns to each point the maximum previous angle. To test for visibility each point only needs to compare its angle to the result of the `max-scan`. Section 6.6 generalizes this problem to finding all visible points on the grid.

This solution has a step complexity (number of program steps) of $O(1)$.

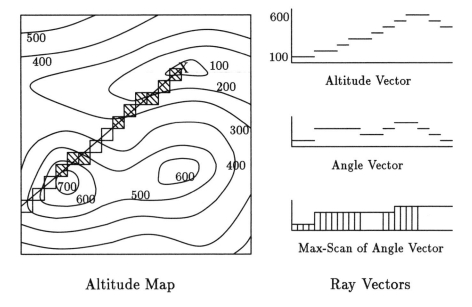

Figure 3.1: The line-of-sight problem for a single ray. The X marks the observation point. The visible points are shaded. A point on the ray is visible if no previous point has a greater angle. The angle is calculated as arctan(altitude/distance).

Flag	=	[T	F	F	T	F	T	T	F]
enumerate(Flag)	=	[0	1	1	1	2	2	3	4]

A	=	[5	1	3	4	3	9	2	6]
copy(A)	=	[5	5	5	5	5	5	5	5]

B	=	[1	1	2	1	1	2	1	1]
+-distribute(B)	=	[10	10	10	10	10	10	10	10]

Figure 3.2:   The enumerate, copy, and +-distribute operations.   The enumerate numbers the flagged elements of a vector, the copy copies the first element across a vector, and the +-distribute sums the elements of a vector.

3.4   Simple Operations

We now consider three simple operations that are based on the scan primitives: enumerating, copying and distributing sums (see Figure 3.2). These operations are used extensively as part of the algorithms we discuss in this chapter and all have an step complexity of $O(1)$.

Enumerating: Return the integer i to the ith true element. This operation is implemented by converting the flags to 0 or 1 and executing a +-scan. We call this the enumerate operation.

Copying: Copy the first element over all elements. This operation is implemented by placing the identity element in all but the first element of a vector and executing a scan.[5] Since the scan is not inclusive, we must put the first element back after executing the scan. The copy operation is useful for distributing information across a vector and often removes the need for a concurrent-read capability.

Distributing Sums: Return to each element the sum of all the elements. This operation is implemented using a +-scan, a vector add, and a backward copy. We call this a +-distribute. We can likewise define a max-distribute, min-distribute, or-distribute and and-distribute. Distributing sums is useful for collecting information from a vector and, as we will see, often removes the need for a concurrent-write capability.

---

[5]One might think of defining a binary associative operator first which returns the first of its two arguments, and use it to execute the copy operation. The problem is that the first operator does not have an identity—a requirement for our definition of a scan.

```
define split-radix-sort(A, number-of-bits){
    for i from 0 to (number-of-bits − 1)
        A ← split(A, A⟨i⟩)}
```

A		=	[5	7	3	1	4	2	7	2]
A⟨0⟩		=	[T	T	T	T	F	F	T	F]
A ← split(A, A⟨0⟩)		=	[4	2	2	5	7	3	1	7]
A⟨1⟩		=	[F	T	T	F	T	T	F	T]
A ← split(A, A⟨1⟩)		=	[4	5	1	2	2	7	3	7]
A⟨2⟩		=	[T	T	F	F	F	T	F	T]
A ← split(A, A⟨2⟩)		=	[1	2	2	3	4	5	7	7]

Figure 3.3: An example of the split radix sort on a vector containing three bit values. The A⟨n⟩ notation signifies extracting the nth bit of each element of the vector A and converting it to a boolean value (T for 1, F for 0).

3.4.1 Example: Split Radix Sort

To illustrate the use of the scans for enumerating, consider a simple radix sorting algorithm. The algorithm is a parallel version of the standard serial radix sort [63].

The algorithm loops over the bits of the keys, starting at the lowest bit, executing a split operation on each iteration. The split operation packs the keys with a 0 in the corresponding bit to the bottom of a vector, and packs the keys with a 1 in the bit to the top of the same vector. It maintains the order within both groups. The sort works because each split operation sorts the keys with respect to the current bit (0 down, 1 up) and maintains the sorted order of all the lower bits—remember that we iterate from the bottom bit up. Figure 3.3 shows an example of the sort along with code to implement it.

We now consider how the split operation can be implemented in the scan model. The basic idea is to determine a new index for each element and permute the elements to these new indices. To determine the new indices for elements with a 0 (F) in the bit, we enumerate these elements as described in the last section. To determine the new indices of elements with a 1 (T) in the bit, we enumerate the elements starting at the top of the vector and subtract these from the length of the vector. Figure 3.4 shows an example of the split operation along with code to implement it.

The split operation has a step complexity of $O(1)$; so for d-bit keys, the split radix sort has a step complexity of $O(d)$. If we assume for n keys that the keys are $O(\lg n)$ bits

```
define split(A, Flags){
        I-down ← enumerate(not(Flags));
        I-up ← n − back-enumerate(Flags) − 1;
        Index ← if Flags then I-up else I-down;
    permute(A, Index)}
```

A	=	[5	7	3	1	4	2	7	2]
Flags	=	[T	T	T	T	F	F	T	F]
I-down	=	[0	0	0	0	$\boxed{0}$	$\boxed{1}$	2	$\boxed{2}$]
I-up	=	[$\boxed{3}$	$\boxed{4}$	$\boxed{5}$	$\boxed{6}$	6	6	$\boxed{7}$	7]
Index	=	[3	4	5	6	0	1	7	2]
permute(A, Index)	=	[4	2	2	5	7	3	1	7]

Figure 3.4: The split operation packs the elements with an F in the corresponding flag position to the bottom of a vector, and packs the elements with a T to the top of the same vector.

long, a common assumption in models of computation [111], then the algorithm has a step complexity of $O(\lg n)$. Although $O(\lg n)$ is the same asymptotic complexity as existing EREW and CRCW algorithms [5, 34], the algorithm is much simpler and has a significantly smaller constant. Note that since integers, characters, and floating-point numbers can all be sorted with a radix sort, a radix sort suffices for almost all sorting of fixed-length keys required in practice.

The split radix sort is fast in the scan model, but is it fast in practice? After all, our architectural justification claimed that the scan primitives bring the P-RAM models closer to reality. Table 3.4 compares implementations of the split radix sort and Batcher's bitonic sort [11] on the Connection Machine. We choose the bitonic sort for comparison because it is commonly cited as the most practical parallel sorting algorithm. I have also looked into implementing Cole's merge sort [34], which is optimal on the P-RAM models, on the Connection Machine. Based on predicted measures, it was determined that it would be at least a factor of 4, and possibly a factor of 10, slower than the other two sorts. The split radix sort is the sort currently supported by the parallel instruction set of the Connection Machine [113].

	Split Radix Sort	Bitonic Sort
Theoretical (Bit Serial Circuit) Bit Time	$O(d \lg n)$	$O(d + \lg^2 n)$
Actual (64K processor CM-1) Bit cycles (sorting 16 bits)	20,000	19,000

Table 3.4: Comparison of the times taken by the split radix sort and the bitonic sort (n keys each with d bits). The constants in the theoretical times are very small for both algorithms. On the Connection Machine, the bitonic sort is implemented in microcode whereas the split radix sort is implemented in macrocode, giving the bitonic sort an edge.

A	=	[5	1	3	4	3	9	2	6]
Sb	=	[T	F	T	F	F	F	T	F]
seg-+-scan(A, Sb)	=	[0	5	0	3	7	10	0	2]
seg-max-scan(A, Sb)	=	[0	5	0	3	4	4	0	2]

Figure 3.5: The segmented scan operations restart at the beginning of each segment. The vector Sb contains flags that mark the beginning of the segments.

3.5   Segments and Segmented Scans

In many algorithms it is useful to break the linear ordering of the processors into segments and have a scan operation start again at the beginning of each segment; we call such scan operations, *segmented scans*. Segmented scans take two arguments: a set of values and a set of segment flags. Each flag in the segment flags specifies the start of a new segment (see Figure 3.5). Segmented scans were first suggested by Schwartz [101]. This book greatly extends the ideas of segments; Section 4.3 discusses how segments are useful for other operations, and Chapter 10 proves a general theorem based on segments.

The segmented scan operations are useful because they allow algorithms to execute the scans independently over the elements of many sets. A graph, for example, can be represented using a segment for each vertex and an element position within a segment for each edge of the vertex. Using this representation, the segmented scans can be used to find the minimum edge of each vertex or to number the edges of each vertex. This graph representation is discussed in more detail in Section 5.1, and algorithms based on it are

Key	=	[24.6	48.1	5.8	3.1	37.8	9.5	48.1	5.8]
Segment-Flags	=	[T	F	F	F	F	F	F	F]
Pivots	=	[24.6	24.6	24.6	24.6	24.6	24.6	24.6	24.6]
F	=	[=	>	<	<	>	<	>	<]
Key ← split(Key, F)	=	[5.8	3.1	9.5	5.8	24.6	48.1	37.8	48.1]
Segment-Flags	=	[T	F	F	F	T	T	F	F]
Pivots	=	[5.8	5.8	5.8	5.8	24.6	48.1	48.1	48.1]
F	=	[=	<	>	=	=	=	<	=]
Key ← split(Key, F)	=	[3.1	5.8	5.8	9.5	24.6	37.8	48.1	48.1]
Segment-Flags	=	[T	T	F	T	T	T	T	F]

Figure 3.6: Parallel quicksort. On each step, within each segment, we distribute the pivot, test whether each element is equal-to, less-than or greater-than the pivot, split into three groups, and generate a new set of segment flags.

discussed in Chapter 7.

It turns out that the segmented scan operations can all be implemented with at most two calls to the unsegmented versions (see Section B.2.3). They can also be implemented directly as described by Schwartz [101] and in more detail in Section 13.2.1.

3.5.1 Example: Quicksort

To illustrate the use of segments, we consider an example: a parallel version of Quicksort. Similar to the standard serial version [56], the parallel version picks one of the keys as a pivot value, splits the keys into three sets—keys lesser, equal and greater than the pivot— and recurses on each set.[6] The algorithm has an expected step complexity of $O(\lg n)$.

The basic intuition of the parallel version is to keep each subset in its own segment, and to pick pivot values and split the keys independently within each segment. The steps required by the sort are outlined as follows:

1. Check if the keys are sorted and exit the routine if they are.

   Each processor checks to see if the previous processor has a lesser or equal value. We execute an `and-distribute` (Section 3.4) on the result of the check so that each processor knows whether all other processors are in order.

---

[6]We do not need to recursively sort the keys equal to the pivot, but the algorithm as described below does. We later discuss how we can remove sets which are already sorted—such as the equal elements.

2. Within each segment, pick a pivot and distribute it to the others elements.

   If we pick the first element as a pivot, we can use a segmented version of the `copy` (Section 3.4) operation implemented based on a segmented `max-scan`. The algorithm could also pick a random element by generating a random number (less than the length) in the first element of each segment and picking out the element with a `copy` of the number, a test and a backwards `max-scan`.

3. Within each segment, compare each element with the pivot and split based on the result of the comparison.

   For the split, we can use a version of the `split` operation described in Section 3.4.1 which splits into three sets instead of two, and which is segmented. To implement such a segmented `split`, we can use a segmented versions of the `enumerate` operation (Section 3.4) to number relative to the beginning of each segment. We can use a segmented version of the `copy` operation to copy the offset of the beginning of each segment across the segment. We then add the offset to the numbers relative to beginning of the segment to generate actual indices to which we permute each element.

4. Within each segment, insert additional segment flags to separate the split values.

   Each element can determine if its at the beginning of the segment by looking at the previous element.

5. Return to step 1.

Each iteration of this sort requires a constant number of calls to the primitives. If we select pivots randomly within each segment, quicksort is expected to complete in $O(\lg n)$ iterations, and therefore has an expected step complexity of $O(\lg n)$. This version of quicksort has been implemented on the Connection Machine and executes in about twice the time as the split radix sort.

The technique of recursively breaking segments into subsegments and operating independently within each segment can be used for many other divide-and-conquer algorithms. The quickhull algorithm described in Section 6.4, and a binary-search routine described in Section 6.1 both use the technique.

3.5.2 Notes on Segments

Although the quicksort algorithm we described is works fine, by building some general-purpose mechanisms, the algorithm can be made simpler, cleaner and more model independent. We mention some such mechanisms here, and later chapters will describe

```
define quicksort(A){
    if A is not sorted
    then
            pivot ← A[0];
            lesser-elements ← quicksort(select A less than pivot);
            equal-elements ← select A equal to pivot;
            greater-elements ← quicksort(select A greater than pivot);
        append(lesser-elements, equal-elements, greater-elements)
    else A}
```

Figure 3.7: A recursive definition of quicksort. Ideally, we could use this definition and it would compile into the segmented code described earlier.

them in detail. The issues discussed here are particularly important when designing and implementing algorithms that are more complicated than the quicksort.

We mention four simplifications. First, programmer's job, could be greatly simplified with a translator that took an unsegmented version of an operator and automatically generated the segmented version. Second, the programmer's job could again be simplified if the segment flags could somehow be hidden. Manipulating segment flags is difficult and can lead to bugs that are hard to find. Third, the definition of quicksort could be made much simpler and more model independent if the quicksort could be defined in a high-level recursive form such as shown in Figure 3.7 and automatically translated into the iterative form described above, or at least a form which has the same complexity. Finally, the performance of the algorithm could be improved if segments are dropped out when they are completed. This optimization is useful when there are more keys than processors.

In Chapter 9 we discuss a compiler for PARALATION LISP [96] which translates a recursive definition of quicksort similar to that shown in Figure 3.7 into a form similar to the iterative version described in the previous section, with the optimization of dropping out sorted segments. All the operations necessary to implement the sort are defined unsegmented and the programmer never has to see a segment flag.

3.6 Allocating Elements

This section illustrates another use of the scan operations. Consider the problem of given a set of processors each with an integer, allocating that integer number of new processors to each initial processor. Such allocation is necessary in the parallel line-drawing routine

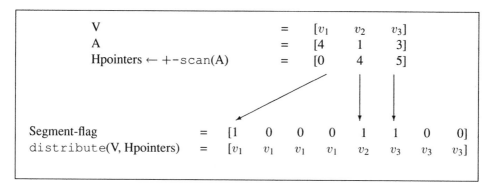

Figure 3.8: Processor Allocation. The vector A specifies how many new elements each position needs. We can allocate a segment to each position by applying a $+$-scan to A and using the result as pointers to the beginning of each segment. We can then distribute the values of V to the new elements with a permute to the beginning of the segment and a segmented copy across the segment.

described in Section 3.6.1. In the line-drawing routine, each line calculates the number of pixels in the line and dynamically allocates a processor for each pixel. Allocating new elements is also useful for the branching part of many branch-and-bound algorithms. Consider, for example, a brute force chess-playing algorithm that executes a fixed-depth search of possible moves to determine the best next move.[7] We can execute the algorithms in parallel by placing each possible move in a separate processor. Since the algorithm dynamically decides how many next moves to generate, depending on the position, we need to dynamically allocate new elements. In Section 3.7.1 we discuss the bounding part of branch-and-bound algorithms.

Defined more formally, allocation is the task of, given a vector of integers A with elements a_i and length l, creating a new vector B of length:

$$L = \sum_{i=0}^{l-1} a_i \tag{3.1}$$

with a_i elements of B assigned to each position i of A. By assigned to, we mean that there must be some method for distributing a value at position i of a vector to the a_i elements which are assigned to that position. Since there is a one-to-one correspondence between elements of a vector and processors, the original vector requires l processors and the new

---

[7]This is how many chess playing algorithms work [16]. The search is called an *minimax* search since it alternates moves between the two players, trying to minimize the benefit of one player and maximize the benefit of the other.

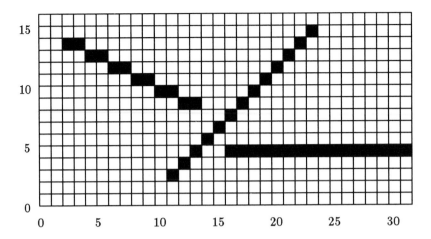

Figure 3.9: The pixels generated by a line drawing routine. In this example the endpoints are (11, 2)–(23, 14), (2, 13)–(13,8), and (16, 4)–(31, 4). The algorithm allocates 12, 11 and 16 pixels respectively for the three lines.

vector requires L processors. Typically, an algorithm does not operate on the two vectors at the same time, so the processors can overlap.

Allocation can be implemented by assigning a contiguous segment of elements to each position i of A. To allocate segments we execute a +-scan on the vector A returning a pointer to the start of each segment (see Figure 3.8). We can then generate the appropriate segment flags by permuting a flag to the index specified by the pointer. To distribute values from each position i to its segment, we permute the values to the beginning of the segments and use a segmented copy operation to copy the values across the segment. Allocation and distribution each require a small constant number of calls to the primitives of the scan model.

Allocation requires $O(\lg n)$ time on a EREW P-RAM and $O(\lg n / \lg \lg n)$ time on a CREW P-RAM based on the prefix sum routine of Cole and Vishkin [36].

3.6.1   Example: Line Drawing

As a concrete example of how allocation is used, consider line drawing. Line drawing is the problem of: given a set of pairs of points (each point is an (x, y) pair), generate all the locations of pixels that lie between one of the pairs of points. Figure 3.9 illustrates an example. The routine we discuss returns a vector of (x, y) pairs that specify the position of each pixel along the line. It generates the same set of pixels as generated by the simple digital differential analyzer (DDA) serial technique [79].

The basic idea of the routine is for each line to allocate a processor for each pixel in the line, and then for each allocated pixel to determine in parallel its final position in the grid. To allocate a processor for each pixel, each line must first determine the number of pixels in the line. This number can be calculated by taking the maximum of the x and y differences of the line's endpoints. Each line now allocates a segment of processors for its pixels, and distributes its endpoints across the segment as described earlier. We now have one processor for each pixel and one segment for each line. We can view the position of a processor in its segment as the position of a pixel in its line. Based on the endpoints of the line and the position in the line (determined with a +-scan), each pixel can determine its final (x, y) location in the grid. Since lines can overlap, some pixels might appear in more than one segment. To actually place the points on a grid, we would need to permute a flag to a position based on the location of the point. In general, this will require the simplest form of concurrent-write (one of the values gets written) since a pixel might appear in more than one line.

This routine has a step complexity of $O(1)$ and requires as many processors as pixels in the lines. The routine has been implemented on the Connection Machine, has been extended to render solid objects by Salem, and is part of a rendering package for the Connection Machine [97].

3.6.2 Notes on Allocating

When an algorithm allocates processors, the number of processors required is usually determined dynamically and will depend on the data. To account for this, we must do one of three things: assume an infinite number of processors, put a bound on the number of elements that can be allocated, or start simulating multiple elements on each processor. The first is not practical, and the second restricting. Section 3.7 discusses the third.

3.7 Long Vectors and Load Balancing

Up to now we have assumed that a P-RAM always has as many processors as elements in our data vectors. In this section we remove this assumption and discuss assigning multiple data elements to each processor. We also discuss how scans can be used for load balancing—keeping the number of elements assigned to each processor balanced.

Simulating multiple elements on each processor is important for two reasons. First, from a practical point of view, real machines have a fixed number of processors but problem sizes vary: we would rather not restrict ourselves to fixed, and perhaps small, sized problems. Second, from both a practical and theoretical point of view, by placing

	Processors	Steps	Processor-Step
Halving Merge	$O(n)$	$O(\lg n)$	$O(n \lg n)$
	$O(n/\lg n)$	$O(\lg n)$	$O(n)$
List Ranking [35]	$O(n)$	$O(\lg n)$	$O(n \lg n)$
	$O(n/\lg n)$	$O(\lg n)$	$O(n)$
Tree Contraction [45]	$O(n)$	$O(\lg n)$	$O(n \lg n)$
	$O(n/\lg n)$	$O(\lg n)$	$O(n)$

Table 3.5:   The processor-step complexity of many algorithms can be reduced by using fewer processors and assigning many elements to each processor.

multiple elements on each processor we can often greatly reduce the number of processors needed by an algorithm, without greatly increasing the step complexity. This makes more efficient use of the processors. Table 3.5 illustrates some examples of such algorithms. Reducing the number of processors is important because processors are likely to have a cost associated with them: we either need a larger machine or need to use processors that someone else could be using. This idea of getting better processor utilization by placing multiple elements in each processor dates back at least to [44].

To operate on vectors with more data elements than P-RAM processors—henceforth called *long vectors*—each processor is assigned to a contiguous block of elements (see Figure 3.10). To execute an arithmetic operation or the `permute` operation on a long vector, each processor loops over the element positions for which it is responsible and executes the operation. To execute a scan operation across all the elements, each processor first sums[8] the elements it is assigned to (see Figure 3.10). Using the results, we execute a single `scan` across the processors. Finally, using the result of the single scan as an offset, each processor scans the elements it is assigned to.

With p processors, all the vector operations can, therefore, be executed on vectors of length n in

$$\lceil n/p \rceil \tag{3.2}$$

steps.

---

[8]Here sum means with respect to the scan operator $\oplus$.

$$[4 \quad 7 \quad 1 \quad 0 \quad 5 \quad 2 \quad 6 \quad 4 \quad 8 \quad 1 \quad 9 \quad 5]$$

processor 0   processor 1   processor 2   processor 3

| Sum | | = | [12 | 7 | 18 | 15] |
| +-scan(Sum) | | = | [0 | 12 | 19 | 37] |

$$[0 \quad 4 \quad 11 \quad 12 \quad 12 \quad 17 \quad 19 \quad 25 \quad 29 \quad 37 \quad 38 \quad 47]$$

processor 0   processor 1   processor 2   processor 3

Figure 3.10: When operating on *long vectors*, each processor is assigned to a contiguous block of elements. To execute a scan, we sum within processors, execute a scan across processors, and use the result as an offset to scan within processors.

3.7.1 Load Balancing

We now turn to the problem of *load balancing* the number of elements assigned to each processor. Load balancing is required in algorithms in which data elements drop out during the execution of a routine. There are three common reasons why elements might drop out. First, some elements might have completed their desired calculations. For example, in the quicksort algorithm described in Section 3.5.1, segments which are already sorted might drop out. Second, the algorithm might be subselecting elements. Subselection is used in the halving merge algorithm discussed in Section 3.7.2. Third, an algorithm might be pruning some sort of search. Pruning might be used in the bounding part of branch-and-bound algorithms such as the chess-playing algorithm we mentioned in Section 3.6. In all three cases, when the elements drop out, the number of elements left on each processor might be unbalanced.

When elements drop out, we can reduce the maximum number of elements a processor is responsible for by balancing the remaining elements across the processors; we call such balancing, load balancing. For m remaining elements, load balancing can be implemented by enumerating the remaining elements, permuting them into a vector of length m, and assigning each processor to m/p elements of the new vector (see Figure 3.11). We call the operation of packing elements into a smaller vector, the pack operation. Once a vector is packed, a processor can determine how many and which elements it is responsible for simply by knowing its processor number and m; m can be distributed to all the processors with a +-distribute.

$$F = [T \quad F \quad F \quad F \quad T \quad T \quad F \quad T \quad T \quad T \quad T \quad T]$$

$$A = [a_0 \quad a_1 \quad a_2 \quad a_3 \quad a_4 \quad a_5 \quad a_6 \quad a_7 \quad a_8 \quad a_9 \quad a_{10} \quad a_{11}]$$

$$\underbrace{\qquad\qquad}_{\text{processor } 0} \quad \underbrace{\qquad\qquad}_{\text{processor } 1} \quad \underbrace{\qquad\qquad}_{\text{processor } 2} \quad \underbrace{\qquad\qquad}_{\text{processor } 3}$$

$$A = [a_0 \quad a_4 \quad a_5 \quad a_7 \quad a_8 \quad a_9 \quad a_{10} \quad a_{11}]$$

$$\underbrace{\qquad}_{\text{proc } 0} \quad \underbrace{\qquad}_{\text{proc } 1} \quad \underbrace{\qquad}_{\text{proc } 2} \quad \underbrace{\qquad}_{\text{proc } 3}$$

Figure 3.11: Load Balancing. In load balancing, certain marked elements are dropped and the remaining elements need to be balanced across the processors. Load balancing can be executed by packing the remaining elements into a smaller vector using an `enumerate` and a `permute`, and assigning each processor to a smaller block.

3.7.2   Example: Halving Merge

To illustrate the importance of simulating multiple elements on each processor and load balancing, this section describes an algorithm for merging two sorted vectors. We call the algorithm, the *halving merge*. When applied to vectors of length n and m ($n \geq m$) on the scan model with p processors, the halving merge algorithm has an step complexity of $O(n/p + \lg n)$. When the $p < n/\lg n$, the algorithm is optimal. The merging algorithm of Shiloach and Vishkin for the CRCW P-RAM model [44, 104] has the same complexity but is quite different. Their algorithm is not recursive. Although the split radix sort and the quicksort algorithms are variations of well-known algorithms translated to a new model, the merging algorithm described here is original.

The basic idea of the algorithm is to extract the odd-indexed elements from each of the two vectors by packing them into smaller vectors, to recursively merge the half-length vectors, and then to use the result of the halving merge to determine the positions of the even-indexed elements. The number of elements halves on each recursive call, and the recursion completes when one of the merge vectors contains a single element. We call the operation of taking the result of the recursive merge on the odd-indexed elements and using it to determine the position of the even-indexed elements, *even-insertion*. We first analyze the complexity of the halving merge assuming that the even-insertion requires a constant number of scan and permute operations, and then discuss the algorithm in more detail.

The complexity of the algorithm is calculated as follows. Since the number of elements halves at each level, there are at most $\lg n$ levels and at level i, $n/2^i$ elements must be merged. With p processors, if we load balance, the most elements any processor is

$$
\begin{aligned}
A &= [1 \quad 7 \quad 10 \quad 13 \quad 15 \quad 20] \\
B &= [3 \quad 4 \quad 9 \quad 22 \quad 23 \quad 26]
\end{aligned}
$$

$$
\begin{aligned}
A' &= [1 \quad 10 \quad 15] \\
B' &= [3 \quad 9 \quad 23]
\end{aligned}
$$

$$
\text{merge}(A', B') = [1 \quad 3 \quad 9 \quad 10 \quad 15 \quad 23]
$$

$$
\text{near-merge} = [1 \quad \boxed{7 \quad 3 \quad 4} \quad 9 \quad \boxed{22 \quad 10 \quad 13 \quad 15 \quad 20} \quad 23 \quad 26]
$$

$$
\text{result} = [1 \quad 3 \quad 4 \quad 7 \quad 9 \quad 10 \quad 13 \quad 15 \quad 20 \quad 22 \quad 23 \quad 26]
$$

Figure 3.12: The halving merge involves selecting the odd-indexed elements of each vector to be merged, recursively merging these elements and then using the result to merge the even-indexed elements (even-insertion). To execute the even-insertion, we place the even-indexed elements in the merged odd-indexed elements after their original predecessor. This vector, the *near-merge* vector, is almost sorted. As shown in the figure, nonoverlapping blocks might need to be rotated: the first element moved to the end.

responsible for is

$$
\lceil n/2^i p \rceil . \tag{3.3}
$$

If the even-insertion requires a constant number of calls to the primitives per element, level i has a step complexity of

$$
O(\lceil n/2^i p \rceil) . \tag{3.4}
$$

The total step complexity is therefore

$$
O\left(\sum_{i=0}^{\lg n - 1} \left\lceil \frac{n}{2^i p} \right\rceil \right) = O\left(\sum_{i=0}^{\lg n - 1} \left(\frac{n}{2^i p} + 1 \right) \right)
$$
$$
= O\left(n/p + \lg n \right) . \tag{3.5}
$$

The merging algorithm of Shiloach and Vishkin for the CRCW P-RAM model [44, 104] has the same complexity but is quite different. Their algorithm is not recursive. When $p \leq n/\lg n$ both algorithms have an asymptotically optimal processor-step complexity— $O(n)$.

We now discuss the algorithm in more detail. Picking every other element before calling the algorithm recursively can be implemented by marking the odd-indexed elements and packing them (load balancing them).

After the recursive call returns, the even-insertion is executed as follows. We expand the merged odd-indexed vector by a factor of two by placing each unmerged even-indexed element directly after the element it originally followed (see Figure 3.12). We call this vector the *near-merge* vector. The *near-merge* vector has an interesting property: elements can only be out of order by single nonoverlapping rotations. An element might appear before a block of elements it belongs after. We call such an element a block-head. A near-merge vector can be converted into a true merged vector by moving the block-head to the end of the block and sliding the other elements down by one: rotating the block by one. The rotation of the blocks can be implemented with two scans and two arithmetic operations:

> define fix-near-merge(near-merge){
>   head-copy ← max(max-scan(near-merge), near-merge)
>   result ← min(min-backscan(near-merge), head-copy)}

The even-insertion therefore requires a constant number of calls to the vector operations.

To place the even-indexed elements following the odd-indexed elements after returning from the recursive call, we must somehow know the original position of each merged odd-indexed element. To specify these positions, the merge routine could instead of returning the actual merged values, return a vector of flags: each F flag represents an element of A and each T flag represents an element of B. For example:

$$
\begin{array}{rcl}
A' & = & [1 \quad 10 \quad 15] \\
B' & = & [3 \quad 9 \quad 23]
\end{array}
$$

$$
\text{halving-merge}(A', B') \quad = \quad [F \quad T \quad T \quad F \quad F \quad T]
$$

which corresponds to the merged values:

$$
[1 \quad 3 \quad 9 \quad 10 \quad 15 \quad 23]
$$

The vector of flags—henceforth the *merge-flag* vector—both uniquely specifies how the elements should be merged and specifies in which position each element belongs.

3.7.3 Notes on Simulating Long Vectors

Simulating multiple elements on each processor can be a major inconvenience to the programmer. The programmer needs to worry about keeping track of how many elements are assigned to each processor, about reassigning the processors after load balancing, about looping over the elements when executing an arithmetic operation or a permutation, and about executing the scan operations as described in Section 3.7. It would be very convenient if the simulation could be hidden. One way to do this is to always operate on vectors, and have a simulator automatically execute the looping when the vectors are longer than the number of processors. The time complexity of an operation on a vector of length n is simply $\lceil n/p \rceil$.

This simulation can also simplify complexity analysis. We can define two complexities based on the vector operations, the first we call s and is the number of operations on a vector, the second we call e and is the sum over the vector lengths during the algorithm execution. For example, for the halving merge algorithm

$$s = O(\lg n)$$

and

$$e = O(n + n/2 + n/4 \cdots) = O(n) \,.$$

In Section 12.2, based on Brent's scheduling principle [28], we show that given these two complexities, the complexity on a P-RAM is:

$$O(e/p + s) \tag{3.6}$$

giving the desired $O(n/p + \lg n)$ for the halving merge. Determining the complexities s and e and using equation 3.6 is easier than doing the analysis given in equations 3.3–3.5.

Yes, we have just reinvented the parallel vector models!!

Chapter 4

The Scan Vector Model

This chapter brings together the contributions of the previous two chapters: the parallel vector models and the scan primitives. It formally defines the *scan vector model* in terms of a set of primitive instructions. The primitive instructions are broken into three classes: scalar, vector and vector-scalar instructions. The vector instructions are further broken into three subclasses: elementwise, scan, and permutation instructions. The scan vector model is introduced both to illustrate a concrete example of a parallel vector model and because its particular primitives are very useful for a wide variety of algorithms and are practical to implement.

As well as defining the scan vector model, this chapter describes a set of vector operations that can be implemented with the primitive instructions of the scan vector model, such as a `pack` operation and an `append` operation (Section 4.2); a set of segmented versions of the primitive instructions, such as a segmented `permute` instruction and segmented `scan` instructions (Section 4.3); and discusses a set of other primitive instructions which are not included in the scan vector model, but might be included in other parallel vector models, such as a `merge` instruction and a set of `combine` instructions (Section 4.5).

4.1 The Scan Vector Instruction Set

This section defines a set of vector primitives. These primitives can be thought of as defining the instruction set of an abstract machine—a scan vector machine. The described instruction set is complete and is sufficient to implement all the algorithms discussed in this book. The particular instruction set was chosen for several reasons. It is small, making it easy to define, implement and understand; it can be implemented on a wide variety of architectures; it is useful for a wide variety of algorithms; and its instructions require

59

Scalar Instructions:

    Arithmetic and Logical Instructions:
        `+, -, and, or, = , <, ...`
    Conditional Instruction:
        `cond-jump`
    Indirect-Access Instructions:
        `move-scalar, move-vector`

Vector Instructions:

    Elementwise Instructions:
        `p+, p-, p-and, p-or, p= , p<, p-select, ...`
    Permutation Instructions:
        `permute, select-permute`
    Scan Instructions:
        `+-scan, max-scan, min-scan, or-scan, and-scan`

Vector-Scalar Instructions:

    `insert, extract, distribute, length`

Figure 4.1: The scan vector instruction set. Input and output instructions are not included because, for the purposes of the book, we consider a scan vector machine as self contained.

approximately equal time on equal-length vectors. All the instructions of the scan vector model have been implemented on the Connection Machine (see Chapter 12).

Figure 4.1 summarizes the instructions of the scan vector model. The instructions are categorized based on which processor of a V-RAM they use—the scalar or the vector processor. Before describing the instructions, we discuss two general issues about the instructions, types and addressing.

So far this book has mentioned nothing about the types of values that can be placed in each element of a vector. To understand why types are important, consider the following questions. Does the operation `p+`, which pairwise adds the elements of two equal-length vectors, add integer values or floating-point values? Can it add integer values in some locations and floating-point values in others? In the scan vector model every instruction assumes that the elements of a vector are all of the same type—we say that the vectors are *homogeneous*—and the instruction set includes two versions of the arithmetic instructions, one for integer values and one for floating-point values.

The book has also mentioned nothing about the types of addressing available to the instruction of a parallel vector machine. In the scan vector model, all but two of the instructions require fixed, absolute addresses. The two exceptions are two move instructions that use indirect-addressing based on addresses in the scalar memory to move a vector or a scalar. The instructions that allow indirect addressing are separated out because indirect addressing presents a problem when trying to prove the replicating theorem in Chapter 10. By only allowing two instructions to use indirect addressing, we can localize this problem.

In many cases it is possible to replace a subset of the instructions with another set of instructions which are equivalent—we will discuss some interesting cases where this is possible.

4.1.1 Scalar Instructions

The scalar instructions are basically the instructions of a standard serial RAM. They include a set of arithmetic and logical operations, a conditional-jump instruction, and the two indirect-addressing instructions. The conditional-jump instruction, cond-jump, jumps to a new location in the program memory if a flag in the scalar memory is true. The scalar indirect-addressing instruction, move-scalar, copies a scalar value from a source location to a destination location. The vector indirect-addressing primitive, move-vector, copies a vector from a source location to a destination location. The move-vector instruction is considered a scalar instruction because both of its arguments are scalars—the source and destination locations.

4.1.2 Elementwise Instructions

Each elementwise instruction operates on equal-length vectors, producing a result vector of the same length. The element i of the result is an elementary arithmetic or logical primitive—such as $+, -, *,$ or or not—applied to element i of each of the input vectors. For example:

A	=	[5	1	3	4	3	9	2	6]
B	=	[2	5	3	8	1	3	6	2]
A p+ B	=	[7	6	6	12	4	12	8	8]
A p× B	=	[10	5	9	32	3	27	12	12]

In addition to the standard elementary operations, the elementwise instructions include an operator p-select. Based on a boolean argument, the p-select function returns either the first or second of its other two arguments. For example:

A	=	[5	1	3	4	3	9	2	6]
B	=	[2	5	3	8	1	3	6	2]
F	=	[T	F	F	F	T	T	F	T]
p-select(F, A, B)	=	[5	5	3	8	3	9	6	6]

As we shall see, this instruction is very useful for implementing simple conditional statements.

4.1.3 Permute Instructions

The permute instruction takes two vector arguments—a *data* vector and an *index* vector—and permutes each element in the data vector to the location specified in the index vector. For example:

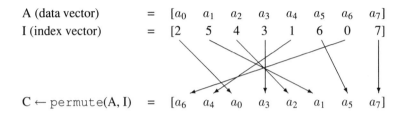

$$
\begin{array}{lclcccccccc}
\text{A (data vector)} & = & [a_0 & a_1 & a_2 & a_3 & a_4 & a_5 & a_6 & a_7] \\
\text{I (index vector)} & = & [2 & 5 & 4 & 3 & 1 & 6 & 0 & 7] \\
\\
\text{C} \leftarrow \text{permute(A, I)} & = & [a_6 & a_4 & a_0 & a_3 & a_2 & a_1 & a_5 & a_7]
\end{array}
$$

It is an error for more than one element to contain the same index—a permutation is a one-to-one mapping. This restriction is similar to the restriction made in the exclusive-read exclusive-write (EREW) P-RAM model, in which it is an error to write more than one value to a particular memory location at a time.

The permute instruction can rearrange elements within a vector of fixed size but cannot rearrange elements into a vector of a different size. The select-permute instruction is included for this purpose. It requires two extra arguments, a *default* vector and a *selection* vector. The default vector specifies the length of the destination vector and puts default values in positions that do not receive any value. The selection vector masks out certain elements so they do not get placed anywhere in the destination vector. For example:

$$
\begin{array}{lclcccccccc}
\text{A (data vector)} & = & [a_0 & a_1 & a_2 & a_3 & a_4 & a_5 & a_6 & a_7] \\
\text{D (default vector)} & = & [d_0 & d_1 & d_2 & d_3] \\
\text{S (selection vector)} & = & [\text{T} & \text{F} & \text{F} & \text{F} & \text{F} & \text{T} & \text{F} & \text{F}] \\
\text{I (index vector)} & = & [1 & 5 & 4 & 6 & 2 & 3 & 7 & 0] \\
\\
\text{select-permute(A, I, S, D)} & = & [d_0 & a_0 & d_2 & a_5]
\end{array}
$$

The pack operation defined in Section 4.2 along with an analogous unpack operation can be used instead of the select-permute operation as instructions for moving values between vectors of different sizes.

4.1.4 Scan Instructions

A scan instruction executes a scan operation on a vector. As defined in Chapter 3, the scan operation takes a binary associative operator $\oplus$ with identity 0, and an ordered set $[a_0, a_1, ..., a_{n-1}]$ of n elements, and returns the ordered set $[0, a_0, (a_0 \oplus a_1), ..., (a_0 \oplus a_1 \oplus ... \oplus a_{n-2})]$. For example:

A	=	[5	1	3	4	3	9	2	6]
+-scan(A)	=	[0	5	6	9	13	16	25	27]
max-scan(A)	=	[0	5	5	5	5	5	9	9]

This book only uses +, `maximum`, `minimum`, `or` and `and` as operators for the scan instructions since these operators are adequate for all the algorithms discussed in the book. We henceforth refer to these scan operations as `+-scan`, `max-scan`, `min-scan`, `or-scan` and `and-scan` respectively. Chapter 13 discusses how all these instructions, including the floating-point versions, can be implemented with just an integer `+-scan` and `max-scan`.

4.1.5 Vector-Scalar Instructions

The scan vector model includes four instructions that take both scalar and vector arguments. The `extract` instruction extracts a scalar value from a vector based on a scalar index. The `insert` instruction inserts a scalar value into a vector based on a scalar index. The `distribute` instruction generates a vector with a scalar copied across the whole vector. The `length` instruction returns the length of a vector. For example:

A	=	$[a_0$	a_1	a_2	a_3	a_4	$a_5]$
V	=	v					
I	=	3					
L	=	5					
insert(A, I, V)	=	$[a_0$	a_1	a_2	v	a_4	$a_5]$
extract(A, I)	=	a_3					
distribute(V, L)	=	[v	v	v	v	v]	
length(A)	=	6					

The vector-scalar instructions are important since they are the only instructions that can move a value between a vector and a scalar, or that generate a vector of a new length (the `select-permute` instruction rearranges elements between vectors of different lengths but cannot generate a vector of a new length). The `insert` instruction is actually redundant—it can be defined using the other instructions (see Section B.3)—but is included for symmetry.

Operation	Other Names	Reference
index	index iota	PARALATION LISP [96] APL [59]
⊕-reduce	reduce vref	APL, COMMON LISP [108] PARALATION LISP
⊕-distribute		
append	catenate concatenate	APL COMMON LISP
pack	pack compress irregular compression	Schwartz [101] APL Batcher [12]
split		
flag-merge		
inverse-permute		
enumerate	enumerate	Christman [31]
max-index		

Table 4.1: A summary of the simple operations and some of the places they have appeared in the past.

4.2   Simple Operations

This section lists a set of simple operations that can all be implemented using a constant number of calls to the scan vector instructions. Many of these operations were introduced in Chapter 3, and many have appeared in various languages and other contexts (see Table 4.1). An attempt was made here to select the clearest name for each operation. The operations are put together in this section partially for reference purposes, but also to show the reader some simple uses of the scan vector instruction set. They are used extensively in this book, and Appendix B shows the implementation of each operations using the scan vector instructions. In practice, where constant factors are important, many of these simple operations might be implemented directly at a lower level rather than implementing them using the scan vector instructions.

index *length*

The index operation takes a scalar *length* and returns a vector of that length with sequential indices. For example:

$$
\begin{array}{lcl}
\text{L} & = & 8 \\
\text{index(L)} & = & [0 \quad 1 \quad 2 \quad 3 \quad 4 \quad 5 \quad 6 \quad 7]
\end{array}
$$

⊕-reduce *values*

The *reduce* operations take a vector of *values* and combine all the elements of the vector using one of five binary operators: +, maximum, minimum, or or and. They return a scalar value. For example:

$$
\begin{array}{lcl}
\text{A} & = & [5 \quad 1 \quad 3 \quad 4 \quad 3 \quad 9 \quad 2 \quad 6] \\
\text{+-reduce(A)} & = & 33 \\
\text{max-reduce(A)} & = & 9
\end{array}
$$

⊕-distribute *values*

The ⊕-*distribute* operations take a vector of *values*, combine all the elements of the vector using one of five binary operators: +, maximum, minimum, or or and, and distribute the values back across the vector. For example:

$$
\begin{array}{lcrrrrrrrr}
\text{A} & = & [5 & 1 & 3 & 4 & 3 & 9 & 2 & 6] \\
\text{+-distribute(A)} & = & [33 & 33 & 33 & 33 & 33 & 33 & 33 & 33] \\
\text{max-distribute(A)} & = & [9 & 9 & 9 & 9 & 9 & 9 & 9 & 9]
\end{array}
$$

append *values1 values2*

The append operation takes two vectors and appends them. For example:

$$
\begin{array}{lcl}
\text{A} & = & [a_0 \quad a_1 \quad a_2] \\
\text{B} & = & [b_0 \quad b_1] \\
\text{append(A, B)} & = & [a_0 \quad a_1 \quad a_2 \quad b_0 \quad b_1]
\end{array}
$$

pack *values flags*

The pack operation takes a vector of *values*, and a boolean vector of *flags*, and packs all the elements with a T in their flag into consecutive elements, deleting elements with an F in their flag. For example:

$$
\begin{array}{llllllllll}
A & = & [a_0 & a_1 & a_2 & a_3 & a_4 & a_5 & a_6 & a_7] \\
F & = & [T & F & T & F & F & T & T & T]
\end{array}
$$

$$
\text{pack}(A, F) \quad = \quad [a_0 \quad a_2 \quad a_5 \quad a_6 \quad a_7]
$$

split *values flags*

The split operation takes a vector of *values* and a boolean vector of *flags*, and packs all the elements with an F in their flag to the bottom of a vector and elements with a T in their flag to the top of the vector. For example:

$$
\begin{array}{llllllllll}
A & = & [a_0 & a_1 & a_2 & a_3 & a_4 & a_5 & a_6 & a_7] \\
F & = & [T & F & T & F & F & T & T & T]
\end{array}
$$

$$
\text{split}(A, F) \quad = \quad [a_1 \quad a_3 \quad a_4 \quad a_0 \quad a_2 \quad a_5 \quad a_6 \quad a_7]
$$

flag-merge *flags values1 values2*

The flag-merge operation takes two vectors of values and a boolean vector of *flags*, and merges the values according to the flags. Positions with a T in their flag will get values from the *values2* vector, and positions with an F in their flag will get values from the *values1* vector. The ordering is maintained. For example:

$$
\begin{array}{lllllllll}
A & = & [a_0 & a_1 & a_2] \\
B & = & [b_0 & b_1 & b_2 & b_3 & b_4] \\
F & = & [T & F & T & F & F & T & T & T]
\end{array}
$$

$$
\text{flag-merge}(F, A, B) \quad = \quad [b_0 \quad a_0 \quad b_1 \quad a_1 \quad a_2 \quad b_2 \quad b_3 \quad b_4]
$$

inverse-permute *values indices*

The inverse-permute operation is similar to the permute instruction but the indices instead of specifying the positions to which the values are written, specify the positions from which the values are taken. The *values* vector must be equal or longer than the *indices* vector. As with the permute instruction, all indices must be unique. For example:

$$
\begin{array}{llllllllll}
A & = & [a_0 & a_1 & a_2 & a_3 & a_4 & a_5 & a_6 & a_7] \\
I & = & [3 & 0 & 7 & 2 & 6]
\end{array}
$$

$$
\text{inverse-permute}(A, I) \quad = \quad [a_3 \quad a_0 \quad a_7 \quad a_2 \quad a_6]
$$

enumerate *flags*

The enumerate operation takes a vector of *flags* and returns unique sequential integers to the elements with T in their flag. We do not care what is returned to elements with an F in their flag. For example:

$$
\begin{array}{lllllllllll}
\text{F} & = & [\text{T} & \text{F} & \text{T} & \text{F} & \text{F} & \text{T} & \text{T} & \text{T}] \\
\text{enumerate(F)} & = & [0 & 1 & 1 & 2 & 2 & 2 & 3 & 4]
\end{array}
$$

max-index *values*

The max-index operation takes a vector of *values* and returns the index of the maximum value. If several values are equal, it returns the leftmost index. For example:

$$
\begin{array}{llllllllll}
\text{A} & = & [2 & 11 & 4 & 7 & \boxed{14} & 6 & 9 & 14] \\
\text{max-index(A)} & = & 4
\end{array}
$$

The min-index operation uses minimum instead of maximum.

4.3 Segments and Segmented Instructions

This section formalizes the notion of a segmented vector, and introduces segmented versions of most of the scan vector instructions. Segments and the segmented versions of the instructions are used extensively in the algorithms discussed in Part II of this book. They are also used to prove the *replicating theorem* in Chapter 10.

Definition: *A segmented vector is an ordered set S of n segments, and an ordered set A of m atomic values (a vector). Each segment s_i $(0 \le i < n)$ of S is mapped onto a consecutive block, possibly empty, of A. The blocks are all adjacent and are in the same order as the segments to which they are assigned.*
    The number of segments in a segmented vector is called the segment count.

The segments of a segmented vector are defined separately over each vector. For example, the third segment of one vector might be much longer than the third segment of another vector.

    We call any structure that describes the segmentation of a vector, a *segment-descriptor*. Figure 4.2 shows three possible segment descriptors: the *head-flags* marks the beginning of each segment, the *lengths* specifies the length of each segment, and the *head-pointers* points to the beginning of each segment. The *head-flags* were introduced in Chapter 3 and are inadequate for describing segments in general because they cannot be used to represent empty segments (empty segments are important for the replicating theorem described in

$$S = [[s_{00} \quad s_{01} \quad s_{02}] \quad [] \quad [s_{20} \quad s_{21}] \quad [s_{30} \quad s_{31} \quad s_{32} \quad s_{33}]]$$

vector elements	=	$[s_{00}$	s_{01}	s_{02}	s_{20}	s_{21}	s_{30}	s_{31}	s_{32}	$s_{33}]$
head-flags	=	$[1$	0	0	1	0	1	0	0	0]

lengths	=	[3	0	2	4]
head-pointers	=	[0	3	3	5]
head-pointer-flag	=	[T	F	T	T]

Figure 4.2: A segmented vector and three ways of describing the segmentation. The *head-flags* marks the beginning of each segment and cannot be used to represent empty segments. The *lengths* specifies the length of each segment. The *head-pointers* point to the beginning of each segment—the *head-pointer-flag* marks the nonempty segments.

Chapter 10). In this chapter we use the *lengths* vector as a segment descriptor. Appendix B shows that any of the segment-descriptors can be generated from any other with a step complexity of $O(1)$.

We now introduce segmented versions of all but three of the instructions of the scan vector model (the cond-jump, move-scalar and move-vector instructions do not have segmented versions). The segmented versions of the instructions execute the original instruction independently within each segment. Figure 4.3 illustrates several examples. Each vector argument in the unsegmented version of an instruction is replaced by a segmented vector in the segmented version, and each scalar argument in the unsegmented version is replaced by a vector in the segmented version. When using a segmented instruction, the segment count of each vector argument must be equal and must equal the vector length of each scalar argument.

All the segmented instructions can be implemented with a constant number of calls to the unsegmented instructions (see Appendix B) and therefore have an step complexity of $O(1)$. Likewise, the element complexity of each segmented instruction is only a constant factor greater than the element complexity of the unsegmented version.

4.4 Segmented Operations

Using the segmented versions of the instructions, we can implement segmented versions of all the operations defined in Section 4.2. Here we mention two additional operations which can be implemented with a constant number of calls to the primitives and which are

C	=	[3	4	7]
D	=	[6	2	3]
C + D	=	[9	6	10]

Scalar Instructions

A	=	[[5	1]	[3	4	3	9]	[2	6]]
B	=	[[1	0]	[2	0	3	1]	[0	1]]
+-scan(A)	=	[[0	5]	[0	3	7	10]	[0	2]]
permute(A, B)	=	[[1	5]	[4	9	3	3]	[2	6]]

Vector Instructions

A	=	[[5	1]	[3	4	3	9]	[2	6]]
B	=	[[1	3]	[2	0	3	1]	[0	1]]
F	=	[[T	T]	[T	T	F	T]	[T	T]]
D	=	[[6	9	2	3]	[3	2	2]	[7	1]]

select-permute(A, B, F, D)

	=	[[6	5	2	1]	[4	9	3]	[2	6]]

Vector Instructions (different size arguments)

A	=	[[5	1	6]	[3	3	9]	[2	6]]
L	=	[4	1	2]
I	=	[0	2	1]
V	=	[3	4	7]
distribute(V, L)	=	[[3	3	3	3]	[4]	[7	7]]
extract(A, I)	=	[5	9	6]
insert(A, V, I)	=	[[3	1	6]	[3	3	4]	[2	7]]

Vector-Scalar Instructions

Figure 4.3: Examples of the segmented versions of the instructions of the scan vector model.

useful when using segments.

split-and-segment *values flags*

The split-and-segment operation is similar to the split operation defined in Section 4.2. It takes a vector of *values* and a boolean vector of *flags*, and returns a segmented vector with two segments: one containing the elements with an F in their flag and the other containing the elements with a T in their flag. For example:

A		=	[5	1	3	4	3	9	2	6]
F		=	[T	F	T	F	F	T	T	T]
split-and-segment(A, F)		=	[[1	4	3]	[5	3	9	2	6]]

c-rank-split *ranks flags*

The rank-split operation is similar to the split-and-segment operation except that the *ranks* argument must be a valid set of indices for the permutation instruction. In addition to splitting these indices, the rank-split operation renumbers the indices so they are valid within the new segments but maintain the same order. For example:

A		=	[5	1	3	4	0	7	2	6]
F		=	[T	F	T	F	F	T	T	T]
split-and-segment(A, F)		=	[[1	4	0]	[5	3	7	2	6]]
rank-split(A, F)		=	[[1	2	0]	[2	1	4	0	3]]

The rank-split operation is used to update pointers when splitting a set of pointers.

4.5   Additional Instructions

In this section we consider the effects of including other primitive instructions in a parallel vector model. The instructions we consider are, a merge-mask instruction, a set of ⊕-combine instructions, a multi-extract instruction, and a set of ⊕-keyed-scan instructions. For each instruction introduced, we briefly discuss how practical the instruction is to implement on a parallel machine, and how the addition of the instruction effects the complexity of various algorithms.

4.5.1   Merge Instruction

The merge-mask instruction takes two sorted vectors of lengths l_1 and l_2, merges them, and returns a boolean vector of length $l_1 + l_2$ with F set in positions in which elements of the first vector belong and T set in positions in which elements of the second vector belong. For example:

$$
\begin{array}{lcl}
A & = & [3 \quad 7 \quad 8] \\
B & = & [1 \quad 4 \quad 5 \quad 9 \quad 11] \\
C \leftarrow \texttt{merge-mask}(A, B) & = & [T \quad F \quad T \quad T \quad F \quad F \quad T \quad T] \\
\texttt{flag-merge}(C, A, B) & = & [1 \quad 3 \quad 4 \quad 5 \quad 7 \quad 8 \quad 9 \quad 11]
\end{array}
$$

We suggest the `merge-mask` instruction instead of a direct merge instruction because a merge operation can be built easily out of the `merge-mask` instruction by using the `flag-merge` operation (Section 4.2), but the opposite is not true. From a practical point of view, it is worth having both instructions.

The `merge-mask` instruction can be implemented on a parallel machine using Batcher's bitonic merge [11]. This operation can be executed deterministically using a single pass of a butterfly network; for n values, the `merge-mask` instruction executes in $O(\lg n)$ time—no more than a `permute` or `scan` instruction.

Algorithms to construct and manipulate the plane-sweep tree data structure [7, 3, 9, 94] are greatly simplified with a merge instruction. The merge instruction is also useful for manipulating sets.

4.5.2 Combine Instructions

The `combine` instructions are similar to the `select-permute` instruction but permit many-to-one mappings: the indices need not be unique. Values with equal indices are combined using a binary associative operator. As with the *scan* operations, we might restrict the combining operators to some simple set such as, $+$, `maximum`, `minimum`, `and` and `or`. The `combine` instructions takes a *default* argument, whose elements get combined and which determines the length of the result vector. For example:

$$
\begin{array}{lcl}
\text{Index} & = & [0 \quad 1 \quad 2 \quad 3 \quad 4 \quad 5 \quad 6 \quad 7] \\
\text{Data} & = & [5 \quad 1 \quad 3 \quad 4 \quad 3 \quad 9 \quad 2 \quad 6] \\
I & = & [2 \quad 5 \quad 3 \quad 3 \quad 1 \quad 0 \quad 3 \quad 5] \\
\end{array}
$$

$$
\begin{array}{lcl}
D & = & [0 \quad 0 \quad 0 \quad 0 \quad 0 \quad 0] \\
\texttt{+-combine}(\text{Data}, I, D) & = & [0 \quad 3 \quad 5 \quad 9 \quad 9 \quad 7] \\
\texttt{max-combine}(\text{Data}, I, D) & = & [0 \quad 3 \quad 5 \quad 4 \quad 9 \quad 6]
\end{array}
$$

The combine instructions are similar to the concurrent-write (CW) instruction of the P-RAM model. The combine instructions are more powerful, however, since as well as permitting many values to be written to a single location, they allow those values to be combined.

For many uses of the combine instructions, the data can be organized so that the reduce operations (based on the scan instructions) can be used instead. This is, for example, the case with the graph data structure described in Section 5.1.

One use of the combine instructions that cannot be replaced with the reduce operations is in histogramming a vector of small integers. In histogramming we are given a vector V of values and we want to determine how many of each value appear in the vector. To implement this, for small integers, we create a vector as long as the largest integer with the integer 0 in each element, create another vector of the same length as V with the integer 1 in each element, and then use the +-combine instruction with the vector V as the index, the 1 vector as the data and the 0 vector as the default. Each element of the result will contain the number of elements of V with that key. Such an implementation of integer histogramming is only efficient if the number of buckets (the largest integer) is on the same order as the length of V. If the number of buckets is significantly larger than V, sorting the values so that equal values are adjacent, and reducing within each segment of values is more efficient.

The hardware implementation of the combine instructions is discussed along with the implementation of the keyed-scan instructions.

4.5.3 Multi-Extract Instruction

The multi-extract instruction takes two vectors, an *index* vector and a *data* vector, of potentially different lengths, and for each index, extracts the corresponding element from the data vector. The indices need not be unique. For example:

Index		=	[0	1	2	3	4	5]		
Data		=	[5	1	3	4	11	9]		
I		=	[2	5	4	3	1	2	3	5]
multi-extract(Data, I)		=	[3	9	11	4	1	3	4	9]

The multi-extract instruction is analogous to the concurrent-read (CR) instruction of the P-RAM model.

For many uses of the multi-extract instruction, the data structure can be organized so that the distribute operation (based on the scan instructions) can be used instead. This is analogous to the use of the reduce operations instead of the combine instructions mentioned in the previous section. In some applications, such as dictionary lookup using small integer keys, the distribute operation cannot be used to replace the multi-extract instruction. Dictionary lookup is the problem of given a "dictionary" of words each with a definition in a vector D, and a vector V of words without definitions, we would like to find the definition for each word in V. Each word may appear multiple times in V, and we assume nothing about the ordering of the words. If each word can be indexed by its position in D, then we can use the multi-extract instruction to extract each definition in D. If the words are long, it might be possible to hash the characters of each word into a small integer and used the hashed value as a key into the dictionary. This requires that we keep multiple dictionary vectors since more than one word might hash to the same location.

The reduce operations cannot be used in histogramming nor the distribute operation in dictionary lookup are for similar reasons. In both cases we are dynamically translating some data into pointers. In histogramming we translate integer values into pointers to locations in the histogram vector, and in dictionary lookup, we translate words into pointers to locations in the dictionary vector. Because of this translation, we know nothing about the organization of the pointers and cannot organize them into segments.

The implementation of the multi-extract instruction is discussed along with the implementation of the keyed-scan instructions.

4.5.4 Keyed-Scan Instructions

The keyed-scan instructions are similar to the combine instructions but return an additional vector: the *scan* vector. The *scan* vector contains the results of executing an independent scan operation for the elements with each index (key). We include a keyed-scan operation for the standard binary associative operators: +, max, min, or and and. For example:

Data	=	[1	1	1	1	1	1	1	1]
Keys	=	[3	2	3	2	0	3	3	2]
Default	=	[0	0	0	0]

+-keyed-scan(Data, Keys)

sum	=	[1	0	3	4]
scan	=	[0	0	1	1	0	2	3	2]

This is analogous to a stable version of the Fetch-and-Op instruction suggested for the Ultracomputer [49], and to the multi-prefix operation suggested by Ranade [93]. By stable, we mean that the scan for each key is executed in the vector order rather than in an arbitrary order.

The +-keyed-scan instruction can be used in a radix sort [19, 93]. For n keys each with d bits, the algorithm requires $O(d/\lg n)$ steps. The algorithm is similar to the split radix sort described in Section 3.4.1 but sorts $\lg n$ bits on each step instead of a single bit. As with the split radix sort, we start by sorting the lowest order bits of the key, and work our way up. Because each step is stable, the keys remain sorted with respect to the lower ordered bits. Each step of the sort works as follows:

> define radix-sort-step(Subkeys, Keys){
>   ones ← distribute(1, length(Keys));
>   intrakey-offset, subkey-sum ← +-keyed-scan(ones, Subkeys);
>   key-offset ← multi-extract(+-scan(subkey-sum), Subkeys);
> permute(Keys, key-offset + intrakey-offset)}

The *Subkeys* argument refers to the $\lg n$ extracted bits of the keys. The basic idea is for each subkey to find its offset within the elements with an equal subkey, we call this the *intrakey-offset*. Each subkey also determines how many elements contain a smaller subkey, we call this the *key-offset*. The position of the subkey in the final ordering is then simply the sum of the key-offset and the intrakey-offset.

The combine instructions, the multi-extract instruction, and the keyed-scan instructions can all be implemented using the routing algorithm suggested by Ranade [92]. This algorithm runs on a butterfly network and for n values, requires $O(\lg n)$ time with very high probability. Each node of the butterfly only requires a constant number of buffers. The implementation of the three types of instructions differ in what is needed in each switch of the network. For the combine and keyed-scan instructions, each switch requires an arithmetic unit to execute the binary associative operator. For the multi-extract and keyed-scan instructions the switches are required to store state from a forward pass of the network, to be used during a backward pass of the network (see [106, 93]).

Part II

Algorithms

Introduction: Algorithms

This part describes a broad variety of data structures and algorithms based on the scan vector model. It contains four chapters. Chapter 5, *data structures*, describes how trees, graphs and multidimensional arrays can be represented using vectors and illustrates how some operations on these data structures can be implemented. Many of these operations have an asymptotic step complexity that is a factor of $O(\lg n)$ less than equivalent operations on either a CRCW or EREW P-RAM model. The next three chapters—*computational geometry algorithms*, *graph algorithms* and *numerical algorithms*—describe a variety of algorithms. These algorithms make extensive use of the data structures and operations defined in Chapter 5.

Chapter 5

Data Structures

This chapter describes data structures for mapping *trees, graphs* and *multidimensional arrays* onto a small number of vectors such that the instructions of the scan vector model can be applied to efficiently manipulate the objects. It also describes the implementation of several operations on the data structures, including finding the maximum value of a neighbor in a graph, finding the depth of each vertex in a tree, or summing the rows in a grid. Many of these operations have an asymptotic step complexity that is a factor of $O(\lg n)$ less than equivalent operations on either a CRCW or EREW P-RAM.[1] The representations and operations described in this chapter are used extensively in Chapters 7 and 8.

5.1 Graphs

This section describes representations of graphs, both directed and undirected, and a set of useful operations that take advantage of the representations. The representations discussed in this section will be called v-graph (vector graph) representations. These representations are used in all the algorithms described in the chapter on graph algorithms (Chapter 7). The v-graph representations are based on segmented vectors in which each segment corresponds to a vertex of the graph, and each element within a segment corresponds to an edge of that vertex. By using segmented operations to operate over the edges of each vertex, the step complexity of many useful operations on graphs can be reduced. For example, each vertex

---

[1] Using the $O(\lg n / \lg \lg n)$ prefix sum routine of Cole and Vishkin [36] and our data structures, some of the operations can execute on a CRCW P-RAM with a step complexity which is $O(\lg n / \lg \lg n)$, instead of $O(\lg n)$, greater than on the scan vector model.

79

Graphs:
Summing Neighbors, Finding the Maximum of Neighbors,
Distributing an Excess,
Deleting Edges, Deleting Vertices, Merging Vertices.

Trees:
Depth of Each Vertex, Size of Each Subtree,
Passing Flag Down Tree, Passing Flag Up Tree,
Merging Trees, Deleting Vertices, Splitting Trees.

Multidimensional Arrays:
Reducing Across Subdimensions, Expanding Across a Dimension,
Extracting a Subplane, Appending Grids.

Table 5.1:   Examples of operations on trees, graphs and multidimensional arrays. All these operations have a step complexity of $O(1)$ in the scan vector model.

summing a value from all neighbors, is reduced from $O(\lg d)$ in the P-RAM models to $O(1)$ (d is the greatest degree of any vertex). The general idea of the representation is that by keeping a graph in a particular form, we can minimize the cost of operations on that graph. Section 5.2 will show that by keeping trees in a particular form, we can similarly reduce the step complexity of many tree operations on trees with n vertices by $O(\lg n)$.

We now consider more precisely how undirected and directed graphs are represented and then illustrate how the representation is used to implement two example operations: neighbor reducing and distributing an excess.

5.1.1   Vector Graph Representations

Undirected Graphs: To represent an undirected graph, we use a single segmented vector. Each segment corresponds to a vertex and each element within a segment corresponds to one of the edges of that vertex. Since each edge is incident on two vertices, it appears in two segments. The actual values kept in the elements of the segmented vector are pointers to the other end of the edge (see Figure 5.1). To include weights on the edges of the graphs, we can use an additional vector that contains the weights of the edges.

Directed Graphs: To represent a directed graph, we use two segmented vectors: one for the incoming edges, and one for the outgoing edges. Each element in the outgoing edges vector is a pointer to a position in the incoming edges vector (see Figure 5.2). As with

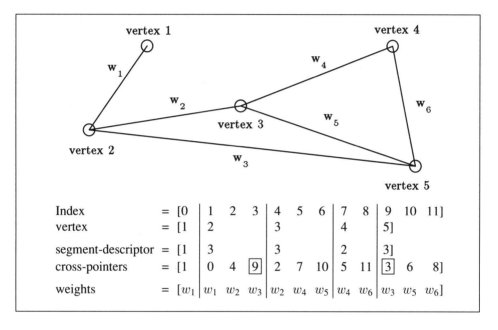

Figure 5.1: An example of the undirected v-graph representation. Each pointer points to the other end of the edge. So, for example, edge w_3 in vertex 2 contains a pointer (in this case 9) to its other end in vertex 5. The segment-descriptor specifies the number of edges incident on each vertex.

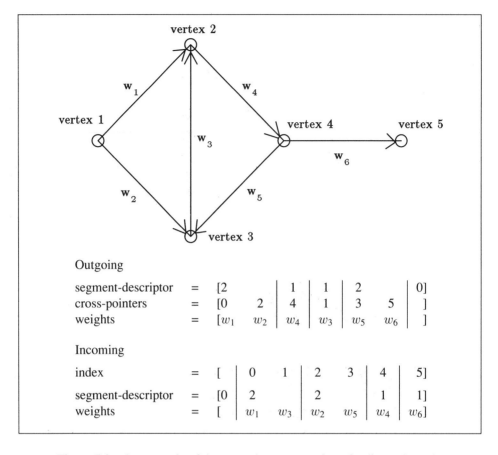

Figure 5.2: An example of the v-graph representation of a directed graph.

undirected graphs, we can represent a weighted directed graph with an additional weight vector.

The operations on graphs discussed in this section assume the graph is already in the v-graph representation. For the representation to be useful, either there must be an efficient routine to generate the representation from another representation, or it must be possible to do all manipulations on graphs using the v-graph representation. A graph can be converted from most other representations into the v-graph representation by creating two elements per edge (one for each end) and sorting the edges according to their vertex number. The split radix sort (Section 3.4.1) can be used since the vertex numbers are all integers less than n. The sort places all edges that belong to the same vertex in a contiguous segment.

We suggest that in the scan vector model graphs always be kept in the v-graph representation. In this representation, most useful manipulations on graphs, such as deleting edges or vertices, or merging vertices (see Section 7.1), can be implemented with an step complexity of $O(1)$.

5.1.2 Neighbor Reducing

We now consider a commonly used operation on graphs: *neighbor reducing*. In neighbor reducing, each vertex applies a binary associative operator over some variable in all of its neighbors. For example, it can be used to determine if any neighbor has a flag set, or to find the maximum of some variable of all neighbors. Neighbor reducing can be executed by (1) distributing the value from each vertex over its edges using the segmented `distribute` operation, (2) permuting these values using the cross-pointers, and (3) "summing" the values on the edges back into the vertices using a segmented `reduce` operation. This routine can be applied to both undirected and directed graphs. For the binary associative operators, `+`, `or`, `and`, `maximum` and `minimum`, neighbor reducing has a step complexity of $O(1)$. The code needed to implement a `+-neighbor-reduce` on an undirected graph is:

```
define +-neighbor-reduce(A, Graph){
      values ← seg-distribute(A, Graph.segment-descriptor);
      neighbors ← permute(values, Graph.cross-pointers);
    seg-+-reduce(neighbors, Graph.segment-descriptor)}
```

On a P-RAM, in general, neighbor reducing requires $O(\lg d)$ time.

5.1.3 Distributing an Excess Across Edges

As another example of the use of the v-graph representations, consider the problem of taking a value (an excess) at each vertex of a directed graph and spreading it across the outgoing edges of that vertex. Each edge has a maximum capacity it can accept, and as long as no edge gets more than its maximum capacity, the excess can be distributed in any way. For example, if a vertex had an excess of 20, and the edges of that vertex had capacities 7, 11, 6 and 14, a valid distribution is to distribute 7, 11, 2 and 0 across the four edges. The maximum-flow algorithm described in Section 7.2, and in [47], uses such a technique.

The distribution of excess can be implemented on the v-graph representation using a segmented `+-scan` and a segmented `distribute` as shown below.

```
define distribute-excess(Excess, Capacity, Graph){
        A ← seg-distribute(Excess, Graph.out-segment-descriptor);
        B ← seg-+-scan(Capacity, Graph.out-segment-descriptor);
        C ← p-maximum(A p− B, 0);
    p-minimum(Capacity, C)}
```

Here is an example for two vertices of a graph:

Capacity	=	[13	5	7	11	6	14]
Excess	=	[15		20]			
A	=	[15	15	20	20	20	20]
B	=	[0	13	0	7	18	24]
C	=	[15	2	20	13	2	0]
Result	=	[13	2	7	11	2	0]

5.2 Trees

This section describes a flexible representation of trees, and a set of useful operations that take advantage of this representation. The representation is based on the Euler-tour order as described by Tarjan and Vishkin [112], but instead of using linked lists, it uses vectors. By using the scan instructions on the vectors, instead of the prefix operations on linked lists, the step complexity for many operations is reduced from $O(\lg n)$ to $O(1)$.

5.2.1 Vector Tree Representation

The Euler-tour order is generated by traversing the tree counter-clockwise, starting at the root, and sequentially numbering each edge passed (see Figure 5.3). Each edge is numbered twice, once on the way down and once on the way up. The Euler-tour ordering can be pictured in a parenthetical form as shown in Figure 5.3. Each matching pair of parentheses corresponds to an edge of the tree and the vertex below it.[2] Our vector representation of a tree is based on this parenthetical form. We use two vectors: one contains the index of the left parenthesis of each vertex, the left-paren vector, and the other contains the index of the right parenthesis of each vertex, the right-paren vector (see Figure 5.3). The vertices are kept in the preorder numbering. We will refer to this representation of a tree as the *v-tree* (vector tree) representation.

In the remainder of this section, we discuss several operations on trees. We describe how the leaffix and rootfix operations [70] can be implemented efficiently using the v-tree

---

[2]Note that we include an edge out of the root.

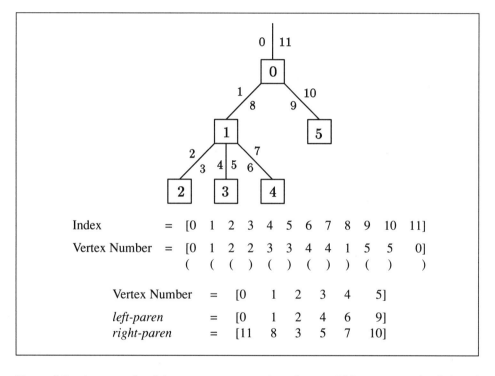

Figure 5.3: An example of the v-tree representation of a tree. This representation is based on the Euler-tour ordering [112].

representation. The leaffix and rootfix operations can, in turn, be used to determine many important properties of a tree, such as the depth of each vertex. We also describe how to delete vertices from a tree, how to split a tree, and how to join trees. For trees with n vertices, all these operations have a step complexity of $O(1)$ and an element complexity of $O(n)$.

Before discussing the operations, we briefly discuss how to generate the v-tree representation from other representations of trees. If a tree is given in the v-graph representation (Section 5.1), perhaps as a result of a graph operations, the tree can be converted to the v-tree representations by hooking the vertices into a linked list and executing a +-list-scan on the list.[3] The list-scan assigns sequential indices to the elements. These indices are then used to permute the tree into the correct order. In the scan vector model, the list-scan operations have a step complexity of $O(\lg n)$ and an element complexity of $O(n)$. Often $O(\lg n)$ operations are required on the tree, therefore, amortizing the cost. If a tree is given in a representation in which each child has a pointer to its parent, a sort might be required to convert it into the v-tree representation—this is also true to get it into a linked list. The sort is used to place all the children who point to the same parent into a contiguous segment.

5.2.2 Leaffix and Rootfix Operations

The leaffix operation takes a binary associative operator $\oplus$, and a tree of values A, and returns to each vertex the result of applying the operator $\oplus$ to all of its descendants. Similarly, the rootfix operation returns to each vertex the result of applying the operator $\oplus$ to all of its ancestors. These operations were introduced by Leiserson and Maggs [70].

Using the v-tree representation, the leaffix and rootfix operations for the operators +, or and and can be implemented with a step complexity of $O(1)$. The implementation of the + version relies on + having an inverse. The implementation of the or and and version is based on the + version[4]. Since maximum or minimum do not have an inverse, and cannot be implemented with the + version, the implementation we describe is not applicable.

Using the leaffix and rootfix computations with the operators +, or and and, we can execute the following useful operations on a tree:

- Determining the depth of each vertex. This is executed by applying a +-rootfix operation on a tree with the value 1 at every vertex.

---

[3] Also called a prefix sum on a linked list or list ranking.

[4] To implement an or with a +, we convert the boolean values T and F to the numbers 1 and 0, execute a +, and if a result is greater than 0, we convert it to T.

- Determining how many descendants each vertex has. This is executed by applying a +-leaffix operation on a tree with the value 1 at every vertex.

- Passing a flag down from a set of vertices to all their descendants. This is executed with an or-rootfix operation on a tree with a flag set to T in vertices that want their descendants marked.

- Passing a flag up from a set of leaves to all their ancestors. This is executed with an or-leaffix operation on a tree with a flag set to T in vertices that want their ancestors marked.

The basic idea of the +-rootfix is to permute the value in A to the *left-paren*, permute the inverse to the *right-paren*, execute a +-scan and get the result from the *left-paren*. Since the inverse of the value cancels out the value, the sum over any subtree is 0. Figure 5.4 illustrates an example. The +-rootfix and +-leaffix operations can be implemented as follows.

```
define +-rootfix(A, Tr){
    I ← distribute(0, 2 × length(Tr));
    L ← select-permute(A, Tr.left-paren, I));
    R ← select-permute(–A, Tr.right-paren, L);
    S ← +-scan(R);
    inverse-permute(S, Tr.left-paren)}
```

```
define +-leaffix(A, Tr){
    I ← distribute(0, 2 × length(Tr));
    L ← select-permute(A, Tr.left-paren, I);
    S ← +-scan(L);
    R-value ← inverse-permute(S, Tr.right-paren);
    L-value ← inverse-permute(S, Tr.left-paren);
    R-value p– L-value}
```

The leaffix and rootfix operations for operators without an inverse, such as maximum, can be implemented with a step complexity of $O(\lg n)$ and an element complexity of $O(n \lg n)$. The method involves finding the sum (relative to the operator) over n overlapping intervals by recursively splitting the vector in halves, finding the sum of the half, and each interval which spans a whole half, adds this sum in. It turns out that this technique requires no permutations; it only requires $O(\lg n)$ scans.

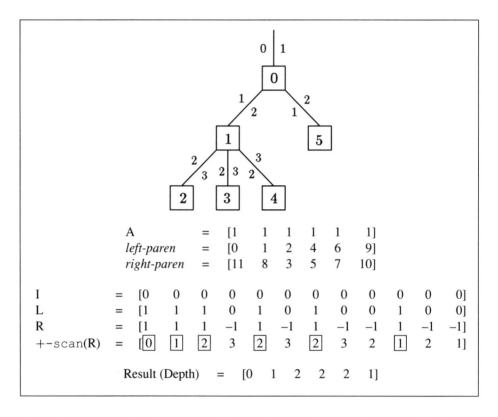

Figure 5.4: An example of a +-rootfix. In this example, since the vector A is all ones, the operation calculates the depth of each vertex.

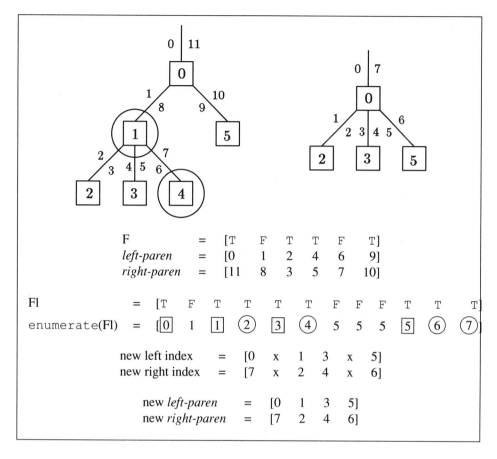

Figure 5.5: An example of deleting vertices of a tree.

5.2.3 Tree Manipulations

In this section we discuss how to delete vertices from a tree, how to split a tree into a set of trees, and how to merge a set of trees. With a total of n vertices, all these operations have a step complexity of $O(1)$ and an element complexity of $O(n)$.

Deleting Vertices: Given a tree, and a boolean vector which marks certain vertices for deletion, we can remove these vertices from the tree by packing the *left-paren* and *right-paren* vectors. We must, however, first renumber the positions. To renumber the positions, we permute the *delete* flag to both the right and left parenthesis of each vertex. We then enumerate this array giving each element which is not being deleted, a unique index.

We permute these indices back to the *left-paren* and *right-paren*, and pack them. Figure 5.5 shows an example. We can use this delete operation to delete all descendants of a set of vertices by marking the descendants with an `or-rootfix` and then deleting the marked vertices.

Splitting a Tree: Using a similar method as used for deleting vertices, we can split a tree into a set of trees. Given a tree and a boolean vector which marks the roots of a set of independent subtrees, the tree split returns each branch, and what remains of the tree, as independent trees each within its own segment.

This *tree-split* operation can be implemented as follows. We distribute the index of the left parenthesis of each root of a branch to all vertices of a branch. Since branches are disjoint, this distribution can be executed with a `+-rootfix` by placing the index in the root of each branch and 0 everywhere else. Every branch vertex subtracts the left parenthesis index of its root from its left and right parenthesis. This returns new indices relative to each vertex's new root rather than the old root. We can reindex the vertices that remain in the original tree using the same method as used for the delete operation. We now use the `split-and-segment` operation (Section 4.4) to split branch vertices from vertices that remain in the original tree. Since the branches are disjoint, the vertices of each branch will be in a contiguous set of elements of the branch segment. We can, therefore, place each branch in its own segment by determining the boundary and generating the appropriate segment descriptor.

Merging Trees: Using almost the inverse of the *tree-split* operation, we can implement a *tree-merge* operation. The *tree-merge* problem is: given a set of trees each in its own segment, and one tree whose vertices contain pointers (segment indices) to the other trees, merge the trees into a single tree. The *tree-merge* is similar to the star-merge operation that will be described in Section 7.1. The principal difference is that in addition to merging the child trees into the parent trees (child vertices into the parent vertices in the case of the star-merge), we must reindex the resulting *left-paren* and *right-paren* vectors so that they correctly describe the tree.

As with the star-merge, each vertex of the parent tree must open enough space to fit its child tree: this is executed with a `+-scan`. We now place each child tree (both its *left-paren* and *right-paren* vectors) in the opened space after its root vertex in the parent tree. To reindex, each vertex of the parent tree determines how many new child vertices will be added below it. This can be calculated with a `+-leaffix`. Each vertex of the parent tree also determines how many new children vertices appear to the left of it using a `+-scan`. The new *left-paren* value of each vertex is the old one plus twice the number of new vertices to the right. The new *right-paren* value of each vertex is the old one plus twice the number of new vertices to the right, plus twice the number of new children. To

$$C = \begin{bmatrix} 5 & 1 & 3 & 4 \\ 3 & 9 & 2 & 6 \end{bmatrix}$$

$$C \quad = \quad [5 \quad 1 \quad 3 \quad 4 \quad 3 \quad 9 \quad 2 \quad 6]$$

$$\text{size} = 4, 2$$

Figure 5.6:   An example of the representation of a two dimensional. The array is mapped onto the vector in row major order.

reindex the children, we distribute the left parenthesis offset of the root of each child tree across the vertices of the child tree and add this offset to the *left-paren* and *right-paren* values of each child vertex.

This operation, as the others, has a step complexity of $O(1)$.

5.3   Multidimensional Arrays

This section describes how multidimensional arrays can be represented with vectors and how several useful array operations, including extracting subdimensions, reducing across subdimensions, and distributing across subdimensions, can be implemented using this representation. These operations have a step complexity of $O(1)$ and an element complexity of $O(n)$—n is the total number of elements. These array operations are important enough that they might be implemented directly rather than being built on the primitives of the scan model [4]. A problem with the direct implementation is that the replicating theorem Chapter 10 does not apply; a segmented version of the array scans would be required.

We represent multidimensional arrays in the scan model in the standard way—by placing all the elements of the array in a single vector, and by keeping a set of scalars which specify the size of each dimension. By using a convention on how elements of the matrix are mapped onto the vector, we can easily determine the location in the vector of a matrix element. So, for example, a two dimensional $m_1 \times m_2$ array could be mapped onto a vector of length $m_1 m_2$ in row-major order (see Figure 5.6).

Based on the array ordering, we can define array versions of the scan primitives (see Figure 5.7). These can be implemented with a constant number of calls to the vector versions by simply permuting the elements before and after the scan operation, and using a segmented scan to separate each row, or each column. With the array versions of the scan primitives, we can implement array versions of all the simple operations defined in Section 4.2. The operations which are particularly useful are the reduce, distribute,

$$C = \begin{bmatrix} 5 & 1 & 3 & 4 \\ 3 & 9 & 2 & 6 \end{bmatrix}$$

$$\texttt{+-scan-row}(C) = \begin{bmatrix} 0 & 5 & 6 & 9 \\ 0 & 3 & 12 & 14 \end{bmatrix}$$

Figure 5.7: Example of a +-scan on a two dimensional array.

$$C = \begin{bmatrix} 5 & 1 & 3 & 4 \\ 3 & 9 & 2 & 6 \end{bmatrix}$$

$$\texttt{+-reduce-rows}(C) = \begin{bmatrix} 13 \\ 20 \end{bmatrix}$$

$$\texttt{extract-row}(C, 1) = \begin{bmatrix} 3 & 9 & 2 & 6 \end{bmatrix}$$

Figure 5.8:   Examples of the simple operations +-reduce and extract on a two dimensional array.

extract and insert operations. Figure 5.8 shows some examples of these operations.

Chapter 6

Computational-Geometry Algorithms

This chapter describes four computational-geometry algorithms: a closest-pair algorithm, two convex-hull algorithms and a line-of-sight algorithm. It first describes two techniques used by these algorithms, a binary-search technique, used in one of the convex-hull algorithms, and a k-D-tree technique, used in the closest-pair algorithm. The algorithms in this chapter are joint work with Jim Little [22]. Table 6.1 summarizes the complexities of the algorithms.

	Complexity	
	Step	Element
n points		
Closest Pair	$\lg n$	$n \lg n$
Quickhull (n points, m hull points)	$\lg m, m$	n, nm
$\sqrt{n}$ Merge Hull	$\lg n$	$n \lg n$
Line of Sight	1	n

Table 6.1: The complexities of the algorithms discussed in this chapter. In the case of the quickhull, the two complexities are the best and worst case complexities.

6.1   Generalized Binary Search

In this section we consider the problem of n elements of a set A each executing a binary search on a binary tree T with m vertices. We first consider a simple binary search in which we start with all the elements at the root and on each step each element either goes to the right or left child. We then consider a generalized binary search in which we can insert new elements at the root on each step, and elements are permitted to remain at a vertex of the binary tree at any step. We assume that the tree T is organized in a vector using the standard heap ordering: the root value is stored at $T[1]$ and the two children of a vertex stored at $T[i]$ are stored at $T[2i]$ and $T[2i + 1]$.

We use a simple routine based on recursive splitting to implement the simple binary search on the scan vector model. We start with all the elements of A in a single segment and then split that segment using a split-and-segment based on whether an element is going to the right or to the left child of the root of T. We then recursively split within each of these segments, based on data from the next level of the tree. Since all the elements of A that are accessing the same vertex of T are in a contiguous segment, we can use a segmented distribute operation to distribute the value from each vertex of the tree to the elements that need it.

We now consider a generalization on the simple binary search. In this generalized binary search, we can insert new elements at the root on each step. This capability might be used to pipeline a search. We also permit elements to remain at a vertex of the binary tree on any step. This capability is required for the $\sqrt{n}$-merge-hull algorithm discussed in Section 6.5. Unlike the simple binary search, in this generalized version there might be elements at every level of the tree on any given step. Figure 6.1 illustrates how the elements of A are stored for this generalized search and shows an example of a step of the search.

To execute a step, we must somehow append the elements at a vertex v that remain with the elements being passed down from the parent of v. To append the elements, we can use a segmented version of the append operation discussed in Section 4.2. The basic idea is first to separate the elements that remain from those that go to a child into two separate vectors using two segmented pack operations. For the example of Figure 6.1 this returns:

$$\text{remain} \quad = \quad [a_0] \quad [] \quad [a_4] \quad [] \quad [a_5 \quad a_6] \quad [] \quad [a_7]$$

$$\text{not-remain} \quad = \quad [a_1] \quad [a_2] \quad [a_3] \quad [] \quad [] \quad [] \quad []$$

We then split the elements going to a child based on whether they are going to the left or right child using a segmented split operation. This returns:

$$\text{split(not-remain)} = [] \ [a_1] \ [a_2] \ [] \ [a_3] \ [] \ [] \ [] \ [] \ [] \ [] \ [] \ []$$

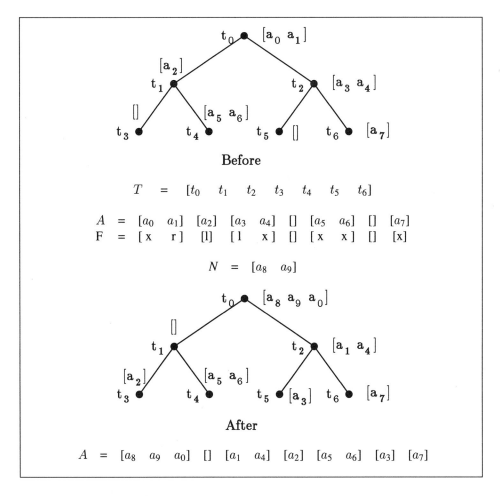

Figure 6.1: An example of a step of the general binary-search technique. We keep a segment in A for each vertex of the tree T such that segment i corresponds to vertex i (remember that the tree is in standard heap order). Each segment contains all elements at the corresponding vertex. The vector F specifies where each element needs to go during a step of the search (r for right, l for left, and x for remain). The vector N contains new elements entering at the root of the search at that step.

We now shift the segments of the split vector right by one and insert the new elements on the left (segments are shifted by shifting the segment descriptor). Because of the heap order of T, this causes each segment to go to its child segment. We also truncate the segments that correspond to children of the leaf vertices. These calculations return:

$$\text{children} \quad = \quad [a_8 \quad a_9] \quad [] \quad [a_1] \quad [a_2] \quad [] \quad [a_3] \quad []$$

We now append the shifted vector (children) to the vector of elements that remained (remain) using the append operation giving the result:

$$[a_8 \quad a_9 \quad a_0] \quad [] \quad [a_1 \quad a_4] \quad [a_2] \quad [a_5 \quad a_6] \quad [a_3] \quad [a_7]$$

The following routine can be used to execute a step of the binary search. The *remain?* flag specifies elements that stay at the current vertex, and the *right?* flag specifies elements that go to the right branch. The vector N contains the new elements to be inserted at the root.

```
define search-step(A, T, N, remain?, right?){
        remain ← pack(A, remain?);
        not-remain ← pack(A, not(remain?));
        children ← shift-segments-right(N, split(not-remain, right?));
    append(remain, children)}
```

Binary search illustrates an important difference between the general programming style used for concurrent-read P-RAM models and for vector models. In the P-RAM model, the problem is best thought of as n independent processes each executing its own search on the tree T. In the scan model, we must think of the n elements as a set and break that set into subsets according to which vertex of T each element is accessing. This might just be a philosophical point, but we believe it is important.

6.2 Building a k-D Tree

A k-D tree is a technique for splitting n points in a k dimensional space into n regions each with a single point [13]. It starts by splitting the space in two along one of the coordinates using a $k - 1$ dimensional hyperplane. It then recursively splits each of the subspaces in two. Figure 6.2 illustrates an example of a 2-D tree. At each step the algorithm must select which dimension to split within each subspace; the criterion for selection depends on how the tree will be used. A common criterion is to select the dimension along which the spread of points is greatest.

The k-D tree is often used as a step in other algorithms. 3-D trees are used in ray tracing algorithms for rendering solid objects. In such algorithms, objects need only be stored in

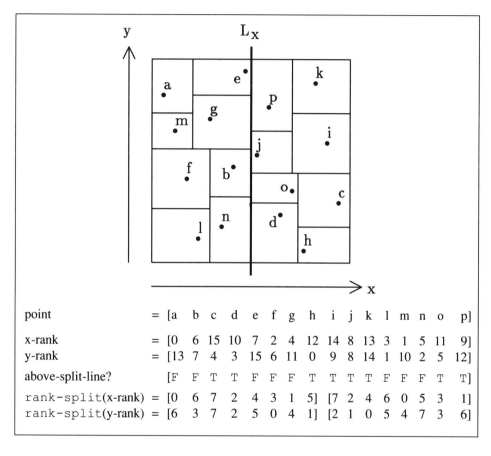

point	= [a	b	c	d	e	f	g	h	i	j	k	l	m	n	o	p]
x-rank	= [0	6	15	10	7	2	4	12	14	8	13	3	1	5	11	9]
y-rank	= [13	7	4	3	15	6	11	0	9	8	14	1	10	2	5	12]
above-split-line?	[F	F	T	T	F	F	F	F	T	T	T	T	F	F	F	T	T]
rank-split(x-rank) =	[0	6	7	2	4	3	1	5]	[7	2	4	6	0	5	3	1]
rank-split(y-rank) =	[6	3	7	2	5	0	4	1]	[2	1	0	5	4	7	3	6]

Figure 6.2: An example of a 2-D tree. The top diagram shows the final splitting. The vectors below are generated during the first step—when splitting along the line L_x.

the regions they penetrate and rays need only examine regions they cross. This can greatly reduce the number of objects each ray needs to examine. k-D trees are also used in many proximity algorithms such as the all-closest-pairs problem [43] or the closest-pair problem (see Section 6.3). k-D trees have also been suggested for use in some machine-learning algorithms [81].

The algorithm we describe here is a parallel version of a standard serial algorithm [88]. For n points, our algorithm has a step complexity of $O(k \lg n)$ and an element complexity of $O(nk \lg n)$. The algorithm is serially time optimal.

Our algorithm consists of one step per split. Each step has a step complexity of $O(k)$. Before executing any steps, the algorithm sorts the set of points according to each of the k dimensions. The sorting can be executed with the quicksort or split radix sort discussed in Chapter 3 or a version of Cole's sorting algorithm [34]. Instead of keeping the actual values in sorted order for each dimension, we keep the rank of each point along each dimension. The rank of a point is the position the point would be located at if the vector were sorted. We call the vectors that hold these ranks, *rank-vectors*—there is one *rank-vector* for each dimension. Figure 6.2 illustrates an example for a 2-D tree, the initial *rank-vectors*, and the result of the first step.

At each step of the algorithm the *rank-vectors* contain a segment for each subspace, and the ranks within each segment are the correct ranks for that subspace. It suffices to demonstrate that we can execute a split along any dimension and generate new ranks within the two subspaces. The algorithm is then correct by induction.

To split along a given dimension the algorithm distributes the cut line and determines for each point whether it is above or below the line[1]. The algorithm now uses the `rank-split` operation defined in Section 4.2 to split each *rank-vector* based on whether a point is below or above the split line. The `rank-split` operation as defined correctly generates the rank within each subspace. Each step therefore requires $O(k)$ calls to the instructions: some operations to determine whether each point is below or above the split, and k `rank-split` operations. Since there are $O(\lg n)$ steps, the whole algorithm has a step complexity of $O(k \lg n)$. Since the vectors are always of length $O(n)$, the algorithm has an element complexity of $O(nk \lg n)$

6.3   Closest Pair

In a two dimensional closest-pair problem, we want to find the pair of points in a plane that are closest to each other (Euclidean distance). The algorithm we describe is a parallel version of an algorithm described by Bentley and Shamos [14]. For n points, it has a

---

[1] As stated earlier, the method for choosing a cut line depends on the particular use of the k-D tree.

step complexity of $O(\lg n)$ and an element complexity of $O(n \lg n)$. The algorithm has an element-space complexity of $O(n \lg n)$ ($\lg n$ vectors of length n)[2] but can be modified to run with a step complexity of $O(\lg n \lg \lg n)$ and element-space complexity of $O(n)$. Atallah and Goodrich have described an $O(\lg n \lg \lg n)$ time $O(n)$ processor algorithm to solve the closest-pair problem in the concurrent-read exclusive-write (CREW) P-RAM model [8].

Our algorithm consists of building a 2-D tree as defined in Section 6.2[3], and then merging rectangles back to the original region. Given two adjacent rectangles and their closest pairs, a merge step can determine the closest pair of the merged rectangle with an step complexity of $O(1)$. Because of segments, we can merge many pairs of rectangles in parallel.

The 2-D splitting was described in Section 6.2 and the merging phase is described here. The merging works on the same principle as described by Bentley and Shamos [14]. We first review the principle and then show how it is implemented on the scan vector model. We will denote the separation of the closest pair in a rectangle R by δ_R.

At each merging step, we know the closest pair within each of a pair of merging rectangles A and B and want to find the closest pair in the rectangle $A \cup B$. The closest pair is either the pair in A, the pair in B, or a pair with one point in A and the other in B. In the last case, the two end points must each lie within $\delta_{min} = min(\delta_A, \delta_B)$ of the boundary between the two rectangles. We call this region AB' (see Figure 6.3).

If we look at a point p in AB', no more than 11 other points in AB' can be less than δ_{min} away from p. Figure 6.3 shows the tightest possible packing. If the points in AB' are sorted along the merge line, each point can determine the minimum distance to another point in AB' by looking at a fixed number of neighbors in the sorted order (at most 11). Once all points in AB' have determined their closest neighbor in AB', we take the minimum of these distances to determine $\delta_{AB'}$ and then calculate the desired result: $\delta_{AB} = min(\delta_{min}, \delta_{AB'})$.

We now show how this technique is applied in the scan vector model. The merge consists of the following steps (each step has a step complexity of $O(1)$):

1. Derive the vector of points in $A \cup B$ sorted along the direction of the split line. To get this vector, we need only keep the appropriate split-flags when executing the 2-D splitting—remember that when building a k-D splitting tree we had the sorted order for all dimensions for all rectangles.

2. Determine δ_{min} by taking the minimum of δ_A and δ_B. Distribute δ_{min} to all points

---

[2]These vectors are all boolean vectors.

[3]In this algorithm it does not matter in what order we pick the dimensions—in fact, we could always split on the same dimension.

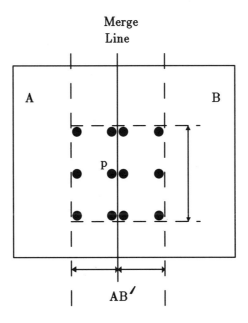

Figure 6.3:   Merging two rectangles to determine closest pair. Only 12 points can fit in the $2\delta_{min} \times 2\delta_{min}$ dashed box such that no two points in either A or B are closer than δ_{min}.

in the sorted vector of $A \cup B$.

3. Pack elements which are within δ_{min} of the merge line using the `pack` operation into a new sorted vector AB'.

4. Shift this vector to the right by one and calculate the distance from each point to its neighbor. Repeat this six times to get the six neighbors on each side.

5. Determine $\delta_{AB'}$ by taking the minimum distance found in the previous step using a `min-reduce`. Take the minimum of δ_{min} and $\delta_{AB'}$ to get δ_{AB}.

The algorithm runs with a step complexity of $O(\lg n)$ because the k-D splitting has a step complexity of $O(\lg n)$ (see Section 6.2) and there are $\lg n$ merge steps each with a step complexity of $O(1)$. To execute the merges with a step complexity of $O(1)$, we must store the split-flags when executing the 2-D splitting. Since there are $\lg n$ levels, this requires that we store $\lg n$ boolean vectors each of length n. If allocating this space is a problem, we can derive the sorted vector for $A \cup B$ on the fly by merging the sorted vectors of A and B. This merge can be implemented as described in Section 3.7.2. If we include a merge instruction in the model, as suggested in Section 4.5.1, the closest-pair algorithm will run with a step complexity of $O(\lg n)$, an element complexity of $O(n \lg n)$, and an element-space complexity of $O(n)$.

6.4 Quickhull

In this section we describe a parallel version of the *quickhull* algorithm [88]. This algorithm is used to solve the planar convex hull problem: given n points in the plane, find which of these points lie on the perimeter of the smallest convex region that contains all points. The quickhull algorithm was given its name because of its similarity with the quicksort algorithm. As with quicksort, the quickhull algorithm picks a "pivot" element, splits the data based on the pivot, and is recursively applied to each of the split sets. Also, as with quicksort, the pivot element is not guaranteed to split the data into equal sized sets, and in the worst case the algorithm can require n steps.

Figure 6.4 shows an example of the quickhull algorithm. The algorithm first splits the points into two sets with a line that passes between the two x extrema—lets call these points l and r. In the scan vector model, this is executed with a few reduce and distribute operations, some elementwise arithmetic calculations, and a `split` operation.

The algorithm now recursively splits each of the two subspaces into two using the following step. It determines for each point p in the subspace the perpendicular distance from the point to the line lr. This can be calculated with a cross product of the lines lr and

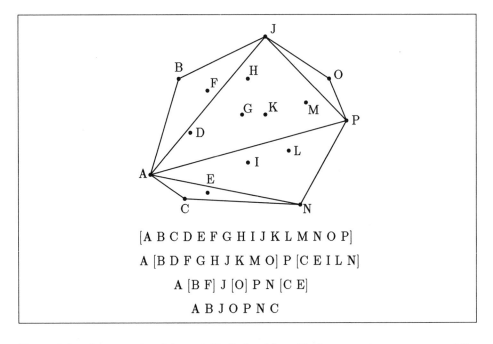

Figure 6.4:   An example of the *quickhull* algorithm. Each vector shows one step of the algorithm. Since A and P are the two x extrema, the line AP is the original split line. J and N are the furthest points in each subspace from AP and are, therefore, used for the next level of splits. The values outside the brackets are hull points that have already been found.

lp. The algorithm selects the furthest point from the line lr and distributes it to all other elements in the subspace—lets call this point t. It should be clear that t lies on the convex hull. Points within the triangle ltr cannot be on the convex hull and are eliminated with a `pack` operation. The point t is now used to further split each segment based on which of the two sides of the triangle, lt or rt, they fall. The algorithm is now applied to the new segments recursively. The algorithm is completed when all segments are empty.

Each step has a step complexity of $O(1)$ and an element complexity of at most $O(n)$: since many points might be deleted on each step, the element complexity could be significantly less. For m hull points, the algorithm runs in $O(\lg m)$ steps for well-distributed hull points, and has a worst case running time of $O(m)$ steps.

6.5 $\sqrt{n}$ Merge Hull

In this section we describe a variation of a parallel algorithm by Aggarwal et. al. [3] and independently by Atallah and Goodrich [8] for solving the convex-hull problem. Their algorithm is based on the concurrent-read exclusive-write (CREW) P-RAM model. We cannot use their algorithm directly because the scan vector model does not permit concurrent access to a single value, a necessary part of their algorithm. The variation we describe keeps all elements that require the same data in a contiguous segment so the data can be distributed using a `distribute` operation. The contribution of our version is showing how the concurrent-read operation can be replaced by the `distribute` operation and involves the binary search method described in Section 6.1. Our variation has a step complexity of $O(\lg n)$ and an element complexity of $O(n \lg n)$. The algorithm is, therefore, serially time optimal. Miller and Stout have shown an exclusive-read exclusive-write (EREW) convex-hull algorithm with an $O(\lg n)$ complexity [76]. Our algorithm, however, is simpler, and the binary search technique it uses in interesting on its own.

We begin by reviewing the CREW algorithm. The algorithm sorts the points according to their x coordinate. It slices this ordering into $\sqrt{n}$ equal sized sets of points and recursively solves the convex hull for each set. It then merges the $\sqrt{n}$ subhulls (see Figure 6.5). The sort and the merge both take $O(\lg n)$ time[4]. The running time of the algorithm thus has the recurrence relation $T(n) = T(\sqrt{n}) + O(\lg n)$ which yields $O(\lg n)$ time.

Since the elements can be sorted using existing algorithms, we concentrate on the merging step. The merge is executed in two parts: one part finds the upper chain of the convex hull and the other part finds the lower chain. The upper chain is the section of the convex hull that runs across the top between the two x extrema. In the CREW algorithm the merge of each chain works as follows.

---

[4]The algorithm of Cole [34] can be used for sorting in the CREW model.

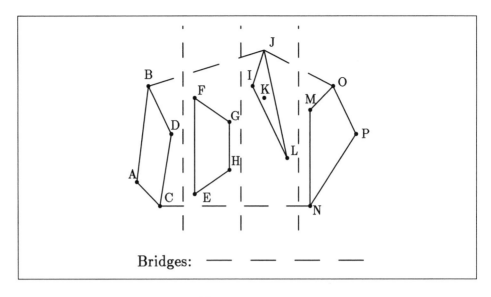

Figure 6.5:   An example of the $\sqrt{n}$ merge hull algorithm. The horizontal dashed lines show the division of the points into $\sqrt{n}$ groups of $\sqrt{n}$ elements each. The subhulls within each group are marked with solid lines. The upper chain is the chain A B J O P.

The algorithm assigns an element (a processor) for each pair of subhulls. Since there are $\sqrt{n}$ subhulls, $O(n)$ elements are sufficient. Each of these pairs independently finds the upper tangent line-segment[5] between its two subhulls using a serial method of Overmars [82]. This method executes a binary search alternating between the two subhulls, and requires $O(\lg n)$ time. At the kth step of the binary search, an element either goes down the left branch, the right branch, or remains in place.

Once the upper tangent lines have been found, the algorithm determines the bridges among the $\sqrt{n}$ subhulls. The bridges are the upper tangent line-segments that belong to the upper chain. To find which of the upper tangent lines are bridges, each subhull finds the highest sloped line in both directions (to a point on the right and to a point on the left). If the joint formed by these lines is convex, then both lines are bridges. If the joint formed by the lines is concave, neither are bridges. All edges on a subhull that lie between bridges of that subhull also belong to the convex hull.

This algorithm cannot be implemented directly on the scan vector model since each pair of subhulls independently finds the upper tangent-line segments using the algorithm

---

[5]An upper tangent line-segment of two sets of points is the line that passes through at least one point from each set so that all other points in the two sets are below the line.

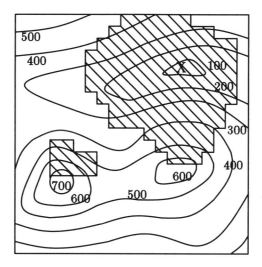

Figure 6.6: An example of a line-of-sight problem. The X marks the observation point. The numbers represent the altitude of each contour line. The elements visible from the observation point are shaded.

of Overmars and , therefore, requires concurrent reads: several pairs, while executing the binary search, will require access to the same elements. To avoid the concurrent read, we place each of the sets of $\sqrt{n}$ points that belong to the same subhull in its own segment. We then use a binary-search method described in Section 6.1. This search requires $O(\lg n)$ time and involves no concurrent-reads.

Our variation of the CREW algorithm runs with the same number of calls to the primitives as the original since, as with the original, the sort runs in $O(\lg n)$ time, and, as shown above, the merge also runs in $O(\lg n)$ time. This variation trades the concurrent-read capability for the scan capability.

6.6 Line of Sight

Given an $\sqrt{n}$-by-$\sqrt{n}$ grid of altitudes and an observation point on or above the surface, a line-of-sight algorithm finds all points on the grid visible from the observation point. Figure 6.6 shows an example. A line-of-sight algorithm can be applied to help determine where to locate potential eyesores. For example, when designing a building, a highway or a city dump, it is often informative to know from where the "eyesore" will be visible. The algorithm is also useful for real time vision applications.

The algorithm we describe in this section has a step complexity of $O(1)$ and an element

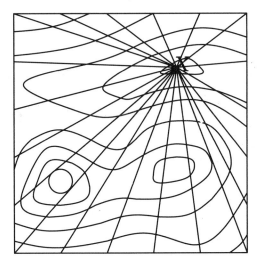

Figure 6.7: Example of some rays propagating from the observation point.

complexity of $O(n)$. The basic idea is to allocate a segment in a vector for every ray that propagates in the plane from the observation point, henceforth referred to as X, to a boundary position (see Figure 6.7). Based on some calculations on the points in each ray, we can determine if the point is visible.

The algorithm consists of four basic steps.

1. Each point p in the grid calculates the vertical angle between the horizontal plane that passes through X (the observation point) and the line from p to X. This is executed by distributing the location of X over all points and calculating the *arctan* of the horizontal difference over the vertical difference.

2. The algorithms allocates a set of rays—one for each boundary grid point—and distributes the angles from each point p in the grid to all the rays it belongs to. Let us call the segmented vector that contains these rays the *ray structure*.

3. Following a ray from X to the boundary, a point p is visible if its angle is greater than all the angles that precede it in the ray. This can be determined for all points in all rays with a single segmented `max-scan`, and a comparison.

4. Visibility information is returned back to the grid points. Since a grid point may belong to many rays, the visibility flags are combined using `or`.

Since steps 1 and 3 should be clear, and step 4 is basically the reverse of step 2, we only describe step 2. To allocate the *ray structure* the algorithm draws a line from the observation point to each boundary element using the routine discussed in Section 3.6.1. Each grid point might belong to several of these rays (points near X belong to more rays than points near the edges). To distribute the angle from a grid point to all the rays it belongs to, the algorithm creates another segmented vector structure—the *copy structure*. In the copy structure, the algorithm allocates a segment for each grid point p. The size of the segment for a point p is equal to the number of rays p belongs to—this can be determined from the relative positions of p, X and the boundary. Each point p distributes its angle to its segment in the copy structure using the `distribute` operation.

There is now a 1-to-1 mapping between positions in the copy structure and positions in the ray structure. The algorithm can calculate the permutation indices needed to execute this mapping based on the location of X. Once the angles are permuted to the ray structure, the algorithm executes step 3. To return the information back to the grid structure after step 3, the algorithm uses the same copy structure but instead of distributing, it reduces using an `or-reduce`. At completion, all points visible from any ray are marked and returned.

The longest vectors required by the algorithm are the vectors of the copy and ray structures. It is not hard to show that for a $\sqrt{n}$-by-$\sqrt{n}$ grid, independent of the location of X, these vectors have length $2n$.

Chapter 7

Graph Algorithms

This chapter describes four graph algorithms: a minimum-spanning-tree algorithm, a biconnected-components algorithm, a maximum-flow algorithm and a maximal-independent-set algorithm. The minimum-spanning-tree algorithm is new. The maximum-flow algorithm is an algorithm of Goldberg's [46]. The maximal-independent-set algorithm and the biconnected-components algorithm are small changes to parallel algorithms designed for the P-RAM models [73, 112].

All the algorithms use the v-graph representation described in Section 5.1 and make frequent use of the operations described in that section. Although most of the algorithms have an optimal step complexity, they are typically not serially time optimal. Table 7.1 summarizes the complexities of the algorithms.

7.1 Minimum Spanning Tree and Connectivity

This section describes a probabilistic minimum-spanning-tree (MST) algorithm. For n vertices and m edges, it has a step complexity of $O(\lg n)$ and an element complexity of $O(m \lg n)$. The best algorithm known for the EREW P-RAM model requires $O(\lg^2 n)$ time [55, 98]. The best algorithm known for the CRCW P-RAM model requires $O(\lg n)$ time [10], but this algorithms requires that the generic CRCW P-RAM model be extended so that if several processors write to the same location, either the value from the lowest numbered processor is written, or the minimum value is written.

All these algorithms are based on the algorithm of Sollin [15], which is similar to the algorithm of Borùvka [27]. The algorithms start with a forest of trees in which each tree is a single vertex. These trees are merged during the algorithm, and the algorithm terminates when a single tree remains. At each step, every tree T finds its minimum-weight edge

	Complexity	
	Step	Element
Graph Algorithms n vertices, m edges		
Minimum Spanning Tree	$\lg n$	$m \lg n$
Maximum Flow	n^2	$n^2 m$
Maximal Independent Set	$\lg n$	$m \lg n$
Biconnected Components	$\lg n$	$m \lg n$

Table 7.1:   The complexities of the algorithms we discuss in this chapter. Some of the algorithms are probabilistic.

joining a vertex in T to a vertex of a distinct tree T'. Trees connected by one of these edges merge. To reduce the forest to a single tree, $O(\lg n)$ such steps are required.

In the EREW P-RAM algorithm, each step requires $\Omega(\lg n)$ time because finding the minimum edge in a tree and distributing connectivity information over merging trees might require $\Omega(\lg n)$ time. In the extended CRCW P-RAM model, each step only requires constant time because each minimum edge can be found with a single write operation. In our algorithm, we keep the graph in the graph representation discussed in Section 5.1 so that we can use the `min-reduce` operation to find the minimum edge for each tree and the `distribute` operation to distribute connectivity information among merging trees with a constant number of calls to the primitives.

As with the Shiloach and Vishkin CRCW P-RAM algorithm [105], trees are selected for merging by forming stars. We define a star as a set of vertices within a graph with one of the set marked as the parent, the others marked as children, and an edge that leads from each child vertex to its parent vertex[1]. A graph might contain many stars. The *star-merge* operation takes a graph with a set of disjoint stars, and returns a graph with each star merged into a single vertex. Figure 7.1 shows an example of a star-merge for a graph with a single star.

The minimum-spanning-tree algorithm thus consists of repeatedly finding starts and merging them. To find stars, each vertex flips a coin to decide whether they are a child or parent. All children check their minimum edge to see if it is connected to a parent. All these edges which are connected to a parent are marked as star edges. Since, on average, half the trees are children and half of the trees on the other end of the minimum edge of a child are parents, 1/4 of the trees are merged on each star-merge step. This random mate

---

[1]This definition of a star is slightly different from the definition of Shiloach and Vishkin [105].

technique is similar to the method discussed by Miller and Reif [75]. Since on average 1/4 of the trees are deleted on each step, $O(\lg n)$ steps are required to reduce the forest to a single tree.

We now describe how a star-merge operation can be implemented in the scan model, such that for m edges, the operation has a step complexity of $O(1)$ and an element complexity of $O(m)$. We define a *star edge* as an edge that connects a child to its parent. The input to the star-merge operation is a graph in the v-graph representation, with two additional vectors: one contains flags that mark every star edge, and the other contains a flag that marks every parent.

To implement a star-merge in the v-graph, each child segment must be moved into its parent segment. The technique we use can be partitioned into four steps: (1) each parent opens enough space in its segment to fit its children, (2) the children are permuted into this space, (3) the cross-pointers vector is updated to reflect the change in structure of the graph, and (4) edges which point within a segment are deleted, therefore deleting edges that point within a tree. Figure 7.2 shows an example of the various intermediate results during a star-merge; we will refer to the figure in the following discussion.

(1) To open space in the parent segments, each child passes its length (number of edges) across its star edge to its parent, so each parent knows how much space it needs to open up for each of its children. Let us call the vector that contains the needed space of each child the *needed-space* vector. A 1 is placed in all the nonstar edges of this vector. We can now use a segmented $+$-`reduce` on the *needed-space* vector to determine the new size of each parent and a segmented `distribute` (Section 4.1.5) to allocate this new space for each parent. We also execute a segmented $+$-`scan` on the *needed-space* vector to determine the offset of each child within its parent segment and the new position of each non star edge of the parent. We call this vector the *child-offset* vector.

(2) We now need to permute the children into the parent segments. To determine the new position of the edges in the child vertices, we permute the *child-offset* back to each child and distribute it across the edges of the child. Each child adds its index to this offset giving each child edge a unique address within the segment of its parent. We now permute all the edges, children and parents, to their new positions.

(3) To update the pointers, we simply pass the new position of each end of an edge to the other end of the edge.

(4) To delete edges that point within a segment, we check if each edge points within the segment by distributing the ends of the segment, and pack all elements that point outside each segment deleting elements pointing within each segment. We must update the pointers again.

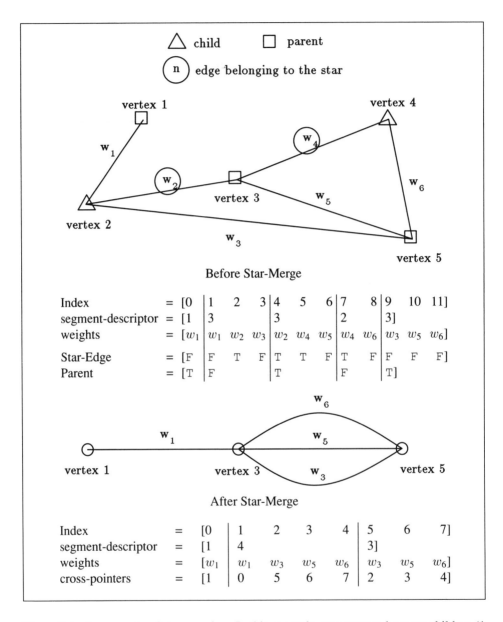

Figure 7.1: An example of star merging. In this example, two parents have no children (1 and 5) and the third (3) has two children (2 and 4). The second diagram shows the graph after the star is merged.

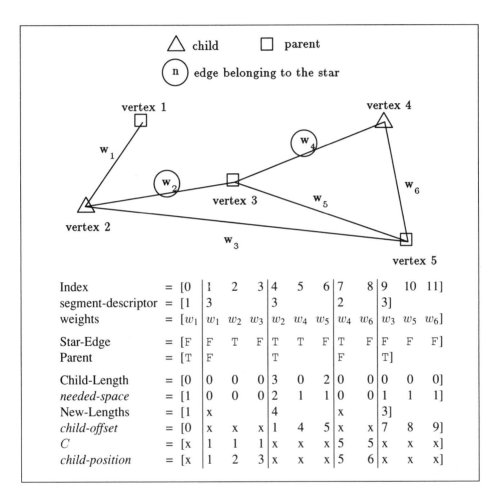

Figure 7.2: The values of the various intermediate results during a star-merge operation.

7.2   Maximum Flow

Goldberg showed [46] that his maximum-flow algorithm could be improved from a step complexity of $O(n^2 \lg n)$ on the EREW and CRCW P-RAM models to a step complexity of $O(n^2)$ with the scan primitives. We review the algorithm here.

Goldberg's algorithm is based on a preflow push method [62] that requires no more than $O(n^2)$ push steps. At each step, every vertex holds an excess value which corresponds to how much more flow is coming in than is leaving (at the end this must be 0), and an effective distance to the sink. Each step works as follows. All edges try to get rid of their excess by passing it off on edges that have residual capacity (the capacity is not used to the maximum) and that are connected to vertices that have a lower effective distance. The edges then reset their effective distance by finding the minimum effective distance of their neighbors that are reachable through a link with positive residual capacity and adding 1 to this value. The new effective distance is passed to the neighbors. This step is repeated until the network settles—the excess is zero at all vertices.

In the scan vector model, each step requires a constant number of calls to the primitive instructions. The distribution of excess is executed as described in Section 5.1.3. The new effective distance calculation can use a `min-reduce`. The passing of the new effective distance requires a `distribute` and `permute`. In the EREW P-RAM model, the effective distance calculation and the distribution of the excess requires $O(\lg n)$ time. In the CREW P-RAM model, the distribution of the excess requires $O(\lg n / \lg \lg n)$ time.

7.3   Maximal Independent Set and Biconnectivity

Luby's maximal-independent-set (MIS) algorithm [73] can be implemented on the scan model. For n vertices and m edges the algorithm has a probabilistic step complexity of $O(\lg n)$ and element complexity of $O(m \lg n)$. His original version for the EREW P-RAM model ran in probabilistic $O(\lg^2 n)$ time.

The algorithm consists of $O(\lg n)$ steps. At each step the algorithm adds some vertices to an initially empty set M, and after $O(\lg n)$ steps, with high probability, M is the MIS. In each step, every vertex not already in M and not a neighbor of a vertex in M, randomly selects itself based on the inverse of its degree. Each such selected vertex then adds itself to M if none of its neighbors of greater degree are also selected. Both determining if a vertex is a neighbor of a vertex in M, and finding if a neighbor of greater degree is selected can be executed with a neighbor reduce (see Section 5.1.2). Each step thus requires a constant number of calls to the primitive instructions.

Tarjan and Vishkin [112] show how the biconnectivity problem reduces to the spanning tree (connected components) problem and some tree manipulations. On the scan model, the tree manipulations can be executed using the techniques discussed in Section 5.2. The connected components can use the minimum-spanning-tree algorithm discussed earlier. The step complexity is, therefore, $O(\lg n)$ and the element complexity is $O(n \lg n)$.

Chapter 8

Numerical Algorithms

This chapter describes five numerical algorithms: a matrix-vector multiply, a linear-systems solver, a simplex algorithm for linear programming, an outer-product, and a sparse-matrix multiply. The first four algorithms assume dense matrices and use the grid versions of the scan vector instructions (see Section 5.3). The linear-systems solver and the simplex algorithms were developed jointly with Ajit Agrawal, Robert Krawitz and Cynthia Phillips [4] and have been run on the Connection Machine giving very high performance. Table 8.1 summarizes the complexities of the algorithms.

8.1 Matrix-Vector Multiplication

To Multiply a matrix by a vector we distribute the vector across the columns of the matrix using a grid `distribute`, execute a elementwise multiply, and then sum across the rows using grid `+-reduce` (see Figure 8.1). Since both the `distribute` and `+-reduce`

	Complexity	
	Step	Element
$n \times m$ Dense Matrices		
Matrix-Vector Multiply	1	nm
Linear-Systems Solver $(n = m)$	n	n^2
Simplex For Linear Programming	1 (per step)	nm

Table 8.1: The complexities of the algorithms discussed in this chapter.

117

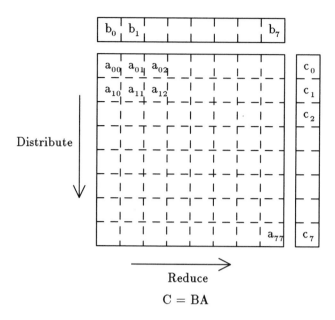

Figure 8.1:   An example of a matrix-vector multiply.

require a constant number of calls to the scan vector instructions, for an $n \times m$ matrix, the step complexity is $O(1)$ and the element complexity is nm. A matrix-vector multiply is therefore serially time optimal.

8.2   Linear-Systems Solver

This section describes an implementation on the scan model of a linear-system solver which uses LU-decomposition with partial pivoting and back solving. For an $n \times n$ matrix, the algorithm has a step complexity of $O(n)$ and an element complexity of $O(n^3)$. Before describing the algorithm, we review LU-decomposition.

Starting from the basic formula $Ax = b$, we compute two matrices L and U such that $A = LU$, where L is lower triangular and U is upper triangular (hence the name LU decomposition). Now we have $LUx = b$, which we rewrite as $Ly = b$ and $Ux = y$. Solving for y is simple since L is triangular [90]; this step is called *forward solution*. Likewise, given y, solving for x is simple, as U is also triangular; this step is called *back solution*. Since for a given system A we may wish to solve x for multiple b vectors, we split the linear-systems solver into two algorithms: LU-decomposition and solution. As the L and U matrices do not share any non-zero elements, we can conveniently store both matrices in a single matrix, known as the *LU matrix*.

When performing LU-decomposition by Gaussian elimination, we select a row and column at each step to eliminate. The process of selecting a row is called *pivoting*. It is needed to improve numerical stability. The partial pivoting technique selects the columns in left-to-right order, and selects the element of the column with the greatest absolute value. Rather than physically exchanging the two rows, which would yield a true lower and upper triangular matrix, we record in a separate vector which row was eliminated in which iteration. This defines a "logical" diagonal to the left and right of which reside the L and U matrices respectively. For example, the following permutation vector corresponds to the following permuted LU-decomposition, where elements labeled L are part of the L matrix, those labeled U are part of the U matrix, and those labeled D are on the diagonal:

$$P = \begin{bmatrix} 2 \\ 4 \\ 1 \\ 3 \end{bmatrix}, \quad LU = \begin{bmatrix} L_{12} & D_{22} & U_{32} & U_{42} \\ L_{14} & L_{24} & L_{34} & D_{44} \\ D_{11} & U_{21} & U_{31} & U_{41} \\ L_{13} & L_{23} & D_{33} & U_{43} \end{bmatrix}$$

The unpermuted LU-decomposition looks like this:

$$LU = \begin{bmatrix} D_{11} & U_{21} & U_{31} & U_{41} \\ L_{12} & D_{22} & U_{32} & U_{42} \\ L_{13} & L_{23} & D_{33} & U_{43} \\ L_{14} & L_{24} & L_{34} & D_{44} \end{bmatrix}$$

The parallel algorithm for LU-decomposition is straightforward. For an $m \times m$ matrix, we execute m steps of Gaussian elimination. Moving left to right through the matrix, we extract the columns in sequence. We find the element with the greatest absolute value, and extract its row. We then divide the pivot column by the pivot element itself, and distribute the pivot row and column across the matrix. We replace the part of the pivot column logically below the pivot element, where it will serve as a column of L. Finally, we execute Gaussian elimination on the part of the matrix logically below and to the right of the pivot row and column. Figure 8.2 illustrates the code for the LU-decomposition.

The forward and back solution phase is also straightforward. We first solve $Ly = b$, divide y and U through by the logical diagonal such that the system has a unit diagonal, and then solve $Ux = y$. A solution step consists of extracting a column, multiplying it by the diagonal element, and subtracting from b. Note that to find the pivot element we compare the permutation vector against the loop index. Figure 8.3 illustrates the required routine.

```
define LU-decomposition(A, P){
    ;A is the original matrix
    ;P is the permutation vector
    for i from 1 to column-length(m) do
        Selecting the rows and columns of A that have not
        been pivoted on
            column ← extract-column(A, i);
            pivot-row ← max-index(column);
            row ← extract-row(A, pivot-row);
            pivot-element ← extract(row, i);
            P ← insert(P, pivot-row, i);
            column ← column p÷ pivot-element;
            column-matrix ← distribute-column(column);
            row-matrix ← distribute-row(row);
            A ← insert-column(A, i, column);
            selecting processors in A that are not in the pivot
            row or column
                A ← A p− row-matrix p× column-matrix;}
```

Figure 8.2: Code for generating the LU-decomposition of a matrix. The results are returned in the matrix A and the vector P.

```
define solve(B, LU, P){
    For i from 1 to m Do
        column ← extract-column(LU, i);
        pivot ← the element of B such that i == P;
        selecting the elements B[j] and column[j] such that P[j] > i
            B ← B p− column p× copy(pivot);
    send the logical diagonal of LU to the first column of temp;
    diag ← extract-column(temp, 1);
        ;At this point B contains y from Ly = b
        ;Divide U and B by the diagonal.
    B ← B p÷ diag;
    temp ← distribute-column(diag);
    Selecting all processors in the logical upper triangle of LU
        LU ← LU p÷ diag;
    For i from m downto 1 Do
        column ← extract-column(LU, i);
        pivot ← the elements of B such that i == P;
        selecting the elements B[j] and column[j] such that P[j] ≤ i
            B ← B p− column p× copy(pivot);
    unpermute B}
```

Figure 8.3: Code for the solving $LUx = B$, given LU, B and the permutation vector P for LU.

8.3   Simplex

We now describe a scan model implementation of a simplex method for solving linear programming problems. The standard form of a linear programming problem is as follows:

$$\text{minimize} \quad c^T x \quad \text{such that} \quad \begin{cases} Ax & = & b \\ x & \geq & 0 \end{cases}$$

where c is an m_2-dimensional integer *objective function* vector, A is an $m_1 \times m_2$ integer *constraint matrix*, b is an m_1-vector of integers, and x is a real m_2-vector of unknowns. Generally we have $m_1 < m_2$.

A vector x such that $Ax = b$ and $x \geq 0$ is called a *feasible solution* because it satisfies all the constraints. If a linear program has an optimal solution, we can always find one such that m_1 of the entries in vector x are equal to 0 [83]. Such vectors, called *basic feasible solutions*, correspond geometrically to corners of the convex $(m_2 - m_1)$-dimensional polytope of all feasible solutions. The simplex method for solving linear programs starts at a basic feasible solution and *pivots* to a new basic feasible solution which improves the objective function. Algebraically, we increase one of the zero-valued *nonbasic* variables (the *entering* variable) until one of the non-zero *basic* variables becomes zero. In the Dantzig method of pivoting, the entering variable is the one that will decrease the objective function by the most (per unit increase in the variable).

All the information necessary to perform the pivoting is kept in a *tableau* where the objective function and all nonbasic variables are represented in terms of the basic variables. At the start, the tableau is the constraint matrix A augmented by the column vector b and the row vector c. We then use Gaussian elimination to eliminate all columns corresponding to basic variables. We do not represent these columns in the tableau since they always form an identity matrix. Since all the nonbasic variables are zero at the basic feasible solution represented by the tableau, the b vector represents values of the basic variables and objective function at the basic feasible solution and the objective function vector c represents the unit change in the objective function per unit increase in each nonbasic variable. To form the tableau for which one basic variable is replaced by a nonbasic variable then involves one step of Gaussian elimination.

The tableau representation is used primarily for linear programs for which the constraint matrix A is *dense*. In practice many linear programs from real applications are sparse. Implementations on sequential computers use special techniques to avoid computing on the whole matrix when only a few elements are non-zero. When the matrix is dense, however, the tableau method (or the revised method which is more numerically stable) can be practical.

The implementation of simplex with Dantzig's rule is fairly straightforward. We first find the index of the most negative coefficient of the objective function; pivoting on this variable will give us the most rapid improvement in the solution per unit increase in the entering nonbasic variable. If there are no negative coefficients, then we cannot make any improvement, and thus have finished successfully. We then extract the indexed column, and select the processors corresponding to real constraints, i. e. only positive coefficients correspond to basic variables that decrease as the entering variable increases. If there are no positive coefficients in the column, then the system is unbounded; we can increase the value of variable without limit and never violate a constraint. To find the limiting constraint, we divide the b vector by the positive elements of the pivot column elementwise and find the index of the smallest ratio. The two indices define the pivot element. We then perform a Gaussian elimination step. We must update the pivot row and column separately since we do not represent the full tableau. Figure 8.4 illustrates the necessary code.

8.4 Outer Product

For a vector v_1 of length m_1, a vector v_2 of length m_2, and a function f of two arguments, the outer product returns a two dimensional array of size $m_1 \times m_2$ with f applied to every pairing of the elements of v_1 and v_2. The outer product is used as a substep in many applications. Some examples include sparse matrix multiplication (see Section 8.5), and finding all closest pairs in a high-dimensional space. We can implement an outer product trivially with a distribute-row, distribute-column and then executing the function f (see Figure 8.5). If the function f has a step complexity of $O(1)$, the outer product has a step complexity of $O(1)$ and an element complexity of $O(m_1 \times m_2)$. The necessary code for a ×-outer-product is:

```
define ×-outer-product(A, B){
    Ad ← distribute-column(A, length(B));
    Bd ← distribute-row(B, length(A));
    Ad p× Bd}
```

8.5 Sparse-Matrix Multiplication

We now consider sparse matrix multiplication of two matrices A and B. We assume that A is ordered in row major order such that each row is in its own segment (we use empty segments for empty rows). We assume that B is ordered in column major order. We now execute an outer-product on each row-column pair. So, for example, each element of row 0 of matrix A is matched with each element of column 0 of matrix B. We use a segmented

```
define simplex(A, B, C){
    ;tableau A ((m₁) + 1 × (m₂ + 1))
    ;constraint vector B
    ;objective function vector C
    repeat forever:
        pivot-column-index ←
                index of element in C with most negative value;
                (if no negative processor, exit simplex successfully)
        pivot-column ← extract-column(A, pivot-column-index);
        selecting processors in Pivotcolumn with positive values
                (if no positive processor, exit simplex unsuccessfully)
            ratio ← pivot-column p÷ B;
            pivot-row-index ←
                    index of element in ratio with smallest value;
        pivot-row ← extract-row(A, pivot-row-index);
            ;update pivot row and column
        pivot-element ← A[pivot-column-index][pivot-row-index];
        pivot-row ← pivot-row p÷ copy(pivot-element);
        row-matrix ← distribute-row(pivot-row);
        column-matrix ←distribute-column(pivot-column);
            ;update the constraint vector and objective function
            ;on their own, even though they get updated later
        value ← A[m, n];
        B ← B p− pivot-column p× copy(value);
        C ← C p− pivot-column p× value;
            ;update the tableau
        A ← insert-row(A, pivot-row, pivot-row-index);
        selecting processors of A that are not part of the pivot row
                or column
            A ← A p− pivot-row p× pivot-column;}
```

Figure 8.4: Code for the simplex method for solving linear programming problems.

$$A \ = \ [1 \quad 2 \quad 3]$$
$$B \ = \ [1 \quad 2]$$

$$Ad = \begin{bmatrix} 1 & 2 & 3 \\ 1 & 2 & 3 \end{bmatrix}$$

$$Bd = \begin{bmatrix} 1 & 1 & 1 \\ 2 & 2 & 2 \end{bmatrix}$$

$$Result = \begin{bmatrix} 1 & 2 & 3 \\ 2 & 4 & 6 \end{bmatrix}$$

Figure 8.5: An example of a ×-outer-product.

version of the outer-product routine described in Section 8.4. The algorithm now runs a sort using the row number appended to the column number as the key. This places elements with the same row and column destination next to each other. In the final step, elements with the same row and column destination are added using a +-reduce. Because of the previous sort, the result is in row major order.

For two $n \times n$ matrices with m_1 and m_2 nonzero elements, respectively, the step complexity of the algorithm is the $O(\lg n)$ required for the sorts (we can use the radix sort described in Section 3.4.1). If e elements are produced by the outer-product step, the element complexity is $O((e + n) \lg n)$.

Part III

Languages and Compilers

Introduction: Languages and Compilers

This part demonstrates that some very-high-level languages are naturally mapped onto the parallel vector models. It contains three chapters. Chapter 9, *collection-oriented languages*, describes a class of high-level languages that map very well onto parallel vector models. These languages include SETL (the Set Theoretic Language) which has been touted as a very high-level programming language which can greatly simplify coding over conventional von Neumann languages. Chapter 10, *flattening nested parallelism*, describes techniques for taking nested parallel routines and mapping them onto a flat homogeneous machine. These techniques are very useful for compiling the high-level collection-oriented languages. These first two chapters are independent and can be read in any order.

Chapter 11, *a compiler for Paralation Lisp*, describes a compiler for a particular collection-oriented language, PARALATION LISP, that compiles into the scan vector instruction set. The chapter brings together ideas from the previous two chapters. Appendix C, *Paralation-Lisp code*, illustrates many algorithms and a relatively large application, Quinlan's ID3 learning algorithm [91], written in PARALATION LISP. All of these algorithms use nested parallelism.

Chapter 9

Collection-Oriented Languages

This chapter presents a framework for comparing a class of high-level computer languages we call *collection-oriented languages*. From a programming standpoint, these languages are excellent languages for cleanly and concisely implementing a broad set of applications. From an implementation standpoint, these languages can be implemented on a broad variety of machines—in particular, as concerns this book, they are naturally implemented on the parallel vector models.

Collection-oriented languages, such as APL [59, 60], APL2 [58], CM-LISP [107], NIAL [77, 99], PARALATION LISP [96], SETL [100], and SQL [39], are centered around data structures which represent collections of elements, and operations for manipulating the collections. Conventional von Neumann languages, such as Pascal and FORTRAN, also support collections, usually in the form of an array data type. Collection-oriented languages, however, differ because their operators focus on manipulating collections as a whole. For example, multiplying all elements of a collection by some constant, sorting the elements of a collection, or summing the elements of a collection are basic collection-oriented operations.

Because the operations of collection-oriented languages operate on whole collections of elements, these languages tend to be much higher level than conventional languages. As argued by the proponents of the collection-oriented languages, the high-level constructs can lead to code that is clearer, easier to write and more concise[1]. Also, the high-level description allows code to be mapped onto a much broader set of architectures—fewer details about the implementation are included in the code, giving more flexibility to a

---

[1]Unfortunately, APL has given much of the computer community the impression that collection-oriented languages are difficult to understand. This is not the fault of the semantics of the language, but rather of the cryptic syntax.

Collections	
Types of Elements	Atomic, Structure, Collection
Homogeneity	Homogeneous, Heterogeneous
Ordering	Unordered, Linear-Ordered,
	Grid-Ordered, Key-Ordered

Collection Operations	
Apply-to-Each	Implicit, Explicit
Collection Operations	Sorting, Summing, Intersecting, ...

Table 9.1: The various dimensions along which to compare the various collection-oriented languages.

compiler. On the other hand, collection-oriented languages have historically been hard to compile to run as efficiently on serial machines as conventional languages, and have therefore never gained great acceptance.

Collection-oriented languages are interesting in the context of this book because most collections are naturally mapped onto vectors and most of the collection-oriented operations are efficiently implemented with vector operations. This chapter compares the various collection-oriented languages based on the types of collections they support and on the types of operations they provide. Table 9.1 illustrates the framework on which we base this comparison. The chapter also illustrates how many of the collection types can be mapped onto simple homogeneous vectors (homogeneous vectors of atomic values).

9.1   Collections

A *collection* is a group of elements viewed as a whole.[2] This section categorizes such collections according to three criteria: the types of elements allowed in a collection, whether the elements of a collection must be of the same type, and the ordering of the elements in a collection. Table 9.2 shows how the collections of various languages fit into the categories.

Types of Elements: We consider three classes of types that can be allowed in a collection: atomic types, structure types, and collection types. If a language allows collection types as elements, we say that the language supports *nested collections*. The languages SETL,

---

[2]The term *collection*, in this context, is taken from a paper by Trenchard More [78].

Language	Relation Among Elements Types	
	heterogeneous	*homogeneous*
CM-LISP	√	
SETL	√	
PARALATION LISP	√	
APL		√
APL2	√	
NIAL	√	
SQL		√

Language	Types of Element		
	atomic	*structure*	*collection*
CM-LISP	√	√	√
SETL	√		√
PARALATION LISP	√	√	√
APL	√		
APL2	√		√
NIAL	√		√
SQL	√	√	

Language	Ordering			
	unordered	*linear-ordered*	*grid-ordered*	*key-ordered*
CM-LISP	xet	xector	—	xapping
SETL	set	tuple	—	map
PARALATION LISP	—	field	—	—
APL	—	—	array	—
APL2	—	—	array	—
NIAL	—	—	array	—
SQL	—	—	—	relation

Table 9.2: The collection types available in various collection-oriented languages. A linear-ordered collection is a vector. In CM-LISP, *xets* and *xectors* are considered special cases of *xappings*. In SETL, *maps* are considered special cases of *sets*: a *map* is a *set* of two element *tuples*.

CM-LISP, and PARALATION LISP all support nested collections, and although APL does not, some of its follow-ups, such as APL2 and NIAL, do. Nested collections are very important for applications with structures more complicated than simple vectors or arrays. If a language only allows atomic types as elements, we say it only supports *simple collections*. APL and SQL both only support simple collections. If a language allows structure types as elements, we say it supports *structure collections*. A structure type is a structure with a fixed number of slots and the only operations allowed on it are removing and inserting elements. We separate structure types from collections because the collection operations cannot be applied to structure types. Relational database languages, such as SQL, and the two lisp based languages, CM-LISP and PARALATION LISP, all support structure collections.

Homogeneity: A *homogeneous* collection is a collection whose elements are all of the same type, and a *heterogeneous* collection is a collection whose elements are of different types. Exactly what constitutes homogeneity depends on how type is defined. For example, if the length of a collection is included in its type, then a collection with subcollections of different sizes is heterogeneous. In this chapter we do not include the length in the type. So, for example, a collection of collections of integers, such as

```
[[3 4 2] [2 8] [4 5 7 1]],
```

is considered homogeneous regardless of the size of the subcollections. All the collection-oriented languages mentioned other than APL and SQL support heterogeneous collections. By only allowing homogeneous collections, we can give every collection a concise type name (for example, collection of collection of integers) and therefore greatly simplify a strongly typed language.

Ordering: We consider four classes of orderings of the elements of a collection: *unordered, linear-ordered, grid-ordered* and *key-ordered*. Unordered collections are basically sets, although for sets we also need to guarantee that no two elements contain the same value. The linear-ordered collections are vectors. The grid-ordered collections are dense arrays— each element is associated with a tuple of integers, one for each dimension of the array. Such grid-ordered arrays form the heart of APL. The key-ordered collections are ordered by a set of keys. A key-ordered collection can be thought of as a mapping in which the keys are the domain and the values the range. The key-ordered collections are clearly the most general of the orderings since the keys can themselves be consecutive integers (making a linear-ordered collection), or tuples of integers (making a grid-ordered collection). Table 9.2 shows the orderings that various different languages support along with the names that the languages give those orderings.

9.2   Collection Operations

All the collection-oriented languages supply a set of *collection-oriented operations* that operate on collections as a whole, and an *apply-to-each* form that applies a function, operation, or body to each element of a collection.

Collection-Oriented Operations: Many of the collection-oriented operations can be associated with a particular ordering. Operations for unordered collections typically include set intersection, set union, and set difference. Operations for linear-ordered collections include sorting, and appending. Operations for grid-ordered collections typically include extractions and insertions of subdimensions, and reductions along subdimensions. Operations on key-ordered collections typically include some form of *join* operation [33]. Certain operations, such as summing the elements of a collection, can be applied to all classes of collections regardless of their ordering. Figure 9.1 shows how two example operations—summing, and removing elements less than 5—are expressed in various collection-oriented languages.

Apply-to-Each: All the collection-oriented languages supply some way of applying a function, operation or body to each element of a collection. Such an *apply-to-each* form is similar to a loop construct in a conventional Von Neumann languages, but is not necessarily iterated sequentially. Also, in the conventional Von Neumann languages, users must supply a start and an end count for a loop, whereas in the collection apply-to-each form, users need only specify that they want to apply the operation to each element of a collection. Figure 9.2 illustrates how apply-to-each is expressed in various collection-oriented languages.

The operations that can be used by an apply-to-each form will depend on the types of collections a language supports. In languages which only support simple collections, such as APL and SQL, all the operations used by an apply-to-each form must be scalar. In languages that support nested collections, the operations can typically be any operation including a collection-oriented operation or another apply-to-each. Since these languages can nest the apply-to-each forms, we say that the languages support nested collection operations.[3] Figure 9.3 illustrates examples of a collection-oriented operation inside an apply-to-each form. Nested collection operations are very useful for expressing a wide variety of algorithms—they allow a user to apply **any** existing function over a collection of elements.

Languages that do not support nested collection operations typically use an implicit apply-to-each form—when a scalar operation is placed between two collections it implicitly

---

[3]Supporting nested collection operations and nested collections go hand in hand—supporting one without the other makes little sense.

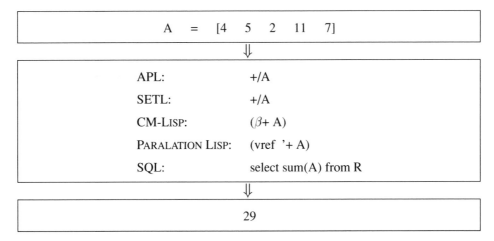

Summing the elements of a collection.

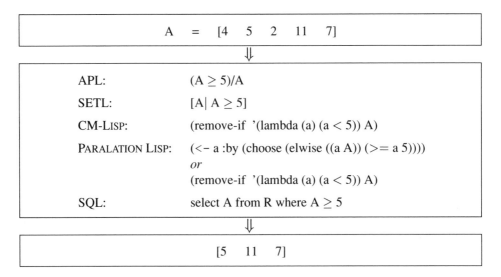

Removing all numbers less than 5 from a collection.

Figure 9.1: Example operations for various collection-oriented languages. In SQL, R is the relation from which A is taken.

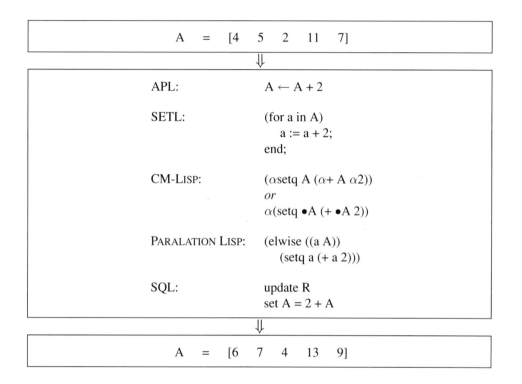

Figure 9.2:   An example of the *apply-to-each* form for various collection-oriented languages. In the example, we are adding 2 to each element of a collection A.

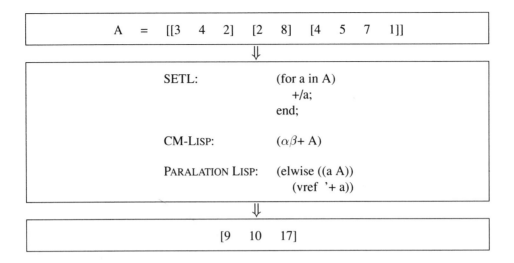

Figure 9.3:   An example of an operation on nested collections. This operation sums the elements of each subcollection of A.

implies that the operation should be applied to each position of the vectors (see Figure 9.1 for the languages APL and SQL). Languages that support nested collection operations, however, must supply an explicit apply-to-each form otherwise the apply-to-each can be ambiguous. For example, consider the statement:

```
A = [[3 4 2] [2 8] [4 5 7 1]]
B = [[7 5 3] [1 9] [6 5 8 2]]

A foo B
```

Does this statement apply `foo` to each of the three subcollections, or does it apply it to each of the nine integers at the bottom level?

9.3   Mapping Collections onto Vectors

This section describes how the various collection types can be mapped onto the vectors supplied by a parallel vector model (simple homogeneous vectors). It describes how to map nested and structure collections, heterogeneous collections, and the four orderings of collections onto vectors. The PARALATION LISP compiler discussed in Chapter 11 will use many of the representations discussed in this section.

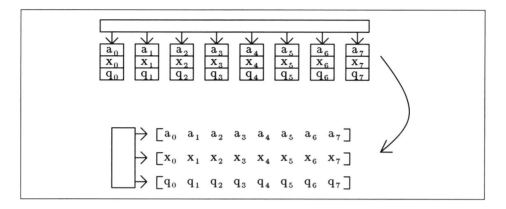

Figure 9.4:   Representing a homogeneous vector of structures with a record of simple homogeneous vectors.

Types of Elements: Segments can be used to represent collections with other collections as elements (nested collections). To represent a collection of depth two, we can use a value vector along with its segment descriptor—each segment is one of the subcollections (see Section 4.3). For example, the nested collection

$$[[2\ 3]\ []\ [4\ 0\ 1]]$$

can be represented with the two vectors:

$$[2\ 3\ 4\ 0\ 1]$$
$$[2\ 0\ 3]$$

The first contains the data and the second is the segment descriptor. To represent collections of depth three we can use a segment descriptor to describe the segmentation of the original segment descriptor. For example, the nested collection

$$[[[2\ 6]\ [9\ 7\ 1]]\ []\ [[3\ 8\ 7\ 2]\ []\ [5]]]$$

can be represented with the three vectors:

$$[2\ 6\ 9\ 7\ 1\ 3\ 8\ 7\ 2\ 5]$$
$$[2\ 3\ 4\ 0\ 1]$$
$$[2\ 0\ 3]$$

The first is the actual values, the second is the segment descriptor of the first, and the third is the segment descriptor of the second. Using this technique, a collection of depth d can be represented with d vectors.

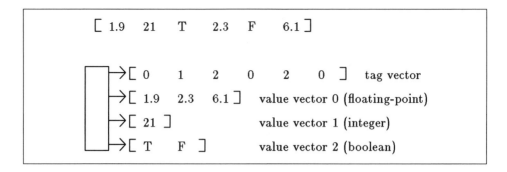

Figure 9.5:   Representing a simple heterogeneous vector with a record of simple homogeneous vectors.

A structure of simple vectors can be used to represent structured homogeneous collections. For example, we can represent a collection of structures each with three slots containing an atomic type, with a single structure with three slots each containing a vector (see Figure 9.4). We call the manipulation of taking structures from inside a collection and dragging them out, *drag-out*.

Homogeneity: To represent heterogeneous collections, we can use a *value* vector for every type that appears in the collection, and a *tag* vector which specifies which elements are of which types. All the elements of a given type are packed into one of the *value* vectors. Figure 9.5 illustrates an example. For unordered collections we do not need a *tag* vector: the *tag* vector is only used to specify the ordering. For a collection with d different types, this representation requires $d+1$ vectors, and when operating on the collection, the run-time code must loop over all the vectors. This is likely not to be a problem in practice since typically only a few types are placed in a single collection.

Ordering: A linear-ordered collection can be mapped directly onto a vector. An unordered collection can also be mapped directly onto a vector if the implementation hides the ordering of the elements. The implementation can take advantage of the unspecified ordering to improve the performance of certain operations. For example, the implementation can keep the elements sorted so that union or intersection operations on sets can be executed with a merge instead of a sort. A grid-ordered collection can be represented by keeping the length along each dimension and having a convention of how grids are laid out on a vector (see using the representation described in Section 5.3). A key-ordered collection can be represented using a pair of vectors, one for the keys (the domain) and one for the values (the range). As with the unordered collections, the keys can be kept in sorted order to improve the performance of certain operations.

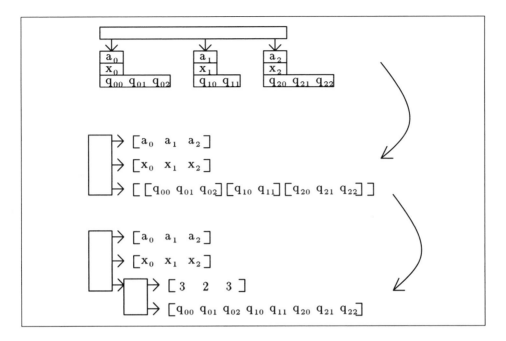

Figure 9.6: An example of the representation of a nested structure. In this example we have a collection with three elements. Each element is a structure with three slots; the first two contain atomic values, and the third contains a collection.

The mappings for nested and structure collections, for heterogeneous collections, and for the various orderings of collections can be combined. Figure 9.6 illustrates an example.

Chapter 10

Flattening Nested Parallelism

Chapter 3 introduced the notion of segments and illustrated how segments can be used to execute the scan operation over multiple sets of data independently and in parallel. Chapter 4 then defined segmented versions of almost all the scan vector instructions, and the algorithms in Part II made extensive use of these instructions. This chapter extracts the important aspect of segments—the application of an operation (perhaps itself parallel) over multiple sets of data independently and in parallel—and separates this aspect from its implementation using segments.

The chapter introduces the notions of *code replicating*—translating a parallel routine that executes an operation on a single set of data into another routine that executes the same operation over many sets of data in parallel—and *flattening nested parallelism*—translating a nested parallel construct into a flat parallel construct. Code replicating (henceforth replicating) is used in flattening nested parallelism. Flattening nested parallelism is important for the implementation of high-level languages since they allow a compiler to translate the high-level description of nested operations onto its low-level implementation on a flat real machine.

The chapter also proves an important theorem: the *access-restricted replicating theorem*. This theorem states that any scan-vector routine that abides by some restrictions on conditional control, can be replicated, and the theorem places important bounds on the element and step complexities of the replicated routine. In particular, it states that the step complexity of a replicated routine is within a constant factor of the original routine applied to the slowest of the inputs, and that the element complexity is within a constant factor of the sum of the element complexities of the original routine applied to each input. The proof of the access-restricted replicating theorem is based on segments and is constructive—it actually defines a replicating translator. This replicating translator generates efficient

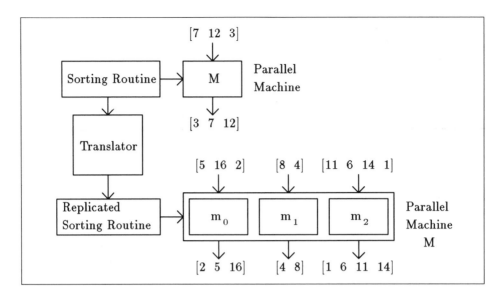

Figure 10.1: Replicating translates a parallel routine that executes an operation on one set of data into another parallel routine that executes the same operation on many sets of data independently but in parallel. The replicated routine runs on the same class of machine as the original routine and effectively simulates multiple machines.

replicated code, and is simple to implement; it forms the heart of the PARALATION LISP compiler discussed in Chapter 11. An important part of the translator is a technique called *branch-packing*. The chapter also introduces the notion of *contained programs*.

It is important to realize that although the proof of the access-restricted replicating theorem is based on segments, the theorem itself is independent of segments. The theorem, as well as the notions of replicating and flattening nested parallelism, have abstracted the important benefits of segments away from the actual implementation. The results of this chapter are particularly important for models with serial control, since we cannot simply spawn off separate control streams for each subproblem, but are also important for models with parallel control since they can greatly simplify scheduling of subproblems.

10.1 Nested Parallelism and Replicating

Replicating is a technique for automatically translating a parallel routine that executes an operation on a set of data, into another routine that executes the same operation over many sets of data in parallel. Both the original routine and the replicated routine run on the same machine model. For example, replicating can translate a parallel sorting algorithm that sorts a vector of keys, into a routine that sorts many vectors of keys in parallel—both can run on a V-RAM (see Figure 10.1). The replicated algorithm effectively simulates multiple machines and takes advantage of two sources of parallelism: sorting for each vector runs in parallel, and the sorts on the different vectors run in parallel.

Why is replicating useful? Replicating can be used to help implement any application or algorithm with *nested parallelism*—code with an inner parallel routine nested inside an outer parallel routine (Table 10.1 lists several examples). To implement a nested parallel application given a parallel routine for the inner parallel part, we can use a replicator to generate another routine that can execute the inner parallel part over multiple sets of data in parallel. We can then use the replicated routine to execute the nested parallelism. For example, to implement a figure drawing algorithm that is based on drawing multiple lines, a user could define a parallel routine that draws a single line given its endpoints and then apply it to multiple lines:

> For each endpoint-pair in endpoint-pairs
> draw-line(endpoint-pair);

The replicator would automatically replicate the *draw-line* routine so that it could run in parallel over all the lines. Note that the line lengths could vary greatly, so just allocating each line to a separate processor could be horribly inefficient—this would also only take advantage of the outer parallelism. The whole process of taking a nested parallel routine and mapping onto a flat parallel model so as to take advantage of both the inner and outer parallelism is called *flattening nested parallelism*. Replicating is the main step of *flattening nested parallelism*.

Nested parallelism also appears in almost all divide-and-conquer algorithms (Table 10.2 shows several examples). A divide-and-conquer algorithm breaks the original data into smaller parts, applies the same algorithm on the subparts, and then merges the results. If the subparts can be executed in parallel, as is usually the case, the application of the subparts involves nested parallelism. As an example, consider quicksort. Quicksort splits a vector into the elements less than, equal to, and greater than the pivot, and forks off a separate quicksort for each set (see Figure 10.2). By flattening the nested parallelism of the quicksort, the quicksort becomes a fully parallel routine. If we only took advantage of parallelism within each quicksort (finding which elements are less than, equal to, and greater than the pivot) and serially looped over the separate invocations of quicksort, we would have a large amount of parallelism at the root but almost none at the leaves of the quicksort. On the other hand, if we only took advantage of parallelism of the separate invocations of quicksort but implemented the internals serially, we would have a large amount of parallelism at the leaves but almost none at the root.

Application	Outer Parallelism	Inner Parallelism
Sum of Neighbors in Graph	For each vertex of graph	Sum neighbors of vertex
Figure Drawing	For each line of image	Draw pixels of line
Compiling	For each procedure of program	Compile code of procedure
Text Formatting	For each paragraph of document	Justify lines of paragraph

Table 10.1: Routines with nested parallelism. Both the inner part and the outer part can be executed in parallel.

Algorithm	Outer Parallelism	Inner Parallelism
Quicksort (Section 3.5.1)	For lesser and greater elements	Quicksort
Mergesort	For first and second half	Mergesort
Closest Pair (Section 6.3)	For each half of space	Closest Pair
Strassen's Matrix Multiply	For each of the 7 sub multiplications	Strassen's Matrix Multiply
Fast Fourier Transform	For two sets of interleaved points	Fast Fourier Transform

Table 10.2: Some divide and conquer algorithms.

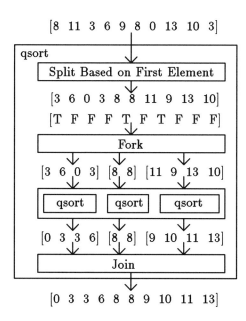

Figure 10.2: In quicksort, after packing the elements less than the pivot to the bottom, the elements equal to the pivot to the middle and the elements greater than the pivot to the top, we need to fork off a quicksort for each set. This involves splitting the original vector into three groups and using a replicated version of quicksort to simulate two separate quicksorts. (The equal elements don't need to be sorted, and the test for completion has been excluded from the diagram.)

Replicating is interesting from both programming and theoretical standpoints. From a programming standpoint, it permits the separation of the high-level notion of nested parallelism from its low-level implementation (typically on a flat uniform machine), and supplies an automatic translation from the prior to the latter. From a theoretical standpoint, the notion of replicating introduces some important questions, such as: Can a parallel routine programmed for some machine always be replicated without a significant increase in complexity? Are any restrictions necessary on the code to allow an efficient replication?

Both the programming and theoretical aspects of replicating are examined in the remainder of this chapter. The approach will be to state a theory of what can be replicated along with complexity bounds, and then to build a replicator that constructively proves the theory. This replicator is very practical, and a variation is used in the PARALATION LISP compiler described in Chapter 11. The chapter will show that restrictions are necessary to replicate algorithms implemented on the scan vector instruction set.

10.2   The Replicating Theorem

Ideally, we would like to prove that any program written in the scan vector model can be replicated without unduly increasing the step and element complexities. Unfortunately, because of difficulties with conditionals and indirect addressing, we cannot demonstrate this for the general case. We will, however, prove that we can go quite far.

We shall prove the following theorem:

Theorem 1 (Access-Restricted Replicating Theorem) *For any access-restricted routine R, with a set of inputs A, an access-restricted routine R_s exists with n sets of inputs $A_0, A_1, \cdots, A_{n-1}$ that executes R independently on each set; and the routine R_s obeys the following relations:*

$$e(R_s, \{A_0, A_1, \cdots, A_{n-1}\}) < k_1 \sum_{i=0}^{n-1} e(R, A_i) \tag{10.1}$$

and

$$s(R_s, \{A_0, \cdots, A_{n-1}\}) < k_2 \max(s(R, A_0), \cdots, s(R, A_{n-1})) \tag{10.2}$$

for some constants k_1 and k_2.

For a routine R with input A, $s(R, A)$ denotes the step complexity and $e(R, A)$ denotes the element complexity. An *access-restricted* routine is a routine implemented on the scan vector model with some restrictions on the use of indirect addressing and conditional branching; these restrictions will be described in Section 10.3.

The access-restricted replicating theorem basically states that for every routine there is a replicated version that can execute the original routine in parallel over many inputs (the number of steps required is within a constant factor of the original routine applied to the slowest of the inputs), without wasting more than a constant quantity of computation (the number of scalar operations executed, the element complexity, is at most a constant factor greater than if the original routine serially looped over the inputs). For example, consider the halving merge described in Section 3.7.2, which for two vectors of length n has an element complexity of $O(n)$ and a step complexity of $O(\lg n)$. The access-restricted replicating theorem states that another access-restricted routine exists that can merge m pairs of vectors each of length n_i $(0 \le i < m)$ with an element complexity of

$$O(\sum_{i=0}^{m-1} n_i) \,,$$

and a step complexity of

$$O(\max_{i=0}^{m-1} \lg n_i) \,.$$

If the vectors where all of equal length m, the complexities would be $O(m^2)$ and $O(\lg m)$ respectively.

The remainder of this chapter is dedicated to proving this theorem. It first defines access-restricted code and discuss how general it is. It then proves a weaker version of the access-restricted replicating theorem, the access-fixed replicating theorem, which is only useful for straight-line code with no indirect addressing. It finally shows how this can be extended to include the restricted forms of conditional branching and indirect addressing allowed by access-restricted code, thus proving the theorem. The proof is constructive and in practice the constants in equations 10.1 and 10.2 are quite small.

Although the proof of the theorem is based on segments, the statement of the theorem says nothing about segments. There might be other methods to prove the theory.

10.3   Access-Restricted Code

This section defines access-restricted code. Every algorithm discussed in this book obeys the restrictions of access-restricted code.

Definition: *A scan vector routine (a routine implemented using the scan vector instruction set) R is* access restricted *if it obeys the following restrictions:*

1. *All conditional control must be of the* fork-and-join *type and each fork must have a constant number of branches. That is to say, all the branches of a conditional fork (where control takes one of a fixed number of paths based on some data), must join at a single point.*

2. *It is contained. This is defined in Section 10.6.2.*

3. *The only forms of memory access permitted must be either (a) absolute, (b) from or to a stack, or (c) absolute relative to a stack.*

4. *All stack pointers must be at the same position at the join point of all branches of a conditional fork-and-join. This means that (pushes − pops) for each stack for each branch must be equal.*

We now consider the applicability of code with these restrictions.

Restriction 1: What sorts of conditionals is the fork-and-join useful for? It can clearly be used for *if-then-else* statements and for *case* statements. It can also be used for *while* and *do* loops by using a two branch fork-and-join with a recursive call in one of the branches to a routine that implements the body of the loop, and with the other branch empty. It cannot, however, be used for a general *goto* statement.

Restriction 2: This restriction will be discussed in detail in Section 10.6.2.

Restrictions 3 and 4: Restricting memory access to absolute addressing and stacks would be a severe drawback for the serial RAM model since it would greatly complicate pointer based algorithms (the machine could no longer access elements via a pointer). It is not, however, a severe problem on a parallel vector machine because pointer based operations are executed within a vector with the `permute` instruction.

The restrictions on access-restricted code are sufficient but not necessary; more lenient and general conditions are possible. The restrictions, however, permit an easy proof, an efficient implementation and are sufficient for most algorithms. Section 10.6.3 shows that every algorithm in this book is contained. Finding the most lenient set of restrictions is an interesting topic for future research.

10.4   Access-Fixed Replicating Theorem

This section proves a special case of the access-restricted replicating theorem, the *access-fixed replicating theorem*. This theorem is valid for any code that does not contain conditionals or indirect addressing (any straight-line code with only absolute addressing). The access-fixed replicating theorem is applicable to all the simple operations defined in Section 4.2, and to some of the example algorithms described in Chapter 3, such as the line-drawing routine, the line-of-sight routine and the split radix sort (assuming a fixed number of bits in each key). The proof of the access-fixed replicating theorem is constructive and is a major part of the proof for the access-restricted replicating theorem.

Definition: *A scan vector routine R is* access fixed *if it does not contain any of the three scan vector instructions* `cond-jump`, `move-scalar`, *or* `move-vector`.

Since an access-fixed routine is just straight-line code (contains no conditional jumps), the step complexity of an access-fixed routine is fixed regardless of the input. We can therefore denote the step complexity of an access-fixed routine R as $s(R)$ instead of $s(R, A)$.

Theorem 2 (Access-Fixed Replicating Theorem) *For any access-fixed routine R, with a set of inputs A, an access-fixed routine R_s exists with n sets of inputs $A_0, A_1, \cdots, A_{n-1}$ that executes R independently on each set; and the routine R_s obeys the following complexity*

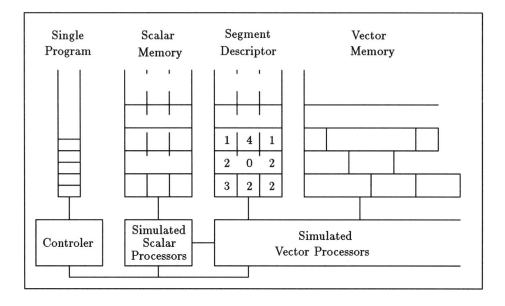

Figure 10.3: A *simulating machine* simulating three *simulated machines*. The scalar memory is expanded into vectors of length 3. The vector memory is expanded into a vector memory of variable width for the values and a vector memory of width 3 for the segment descriptors.

relations:

$$e(R_s, \{A_0, A_1, \cdots, A_{n-1}\}) < k_1 \sum_{i=0}^{n-1} e(R, A_i) \qquad (10.3)$$

and

$$s(R_s) < k_2 s(R) \qquad (10.4)$$

for some constants k_1 and k_2.

Proof: The proof is constructive. We will demonstrate how to build a *simulating machine* out of a V-RAM that can simulate n *simulated machines*. Figure 10.3 illustrates the simulating machine. We make the following changes to the original routine R to have it act as the simulating machine. We replace all calls to the access-fixed instructions with their segmented versions, replace all vectors with segmented vectors, and replace all scalars with vectors. In our simulating machine the original scalar memory becomes a vector memory, and the original vector memory becomes two vector memories, one for the value vectors and one for the segment descriptors (see Figure 10.3). We must somehow accommodate these extra vector memories in our simulating machine. To do this we triple all of the addresses in the following way. Each vector memory location Mv[j] used in R is replaced by the locations Mv[$3j$] and Mv[$3j + 1$]—one for the value vector and one for the segment-descriptor. Each scalar memory location Ms[j] is replaced by the vector memory location Mv[$3j + 2$] in R_s. This memory address translation relies on the addresses being absolute.

Now to execute R_s over the inputs A_i, we place each input A_i in segment i of a segmented vector and assign segment i of each vector to the ith simulated machine. Since all the segmented instructions work independently within each segment, each input gets operated on independently. Equation 10.4 holds because each segmented instruction requires at most a constant number of calls to the unsegmented instructions. To show that equation 10.3 holds, we need only show that it holds for each step since we know the number of steps is the same order. As stated in Section 4.3, the element complexity of a call to a segmented instruction is at most a constant factor greater than the total length of the segmented vector. Since the data for each input A_i is in a contiguous segment, the total length of any segmented vector is the sum of the lengths of the values in each segment. □

To prove the access-restricted replicating theorem, the above proof must be extended to include the restricted forms of indirect addressing and conditional jumps. This is done in the following two sections.

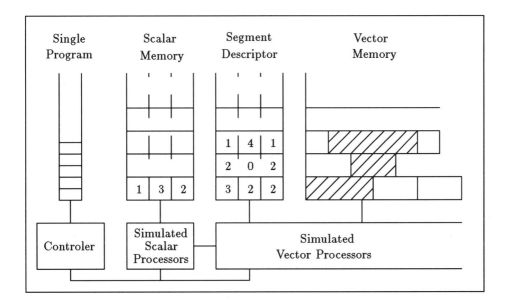

Figure 10.4: A simulating machine executing indirect addressing for 3 simulated machines. Each simulated machine is accessing a different vector memory location specified in the scalar memory (the values 1, 3 and 2 are addresses). The segment each machine is accessing is shaded. Accessing the three locations will require at least three steps.

10.5 Indirect Addressing

This section illustrates how segmented versions of stack operations can be implemented, but it first exposes the problem with general indirect addressing. In a scan vector machine, the indirect addressing primitives (`move-scalar` and `move-vector`) are used to access a location of the scalar or vector memory based on a pointer (index) in the scalar memory. The simulation described in the previous section (Section 10.4), relies on the fact that each simulated machine is accessing the same memory location at the same time, while with indirect addressing each simulated machine might access different memory locations at the same time (see Figure 10.4). To simulate the indirect addressing the simulating machine must, therefore, serially loop over all the locations that appear in different simulated machines. This would clearly ruin our bounds on the step complexity. When indirectly accessing a vector, the simulating machine would also have to pack and merge the appropriate segments from each vector (patch them together). This would ruin our bounds on the element complexity.

Unlike general indirect addressing, with stacks all machines always access the same location, since they push and pop at the same time and therefore contain the same stack pointer. We can include any fixed number of stacks as long as all machines are pushing or popping from the same stack. We can also include absolute access relative to a stack because, again, all machines would access the same location. The one problem with a stack is in its interaction with conditionals. If two branches of a conditional fork-and-join include different numbers of pushes to and pops from a stack, then the stack pointers will be different at the join point. This is the motivation for condition 4 of access-restricted code. So with restrictions 3 and 4 the simulating machine still works with constant slow-down.

10.6 Conditional Control

This section illustrates how a segmented version of the conditional fork-and-join can be implemented, but, again, it first exposes the problem with conditional control in general. The problem with implementing a segmented version of a conditional control instruction, is that different simulated machines will want to jump to different instructions, while the simulating machine can only execute a single stream of control. This is the standard problem of implementing functions with conditionals on SIMD computers: even though all processors might start executing the same code, because of data-dependent branches they might all end up taking different paths and executing different code.

This section illustrates how by placing restrictions 1 and 2 of access-restricted code we can prove the desired complexity bounds for the access-restricted replicating theorem. The element complexity is bounded by *branch-packing*: packing all the variables used in a branch of a conditional fork-and-join, so that only the segments of the simulated machines that take that branch remain (other segments are deleted). The step complexity is bounded by only considering *"contained programs"* (restriction 2). We first discuss branch packing and then discuss containment.

10.6.1 Branch-Packing

The following discussion is based on the *if-then-else* statement; all other conditional fork-and-joins can be implemented by nesting the if-then-else statement. The basic idea of *branch-packing* is that all variables accessed in a branch are packed so they only include values for the simulated machines that take that branch. This means that each branch does no more element computations than it must. The if-then-else statement is implemented with branch-packing as follows (the description will refer to the example code shown in Figure 10.5).

- Evaluate the condition, returning a T or F to each simulated machine.

if Flag											
then +-reduce(B);											
else A − 5;											

input:
Flag	=	T	T	F	T						
A	=	3	4	9	6						
B	=	[4	6	1]	[2	1]	[7	2	8	3]	[6]

then-expression:
pack-segments(B, Flag)	=	[4	6	1]	[2	1]	[6]	
+-reduce(B)	=	11	3	6				

else-expression:
pack(A, not(Flag))	=	9	
A − 5	=	4	

result:
flag-merge(then, else, Flag)	=	11	3	4	6

Figure 10.5: An example of an if-then-else statement and the values during its execution. The statement is being executed on four simulated machines. Three of the simulated machines execute the *then* part and one of them executes the *else* part.

We call machines with a T, *T-machines*, and machines with an F, *F-machines*.

In the example, we have three T-machines and one F-machine.

- If there are any T-machines, go through all the variables used in the then-expression and pack the segments corresponding to T-machines deleting the other segments. If there are no T-machines, skip this step.

  If the variable is a scalar, we use the `pack` operation defined in Section 4.2 for the packing. If the variable is a vector, we need to use a pack that packs whole segments. We call this version a `pack-segments` operation; its implementation is given in Section B.2.4. Both have a step complexity of $O(1)$ and an element complexity proportional to the total length of the original vector.

  In the example, B is packed using the `pack-segments` operation.

- Execute the then-expression using the packed variables.

  In the example, this consists of a `+-reduce`.

- Execute the analogous operations used on the then-expression on the else-expression: go through all the variables used in the else-expression and pack the segments corresponding to F-machines deleting the other segments.

  In the example, A is packed using the `pack` operation.

- Execute the else-expression using the packed variables.

  In the example, this subtracts 5 in the single F-machine.

- Merge the results of the then-expression and else-expression.

  If a result is a scalar, we use the `flag-merge` operation defined in Section 4.2. If the result is a vector, we use a version that merges whole segments. We call this version the `flag-merge-segments` operation; its implementation is given in Section B.2.4. Both have a step complexity of $O(1)$ and an element complexity proportional to the total length of the result vector.

  In the example, we use the `flag-merge` operation to merge the results.

Since the vectors used in both the then-expression and the else-expression are packed, both expressions only execute their body on the simulated machines that follow their branch. The element complexity for each branch therefore only includes the sum of the element complexities for the simulated machines taking that branch, thus enforcing equation 10.3.

The only problem might be the cost of the packing itself. We, however, make the following argument that the cost of packing causes at most a constant-factor slow-down.

We claim that any vector only needs to be packed a constant number of times. This is because the only way of getting more than constant depth nesting of conditionals is through recursive calls, and then the packing happens in the recursive call itself when passing in the variables. With a fixed-depth nesting, the number of branches is constant and therefore the number of packs is constant. If we assume that every vector was created at some point, a reasonable assumption, the element complexity of packing is no more than a constant factor greater than the element complexity of creating the vector.

10.6.2 Contained Programs

This section defines a class of programs, *contained programs*, and for this class proves the second part of the replicating theorem (10.2), the bound on the step complexity. All algorithms in book are contained and can therefore be replicated efficiently (see Section 10.6.3). To discuss containment, we must first have a notion of the path taken by a program p. For this purpose, we define an *evaluation tree*.

Definition: *An evaluation tree $T(p, a)$ is the ordered tree generated by applying the program p to the data a. By this we mean that we draw a tree with each vertex being a function and the children being all the functions it calls, in the order it calls them. The leaves of such a tree are primitive operations.*

Figure 10.6 shows examples of evaluation trees for three programs, each for two sets of data. For the definition of containment, we only consider deterministic programs. For probabilistic algorithms, any random bits must be passed in as arguments to the programs. Any deterministic program has a many to one correspondence from its input to evaluation trees—every possible input has exactly one evaluation tree, but one evaluation tree could correspond to many different inputs.

We now return to the notion of containment. If we look at the examples in Figure 10.6, we notice that in the first program, `gloop`, every evaluation tree for this program must always be either a subtree or supertree of all other evaluation trees. As the argument n gets larger, the evaluation tree grows and subsumes all evaluation trees for lesser n. This is not true with the second program, `hloop`, since some trees will have an f function while others will have the g function depending on the outcome of (p v). It is also not true with the last example, `floop`, since the evaluation tree of (`floop 2 1 v`) is neither a subtree nor a supertree of (`floop 1 2 v`). We say that `gloop` is contained while the other two are not. We now define containment formally, but must first define what it means for one invocation of a program to be contained within another.

Definition: *We define $p(a)$ to mean the application of the program p to the data a with*

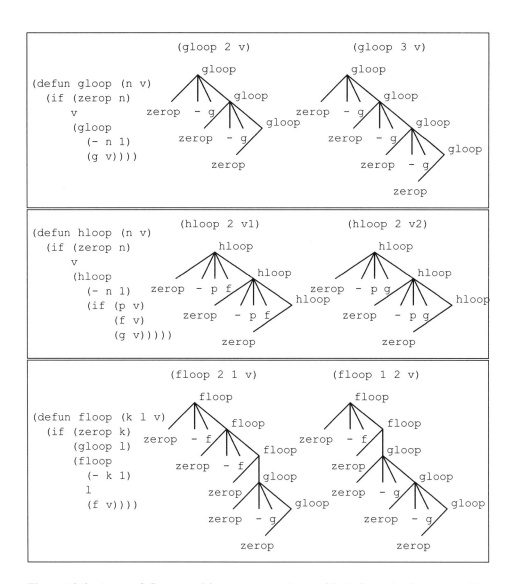

Figure 10.6: A set of Common Lisp programs along with their evaluation trees. The function gloop is contained while the other two functions are not. An evaluation tree can be generated by tracing the program p running on the data a.

the following relation:

$$p(a) \sqsubseteq p(b) \tag{10.5}$$

if and only if $T(p, a)$ is a subtree of, or the same tree as, $T(p, b)$. The relation $\sqsubseteq$ is called the containment relation, and $p(a) \sqsubseteq p(b)$ can be read, the application of p to a is contained within the application of p to b.

The application $p(a)$ is homomorphic with $T(p, a)$ and is used to abstract away from the trees.

Lemma 1 *For every program p the relation $\sqsubseteq$ places a partial order on its inputs.*

Proof: For a relation over a set to satisfy a partial order, the relation must be reflexive and transitive.

1. (reflexive) $p(a) \sqsubseteq p(a)$ is true since p is deterministic and will generate the same tree for the same data.

2. (transitive) $p(a) \sqsubseteq p(b)$ and $p(b) \sqsubseteq p(c)$ implies $p(a) \sqsubseteq p(c)$ since tree containment is transitive: if tree 1 is a subtree of tree 2, and tree 2 is a subtree of tree 3, then tree 1 must be a subtree of tree 3.

□

We now define the containment of a program.

Definition: *A program p is contained whenever the relation $\sqsubseteq$ places a total order on its inputs, that is, for any inputs a and b, either $p(a) \sqsubseteq p(b)$ or $p(b) \sqsubseteq p(a)$.*

This definition corresponds to the notion of any evaluation tree being either a subtree or a supertree of every other evaluation tree for the program. Returning to Figure 10.6, the program `gloop` is contained by this definition, but the other two programs in the figure are not.

We now show that contained functions satisfy the second part of the replicating theorem (10.2), in particular:

Lemma 2 *For any access-restricted routine R, with a set of inputs A, an access-restricted routine R_s exists with n sets of inputs $A_0, A_1, \cdots, A_{n-1}$ that executes R independently on each set; and the routine R_s obeys the relation:*

$$s(R_s, \{A_0, \cdots, A_{n-1}\}) < k \max(s(R, A_0), \cdots, s(R, A_{n-1})) \tag{10.6}$$

for some constant k.

Proof: If R is access restricted it is contained (by definition). This means that there is an ordering on the $R(A_i)$ and that for some j and for all i, $R(A_i) \sqsubseteq R(A_j)$. All the execution trees are therefore subtrees of $T(R, A_j)$. This means that the replicated version R_s need just execute all of $T(R, A_j)$. Whenever we reach a fork in a condition, R_s can turn off any of the R which do not need to go deeper in the tree, and turn them back on during the join. Since the branch packing technique turns off (deletes the entry) of routines which don't take a branch, the implementation discussed in the last section is sufficient. $\square$

10.6.3 Containment of Functions in Book

It turns out that all algorithms described in this book are contained.[1] In this section we go through the algorithms to show that they are contained. The discussion is informal; finding a way to formally prove that functions are contained is an interesting direction for future research.

We categorize the algorithms into three classes (see Figure 10.7):

Non Conditional Functions: These are functions that have no conditionals (straight-line code). The evaluation tree for these functions is fixed regardless of the input, so they are clearly contained.

Singly Recursive Functions: These are functions that only have a single call to a recursive function in their body, and the single call must also be to a singly recursive function. This call could be to a different function or to the function itself. All singly recursive functions can be converted to be contained, as shown below.

Multiply Recursive Functions with Equal Depth: These are functions that might make calls to multiple recursive functions, but in which it can be proved that the depth of each recursive call increases over the same data.

We first argue that all *singly recursive functions* can be converted to be contained at a constant cost. Since the depth of nesting is at most constant without a recursive call, at any vertex only one branch of the evaluation tree of a singly recursive function can be more than constant depth (the constant depends on the code not the data). All branches that are constant depth can be evaluated completely; this will impose a constant overhead. Now the one branch which is not constant depth will be the same for all data, so the one invocation which goes deepest will always contain all other invocations. It turns out that all

---

[1]This assumes we pass in the random bits as arguments for the probabilistic algorithms, such as the minimum-spanning-tree algorithm.

Non Conditional:

All the Simple Operations
Neighbor-Reduce, Distribute-Excess
+-Rootfix, +-Leaffix, Tree-Vertex-Delete
Line-Drawing, Line-of-Sight

Singly Recursive:

Split-Radix-Sort, Quicksort, Halving-Merge,
KD-Tree, Quickhull,
Minimum-Spanning-Tree, Maximal-Independent-Set,
Sparse Matrix-Matrix Multiply (assuming single sort),
Simplex, Dense Matrix-Matrix Multiply

Doubly Recursive, Equal Depth:

Binary-Search, $\sqrt{n}$-Hull, Closest-Pair,
Maximum-Flow, Biconnected-Components,
Linear-Systems Solver

Figure 10.7: A list of the algorithms in the book and in which way they are contained.

the constant depth branches, for the singly recursive functions in this book, do not impose any overhead. This is because these branches do not have any conditionals.

The only functions left are the multiply recursive functions. In all the multiply recursive functions in this book (see Figure 10.7), the branches all depths that increase over the same data. Here we just consider the $\sqrt{n}$-hull, the others are straightforward. In the $\sqrt{n}$-hull, the main procedure makes two recursive calls. The first is to itself, and the second is to the binary-search routine which is used to find the bridges. The binary search routine is singly recursive and for n points has depth $O(\lg n)$, and is therefore increasing with the size of the problem. The recursive call to $\sqrt{n}$-hull also has depth that is increasing with the size of the problem, so both recursive calls grow in depth with the size of the problem, and therefore increase over the same data.

10.6.4 Round-Robin Simulation

We now consider another technique that could be used to limit the step complexity of a replicated routine, *round-robin simulation*, and discuss why it is impractical.

The idea of *round-robin* simulation is that we simulate a MIMD model on the SIMD model. The SIMD machine must have the capability of disactivating and reactivating any processor. The SIMD machine continually loops over all the instructions of the MIMD machine and each processor only executes the instruction when the right instruction comes around. If the MIMD machine being simulated has k instructions, then this simulation causes a factor of k slow-down. Although in theory the number of instructions k is constant, such a simulation is impractical for most machines since the number of instructions k is usually at least on the order of 100.

One way to minimize the simulation cost is to reduce the number of instructions (k) to a small number. This can be done by breaking each instruction into even more primitive parts (we could for example create a machine with only a logical NAND instruction). The idea of reducing the number of instructions was used by Hudak [57] to implement a laze functional language on the Connection Machine. He was able to reduce the process of graph reduction to 5 primitive operations. He implemented this reduction machine on the Connection Machine and took several timings. The running times he measured were extremely inefficient, often running slower on the Connection Machine than on a serial machine. The problems he found with this technique was that the simulation overhead was large and that breaking the operations into the five primitives added significant costs.

Chapter 11

A Compiler for Paralation Lisp

This chapter discusses a compiler that translates a subset of PARALATION LISP, a collection-oriented language of Sabot's [96], into the scan vector instruction set.[1] As mentioned in the introduction to the book, a PARALATION LISP version of quicksort translated by the discussed compiler onto the Connection Machine runs within a factor of two of the fastest sort implemented on the Connection Machine. This result lends practical credence to many of the methods and techniques discussed in this book, and asserts concrete support for the general use of high-level collection-oriented languages for programming applications and algorithms, and powerful compilers for mapping these languages onto a gamut of parallel and serial machines.

The compiler described in this chapter ties together many of the independent contributions of the book. The compiler makes use of the scan vector model as an intermediate language; it makes use of many of the simple operations discussed in Section 4.2 to implement some of the language forms; it makes use of the implementation of the scan vector model on the Connection Machine discussed in Section 12.1 as the back end; it makes use of segments, the replicating theorem, and packing nested conditionals discussed in Chapter 10 to implement nested parallel constructs; and it makes use of the representation of collections discussed in Section 9.3 to map the PARALATION LISP collection type, the *field*, onto vectors. Figure 11.1 illustrates the stages of compiling and how they fit into the book as a whole.

The most original contribution of the described compiler is its ability to flatten nested parallelism. Although compilers have been implemented that compile collection-oriented languages that support nesting onto parallel machines, such as the compiler for CM-

---

[1] Some of the work described in this chapter is joint work with Gary Sabot and is described in more detail in [24].

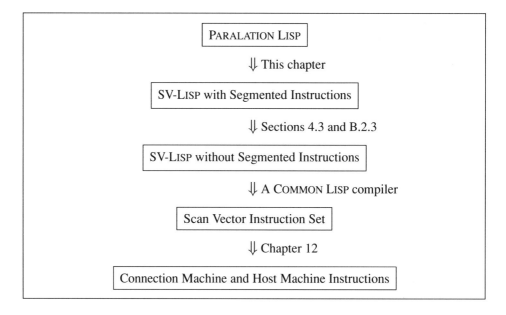

Figure 11.1: The stages of compiling a PARALATION LISP program onto a target machine. Scan Vector Lisp is basically the scan vector instruction set buried in Lisp Syntax with some of COMMON LISP's higher level forms.

LISP [119], these compilers only compile for parallelism at the leaves of the nesting. For example, a compiled routine that draws a set of lines would draw each line in parallel but would serially loop over the lines. By taking advantage of segments and the replicating theory, the implementation of nested parallelism by the described compiler is straightforward and can be broken into the following major parts:

- Nested *fields* (the collection type of PARALATION LISP) are represented based on a *pfield* data structure. This data structure has two slots: one contains a segment descriptor and the other either a vector of data, if the field is not further nested, or another *pfield*, if the field is further nested.

- The compilation of two versions of every function: one for use when called at top level, and one for use when called inside a nested form.

- The insertion of *stepping-down* code at the entry of each `elwise` form (the apply-to-each form of PARALATION LISP), which at run time strips off the top *pfield* of each variable passed into the `elwise`; and the insertion of *stepping-up* code at the exit of each `elwise` form, which at run time appends a *pfield* back onto the value being returned.

- The insertion of code that at run time packs all active segments when entering either branch of an `if` special-form, so that segments which are not being executed are eliminated. The results of the two branches are joined when the else-expression completes.

The compiler also shows the power of parallel vector models as an intermediate instruction set on which to compile a collection-oriented language. The techniques used by the described compiler can can be applied to other collection-oriented languages that support nesting such as CM-LISP or SETL.

Figure 11.2 illustrates the organization of this chapter. The chapter is separated into three parts: 1) an outline of the source language, the subset of PARALATION LISP; 2) an outline of the target language, SV-LISP; and 3) the important translation techniques used by the compiler. Each of these parts is split into data structures, and operations.

11.1 Source Code: Paralation Lisp

This section summarizes the PARALATION LISP language; for more details the reader should see [96]. PARALATION LISP consists of a new data structure, three primitive operators, and a set of other operators built on the primitive operators, all added to COMMON LISP.

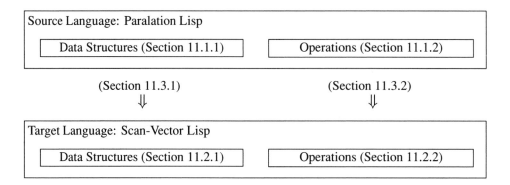

Figure 11.2: Organization of the compiler. To translate PARALATION LISP onto scan-vector lisp both the data structures and the operations must be translated.

11.1.1 Data Structures

The data objects permitted in PARALATION LISP are all the standard COMMON LISP data objects with one additional object, the *field*. The *field*, is a linear-ordered collection of elements. A field can be heterogeneous and the elements can be any PARALATION LISP value—including another field, allowing nested collections. Here are some examples of fields.

A homogeneous field:

```
#F(7 2 11 19 6 12 9)
```

A nested homogeneous field:

```
#F(#F(4 8 3) #F(9 1 12 7) #F(2 9))
```

A heterogeneous field:

```
#F(7 #F(4 Nil 3) T "horse")
```

A structure field:

$$\#\mathrm{F}\left(\begin{array}{|c|}\hline u:u_{00}\\ v:v_{00}\\\hline\end{array}\begin{array}{|c|}\hline u:u_{01}\\ v:v_{01}\\\hline\end{array}\begin{array}{|c|}\hline u:u_{02}\\ v:v_{02}\\\hline\end{array}\right)$$

11.1.2 Operators

The operations permitted in PARALATION LISP are all the standard COMMON LISP operations with three additional operations: an iteration operator and two field operators. The iteration operator, `elwise`, is used to iterate any PARALATION LISP code, including another `elwise`, over all elements of a field. The two primitive field operators, `match` and `<-`, perform communication among the elements of fields: `match` encapsulates a communication pattern into a *mapping*, and `<-` transfers a field according to a *mapping*. Several other operations are supplied by PARALATION LISP but can be defined in terms of `match` and `<-`. All the COMMON LISP sequence functions can also be used on fields.

The operators of PARALATION LISP that are needed for the compilation examples are outlined below. The ideas behind paralations and mappings, which are both important concepts of the language, are not discussed because they are not germane to a discussion of compiler issues.

Elwise: The `elwise` operator is used to apply a body over each element of a field, or set of fields. The body can include any valid PARALATION LISP form. The form:

```
(elwise bindings
    body)
```

executes the body elementwise over the elements of each field in the bindings. For example:

```
(elwise ((a #F(4 7 1 3))
         (b #F(6 2 5 8)))
   (+ a b))
 ⇒ #F(10 9 6 11)
```

pairwise adds the elements of a and b. Each binding of an `elwise` must be from the same paralation (of the same length).[2]

Match and Move: The `match` operation takes two key fields as arguments—one from a source paralation and one from a destination paralation—and returns a *mapping*. A mapping can be thought of as a bundle of one-way arrows that connect certain sites of the source paralation to certain sites of a destination paralation. Two sites are connected if their key field values are equal. A mapping is an encapsulated communication pattern.

The `<-` (move) function accepts a mapping and a field from the source paralation of the mapping as its arguments. `<-` simply pushes this source data field into the tails of the mappings arrows, causing a field in the destination paralation to pop out at the other end of the mapping. The elements in this field are calculated based upon what arrived over

---

[2]The example is actually not quite correct since the two fields given to the `elwise` will be from different paralations, but for the sake of simplicity in the examples we assume that the two fields passed to the `elwise` are from the same paralation if they are the same length. This assumption will be made in some of the other examples.

the arrows. If a single arrow arrives at a destination site, it is clear what that element's value should be. Of course, in many cases, arrows can conflict. Simple rules govern the resolution of the conflicts.

When the mapping indicates that source data is needed in multiple destination sites, because a particular key occurred several times in the destination, a concurrent-read automatically takes place, thus giving each destination site the data it needs. On the other hand, if a destination site receives no incoming values, a value is taken from a user-specified default field in the destination paralation.

The most interesting case arises when many source data items arrive at a single destination, because a particular key occurred several times in the source. The multiple incoming values are reduced into a single value by repeatedly applying a user-specified, two-argument combining function. Combining will not be needed for the examples presented in this chapter, but it is an important part of the paralation model.

Composite Operations

Many operations can be defined using the `elwise`, `match` and `<-` operations, and are important enough that they are worth mentioning here.

Vref: The `vref` operation "sums" the elements of a field according to any binary operator. So, for example:

```
(vref #F(7 4 1 11 2 6) :with 'max)
  ⇒   11
```

Collapse and Collect: The `collapse` operator takes a set of *keys* and generates a mapping in which all elements with equal valued keys are mapped to the same position. The `collect` operator takes a mapping and a field and appends all the elements which are mapped into the same position into a subfield. This can be implemented using a `<-` with a combiner of `concatenate`. The `collect` operator returns a field of fields. As an example of `collect` and `collapse` consider the following operation:

```
(let ((A #F(a_0 a_1 a_2 a_3 a_4 a_5))
      (B #F(k_0 k_1 k_0 k_2 k_1 k_1)))
  (collect A :by (collapse B)))
  ⇒   #F(#F(a_0 a_2) #F(a_1 a_4 a_5) #F(a_3)))
```

Expand: The `expand` operator takes a field of fields and appends all the subfields into a single field. So, for example:

```
(expand (collect A :by (collapse B)))
```
$\Rightarrow$ #F(a_0 a_2 a_1 a_4 a_5 a_3)

11.1.3 Restrictions

The compiler implements a small enough subset of PARALATION LISP that the subset is more concisely described by what it does include rather than what it does not include.

The subset only supports homogeneous fields and the data type of each elements of a field must be either an integer, boolean, field or structure. Since the elements can be fields, the subset supports nested fields. Many other data types, such as floating-point numbers or characters, would be straightforward to include, but were left out for the sake of simplicity.

The subset supports the following operations. It supports the three primitive operations of PARALATION LISP, elwise, match and <-. It, however, only knows how to match integer and boolean keys. The subset supports most of the operations on integer and boolean values inside an elwise. It also supports nested operations on fields. The only conditional the subset supports is the *if* special form, and it places the restriction that the results returned from both the then-expression and the else-expression must be of the same type. The subset includes the composite operations, vref, collect, collapse, and expand. The subset supports the following sequence operations on fields: elt, length, sort, reduce, and concatenate. Many other sequence operators would be straightforward to include, but these were the only ones needed for the test code.

These restrictions allow the application of the access-restricted replicating theorem described in Chapter 10 so that any function written using these restrictions can be used either at top level or nested within an elwise.

11.2 Target Code: Scan-Vector Lisp

This section describes the target code of the compiler, *scan-vector* Lisp (SV-LISP). SV-LISP is a subset of COMMON LISP with the addition of a set of functions that implement the vector and vector-scalar instructions of the scan vector instruction set (the scalar instructions are included in COMMON LISP).

Translating PARALATION LISP to SV-LISP rather than directly onto a parallel machine, such as the Connection Machine, has some important advantages. First, it separates the novel techniques of compiling collection-oriented languages onto a set of vector instructions from standard compiler techniques. The novel techniques, such as flattening nested parallelism, are implemented in translating from PARALATION LISP into SV-LISP while the standard techniques, such as memory allocation or compiling recursive routines, are im-

---

COMMON LISP Data Types
Integers, Booleans, Structures

Pvector Data Types
Integer-Pvectors, Boolean-Pvectors

Figure 11.3:   The data types of SV-LISP.

plemented in translating from SV-LISP into actual machine instructions. Second, assuming a COMMON LISP compiler exists for a machine, PARALATION LISP can be ported to that machine simply by implementing a subroutine for each of the pvector instructions, and interfacing these subroutines into COMMON LISP. This allows great portability.

11.2.1   Data Structures

SV-LISP has five data types, three from COMMON LISP—integers, booleans and structures—and two additional data types—boolean pvectors and integer pvectors. Pvectors are arbitrarily long linear-ordered collections of atomic values—boolean values for the boolean pvectors and integers for the integer pvectors.[3] Every pvector can have a different length and the only operations that can create or manipulate the pvector data types are the pvector instructions discussed in Section 11.2.2. If one was to implement a complete PARALATION LISP rather than the subset discussed in this chapter, SV-LISP would need to be augmented with some other types, such as floating-point numbers and floating-point pvectors.

11.2.2   Operations

Figure 11.4 lists the operations of SV-LISP. These operations are broken into two classes, operations from COMMON LISP and the parallel vector instructions discussed in Section 4.1. The COMMON LISP operations are defined in the COMMON LISP reference manual [108].

11.3   Translation

This section discusses how PARALATION LISP is translated into SV-LISP. In keeping with the rest of the chapter, it first describes data structures and then describes operations.

---

[3]The term pvector is used instead of vector so as not to confuse it with the COMMON LISP vector data type—a linear-ordered collection whose elements can be of any type.

COMMON LISP Operations

Special Forms and Macros:

```
if, defstruct, defun, let, let*, progn, setq
```

Scalar Arithmetic and Logical Operations:

$+, -,$ and, or, $=, <, ...$

Pvector Instructions

Elementwise Instructions:

```
p+, p-, p-and, p-or, p=  , p<, p-select, ...
```

Permutation Instructions:

```
permute, select-permute
```

Scan Instructions:

```
+-scan, max-scan, min-scan, or-scan, and-scan
```

Vector-Scalar Instructions:

```
insert, extract, distribute, length
```

Figure 11.4:   The operations of SV-LISP.

pfield
    segdes: segment-descriptor
    values: boolean pvector, integer pvector, structure, pfield

Figure 11.5:   The definition of the *pfield* structure. Each line of the structures includes the slot name followed by the type of values that can be placed in the slot.

11.3.1   Data Structures

In collection-oriented languages, different mappings of the high-level collections onto the target architecture can give rise to orders of magnitude differences in the efficiency of code on the architecture. A compiler must therefore pay special attention to how the mappings effect the efficiency of code. This section discusses how the compiler maps the collections of PARALATION LISP, fields, onto the primitive data structures of SV-LISP, pvectors. The mapping discussed allows a particularly efficient manipulation of nested fields by the vector instructions of SV-LISP. The representation of nested fields is based on segments as introduced in Section 4.3 and allows the generated code to operate over all subfields in parallel.

All fields are constructed from the *pfield* structure—a COMMON LISP structure type with two slots (see Figure 11.5). The first slot stores a *segment-descriptor*, which describes the length or segmentation of the field (see Section 4.3).[4] The second slot stores the actual values. This slot contains a pvector if the field contains only atomic values, contains another *pfield* if the field is nested, and contains a user-defined structure if the field is a field of user-defined structures. Each of these cases is discussed below. Since the subset of PARALATION LISP considered only supports homogeneous fields, heterogeneous fields are not considered.

Simple Field: To represent a simple field—a field whose elements are all atomic—we use a single *pfield* structure. The first slot contains a definition of a single segment—its length. The second slot contains a pvector with the values of the field. For example:

$$\#F \; (a_0 \;\; a_1 \;\; a_2 \;\; a_3 \;\; a_4)$$

$$\Downarrow$$

pfield
segdes: [5]
values: [$a_0 \;\; a_1 \;\; a_2 \;\; a_3 \;\; a_4$]

We use a *pfield* structure instead of using a pvector directly since it allows us to check if two equal length fields belong to the same paralation.[5] Using the *pfield* structure also permits a more homogeneous implementation of the stepping-up and stepping-down manipulations to be discussed in Section 11.3.2.

Nested Field: We represent a nested field—a field whose elements are themselves fields— by nesting the *pfield* structures and using segments of a single pvector to represent each subfield. For example:

---

[4]In the actual compiler the segment-descriptor is itself a structure which contains several slots each with one of the segment descriptors defined in Section 4.3 For the purposes of this chapter, we assume the segment-descriptor only contains the *lengths* segment-descriptor (the length of each segment).

[5]Since the segment-descriptor is actually a structure, we can check if two fields are from the same paralation by seeing if the two segment-descriptors are eql.

$$\#\text{F} \; (\#\text{F} \; (a_{00} \; a_{01}) \quad \#\text{F} \; (a_{10} \; a_{11} \; a_{12}) \quad \#\text{F} \; (a_{20}) \;)$$

$$\Downarrow$$

pfield
    segdes: [3]

                    pfield
    values: segdes: [2 3 1]
                    values: $[a_{00} \; a_{01} \; a_{10} \; a_{11} \; a_{12} \; a_{20}]$

In this example, the *segdes* slot of the inner *pfield* describes the segmentation of the *values* slot. This technique can be applied recursively to represent a nesting of any depth. A field nested n deep can be represented with n segment-descriptor structures and n *pfield* structures.

The purpose of representing nested fields with a single value pvector is to get both the parallelism on operations within each bottom level field and the parallelism over all the bottom level fields.

Structure Field: We represent a structure field—a field whose elements are each a user defined structure—by pulling the structure out from inside the field. For example:

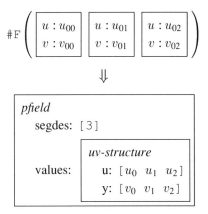

In this example, the field of three uv-structures is mapped onto a single uv-structure whose slots contain a pvector with the values of all three of the original uv-structures. Figure 11.6 illustrates a final example of a field with both nesting and structures.

Mappings in PARALATION LISP can be represented in canonical form as a pair of integer vectors: the first vector are indices into the destination from the source, and the second are indices into the source from the destination (see [96] for more details).

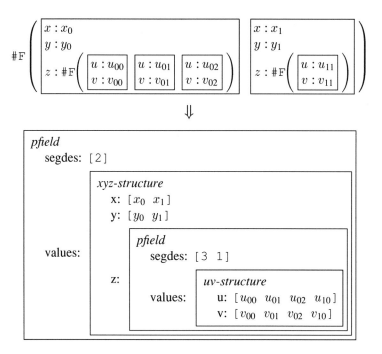

Figure 11.6: An example of how a nested field with structures is represented. In the example, the *xyz-struct* and the *uv-struct* are user-defined structures.

```
                    (defun plus-times (a b)
                      (* a (+ a b))))

        Called at top level              Called within an elwise

(plus-times 5 2)                   (elwise ((a #F(2 1 6))
   ⇒ 35                                     (b #F(3 5 2)))
                                     (plus-times a b))
                                    ⇒ #F(10 6 48)
```

Figure 11.7: Any routine in PARALATION LISP can be called either at top level or within an elwise.

11.3.2 Operations

This section discusses the manipulations necessary to translate code from the subset of PARALATION LISP into SV-LISP. The discussion is broken into four parts: 1) compiling two versions of all code, one parallel and one serial; 2) compiling the elwise form; 3) compiling conditionals; 4) and implementing the PARALATION LISP collection operations.

Compiling Two Versions

When a function is defined in PARALATION LISP, it must work both if called at top level (not within an elwise), and if called within an elwise. Consider the example of Figure 11.7. In the first case, the compiler uses a serial version of plus-times while in the second case the compiler uses a parallel version of the routine. The serial version uses the standard COMMON LISP + and * operations while the parallel version uses the pvector primitives p-+ and p-*. Figure 11.8 illustrates an example of the translation of a PARALATION LISP routine into the two SV-LISP routines.

The compiler keeps two versions of every user-defined function and every function supplied by PARALATION LISP: the top level version and the replicated version (the version called inside a nested parallel form). When compiling the replicated version of a new function, the function calls inside the routine are simply replaced with their replicated version (see Figure 11.8). The *special forms*, however, cannot in general be replaced with a parallel function. This is because the arguments of special forms in COMMON LISP are not necessarily all evaluated (for example, the if form only evaluates the second argument if the first evaluates to T). Furthermore, COMMON LISP does not permit user definitions of special forms. Special forms can therefore require some extra manipulations. The translation of the if special form is discussed in Section 11.3.2. The let, let* and

```
                    (defun plus-times  (a b c)
                       (+ a (* b c)))
```

⇓

```
                    (defun s-plus-times (a b c)
                       (+ a (* b c)))

                    (defun p-plus-times (a b c)
                       (p-+ a (p-* b c)))
```

Figure 11.8:   Compiling both a parallel and a serial version of a routine. The parallel
version replaced all function calls with their parallel versions.

`progn` special forms require no manipulations.

Compiling Elwise Forms

The compiler applies several manipulations to translate an `elwise` form. First, it executes
the same manipulations required when creating a parallel form of a function as discussed
in the last sections. Second, it inserts code that copies all the free variables—variables that
appear in the body but not in the binding list—across the elements of the `elwise`. Third,
it inserts code that steps-down all the values bound in the binding list, and steps-up the
result of the body.

   We first discuss copying free variables. In PARALATION LISP, if a variable appears in
the body of an `elwise` but not in the binding list, the variable in implicitly copied across
the elements of the `elwise`.[6] For example, in the form:

```
(let ((b 3))
  (elwise ((a #F(4 1 2)))
    (+ a b)))
⇒ #F(7 4 5)
```

the value of the variable b is implicitly copied across the three elements and added to
each. When translating from PARALATION LISP to SV-LISP, the translator inserts code to
execute this copy at run time. The particular code inserted depends on the type of value
that needs to be copied. If the value is a scalar, the `distribute` pvector primitive (see

---

[6]This is similar to *scalar extension* in APL [59], but in PARALATION LISP any value will be extended, not just
scalars.

```
                    (elwise ((a A))
                      (+ a b))
```

⇓

```
    (simp-elwise ((a A)
                 (b (distribute b (pfield-segdes A))))
        (+ a b))
```

Figure 11.9: An example of the code inserted for copying free variables. All free variables are removed by this manipulation. The `simp-elwise` form is a version of `elwise` that does not accept free variables.

```
                 (simp-elwise ((a A)
                              (b B))
                    (+ a b))
```

⇓

```
    (let ((a (pfield-values A))
          (b (pfield-values B))
          (current-segdes (pfield-segdes A)))
       (make-pfield
           :segdes current-segdes
           :values (p-+ a b)))
```

Figure 11.10: An example of the stepping-down and stepping-up manipulations.

Section 11.2.2) is inserted. Figure 11.9 illustrates an example of this manipulation. If the value is a structure of scalars, a `distribute` primitive is inserted for each slot of the structure. If the value is a field, a `distribute-segment` operation is inserted that creates a nested field with the original field in each element. The type of the variable to be copied can often be inferred at compile time so that the correct code can be inserted at compile time (in the above example b must be a scalar since it is being added). If the type cannot be inferred at compile time, the compiler inserts code that executes a type dispatch at run time.

We now discuss *stepping-down* and *stepping-up*. Stepping down and up are crucial to the implementation of operations on nested fields. Stepping-down consists of stripping off the top *pfield* from each value being bound in the `elwise` bindings, and setting a variable called the *current-segdes* to this value. So for a nested field, each time the field is passed inside another `elwise` another of its *pfield* structures is stripped off. Stepping-up is the inverse of stepping-down. When leaving an `elwise`, stepping-up consists of tagging on a *pfield* structure to the result returned from the body of the `elwise`, and restoring the value of the *current-segdes*. Figure 11.10 illustrates the code inserted by these manipulations.

To see how stepping-down and stepping-up are used, consider the following code:

```
(let ((field-of-fields #F(#F(7 4) #F(11) #F(8 1 17))))
  (elwise ((field field-of-fields))
    (elwise ((value field))
      (+ value value))))
  ⇒    #F(#F(14 8)  #F(22)  #F(16 2 34))
```

Based on the representation discussed in Section 11.3.1, the original field is represented as:

field-of-fields =

| *pfield* |
| segdes: [3] |
values:	*pfield*
	segdes: [2 1 3]
	values: [7 4 11 8 1 17]

When entering the outer `elwise`, the stepping-down code strips off the top *pfield* leaving:

field =

| *pfield* |
| segdes: [2 1 3] |
| values: [7 4 11 8 1 17] |

And when entering the inner `elwise`, the next *pfield* is stripped off leaving:

field = [7 4 11 8 1 17]

Now when `p-+` is applied to `field`, the result is:

[14 8 22 16 2 34]

When exiting the inner `elwise` the stepping-up code appends a *pfield* back on, returning:

| *pfield* |
| segdes: [2 1 3] |
| values: [14 8 22 16 2 34] |

And when exiting the outer `elwise` another *pfield* is appended, returning:

```
┌──────────────────────────────────────────────────┐
│ pfield                                            │
│    segdes: [3]                                    │
│           ┌──────────────────────────────────┐   │
│           │ pfield                           │   │
│    values:│    segdes: [2 1 3]               │   │
│           │    values: [14 8 22 16 2 34]     │   │
│           └──────────────────────────────────┘   │
└──────────────────────────────────────────────────┘
```

Which is the representation of the desired result:

```
#F(#F(14 8) #F(22) #F(16 2 34))
```

In this example, the code that executes the addition runs in parallel over all elements therefore taking advantage of the parallelism within each subfield and also the parallelism among the subfields. This technique works regardless of the depth of the nesting and regardless of the complexity of the operations executed within the `elwise`.

One way of thinking about what is going on is that the compiler converts an `elwise`, which is a mapping of a function over many sets of data, into a new "composite" function over one larger set of data—the data sets all appended together. The effect of stripping off a *pfield* by the translated `elwise` is to remove a level of dividing boundaries and therefore effectively appending the data sets. The "composite" function (the replicated function) can then be applied to this appended data set. So, in the above example, inside the inner `elwise` there are no longer any dividing boundaries—all the original values are appended into one long vector—and the parallel vector version of + is then applied over all the elements.

Compiling Conditionals

This section describes the translation used for the `if` special form. Many of the other COMMON LISP control forms, such as `cond`, `when`, and `do`, can be implemented with the `if` special form. The general `throw`, `catch` and `go` special forms, however, cannot be implemented with just the `if` form and are not supported by the subset of PARALATION LISP accepted by the compiler. The translation described in this section is based on the methods discussed in Section 10.2.

The problem with the parallel (replicated) version of a routine with an `if` form is that, some of the segments might take one branch while others might take the other. The parallel version therefore might need to execute both branches. It, however, cannot simply evaluate both branches and select the appropriate result based on the conditional flag. This would render the program incorrect for the following two reasons:

- if there are any side effects (such as a `setq`) in the then-expression or else-expression, these side effects might be evaluated in segments in which they should not be;

- if there is a recursive call in one of the branches, the recursion would never terminate—the branch would be executed in the recursive call and again in the next recursive call with no termination condition.

It would also make the program inefficient for the following reason:

- If both branches are executed for all segments, computation is performed on the segments which were not supposed to take a branch and therefore wasted. This can be particularly bad when conditionals are nested.

The first problem can be solved by guaranteeing that side effects are only executed in segments which should be taking the current branch. The second problem can be solved by only executing a branch if there is at least one segment that needs to execute that branch. The third problem can be solved by packing the active segments in each branch and merging the results as discussed in Section 10.2. The compiler inserts code for all these manipulations.

Figure 11.11 illustrates an example of the translation executed by the compiler for the `if` special form. Each `or-reduce` is inserted to check if any segment needs to execute that branch. This code guarantees that at run-time a branch will only be executed if there are segments taking the branch. The `recursive-pack` function packs the segments of a variable so that inactive segments are dropped out. This function is applied to every variable that appears in a branch. Unlike the `pack` operation described in Section 4.2, this version can pack nested fields: it recursively packs the levels of a nested field and returns when it reaches the leaves. The `recursive-flag-merge` function merges two segmented values based on the conditional flags. As with the `recursive-pack`, it can be applied to nested fields. To merge in variables that are side effected in one of the branches (with a `setq`), a `recursive-unpack` routine is inserted at the exit of each branch. At run-time, this routine replaces the altered segments with the new values but leaves the unaltered segments unchanged.

Since our subset of PARALATION LISP only manipulates homogeneous fields, the results from the two branches of an `if` special-form must be of the same type so that the `recursive-flag-merge` will return a homogeneous field.

Operations

This section has covered everything except how the PARALATION LISP operations defined in Section 11.1.2 are implemented. The operations considered here are the `elt`,

```
                        (if flag
                             (func1 a)
                             (setq a (func2 b)))
```

⇓

```
(if (or-reduce flag)
     (if (or-reduce (p-not flag))
          (recursive-flag-merge flag
               (let ((temp-a (recursive-pack a flag)))
                    (func1 temp-a))
               (let ((temp-b (recursive-pack b (not flag))))
                    (let ((result (func2 temp-b)))
                         (setq a (recursive-unpack
                                        result a (not flag)))
                         result)))
          (func1 a))
     (func2 b))
```

Figure 11.11: Translating the parallel version of the if special form. If the flag is NIL in all of the segments, only func2 is executed. If the flag is T in all of the segments, only func1 is executed. If some flags are T and other NIL then the respective segments are packed before execution and merged after execution.

collapse, collect, and expand. A full description of the implementation of these functions is not within the scope of this chapter, but the code is provided and the basic ideas are outlined. Only one version of each function needs to be written because the compiler itself can be applied to this group of library of functions to generate the nested parallel versions automatically.

```
 0  (defun elt (sequence index)
 1    (extract sequence index))
 2
 3  (defun collapse (field)
 4    (make-map
 5       :pointers (rank field)
 6       :length (value-count field)
 7       :segdes (elements-counts field)))
 8
 9  (defun collect (field &key by)
10    (make-pfield
11       :values (make-pfield
12                  :values (permute field (map-pointers by))
13                  :segdes (map-segdes by))
14       :segdes (map-length by)))
15
16  (defun expand (field)
17    (let ((child-field (pfield-values field)))
18      (make-pfield
19         :values (pfield-values child-field)
20         :segdes (+-reduce (pfield-segdes child-field)))))
```

The collapse routine generates a mapping which can then be used to move data using the collect routine. The mapping is represented with two vectors and a scalar. The *pointer* vector contains pointers from the original field into a new vector so that equal values in the original field are adjacent. This pointer vector is generated by executing a rank on the original field. For example:

(rank #F(2 5 3 8 2 2 8))

$\Rightarrow$ #F(0 4 3 5 1 2 6)

If the field is an number field, the implementation of rank requires a sort. If the field is a boolean field, however, the rank can be implemented with two scans and a permute (because a single partition phase of quicksort always suffices for a boolean key).

The *segdes* vector of the mapping contains the number of occurrences of each distinct value in the source field. It is generated with the `elements-counts` routine; for example:

```
(elements-counts #F(2 5 3 8 2 2 8))
  ⇒   #F(3 1 1 2)
```

If the field is a boolean field, this requires two calls to the `+-scan` primitive. The *length* slot of the map contains the number of distinct values and is generated with the `value-count` routine. For example:

```
(value-count #F(2 5 3 8 2 2 8))
  ⇒ 4
```

This is just the length of the `segdes` vector.

The `collect` routine extracts the pointers from the map structure and permutes its input to those pointers. Collect creates a field of fields from a field, using the *length* slot as the top level segment-descriptor and the *segdes* slot as the next level segment-descriptor.

The `expand` removes a level of nesting. It strips off two levels of segment descriptors, sums the lengths of the subfields, and creates a new segment descriptor with the length specified by this sum.

Part IV

Architecture

Introduction: Architecture

This part contains two chapters. Chapter 12, *implementing parallel vector models*, describes the implementation of the parallel vector models on the Connection Machine and describes how the models can be simulated on the P-RAM models. Chapter 13, *implementing the scan primitives*, illustrates how the scan operations can be implemented in hardware. This illustration is important because although there has been considerable theoretical and practical research on how to implement the permutation operations (routing), and there has been theoretical research on how to implement the scan operation [65, 41], there has been little research on how to implement the scan operation on real hardware.

The purpose of this part is to illustrate that the parallel vector models can be implemented on parallel machines. Many of the techniques described in this part can be used for machines other than the Connection Machine.

Chapter 12

Implementing Parallel Vector Models

This chapter describes how parallel vector models in general and the scan vector model in particular can be simulated on a real machine, the Connection Machine, and how they can be simulated on another theoretical model, the P-RAM model. The general simulation techniques described should be applicable to a wide range of parallel machines, both with serial control and with parallel control. In particular the chapter shows:

1. All the scan vector instructions can be implemented on the Connection Machine (CM-2). The running times are tabulated in Table 12.1.

2. Any scan vector algorithm with an element complexity of e and a step complexity of s, can be simulated on a synchronous EREW P-RAM with scan primitives with asymptotic complexity $t = O(e/p + s)$.

12.1 Implementation on the Connection Machine

In this section we describe an implementation of the scan vector model on the Connection Machine. Much of the description is useful for parallel vector models in general. In Section 12.1.4 we tabulate the running times of the instructions for vectors of various lengths. We start with a brief description of the Connection Machine; more detailed descriptions can be found in Hillis's book on the Connection Machine [53] or in a Thinking Machines Corporation technical summary [114].

The CM-2 Connection Machine is a fine-grained data-parallel computer with between

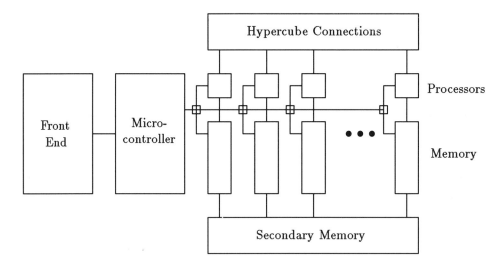

Figure 12.1:   Block diagram of the Connection Machine.

8K and 64K processors (see Figure 12.1). Each processor is a 1-bit serial processor, with 64K bits of local memory, and optional floating-point hardware. Each processor can access its memory with independent addresses. All the processors are controlled by a microcontroller, which is attached to a front end computer. The processors are organized into a hypercube network with 16 processors at each node (corner) of the hypercube. The wires of the hypercube network are shared by the scan instructions and the permutation instructions.

We now consider how the general architecture of a V-RAM can be mapped onto the Connection Machine. The scalar processor of the V-RAM can be mapped onto the front end of the Connection Machine, and the vector processor can be mapped onto the processor array of the Connection Machine. Since vectors in a V-RAM can be arbitrarily long, we must somehow simulate them on the Connection Machine which has a fixed number of processors. In the following discussion we first discuss how the vector memory of a V-RAM is mapped onto the Connection Machine and then discuss how the specific instructions of the scan vector model are mapped onto the Connection Machine.

12.1.1   The Vector Memory

To support the vector memory on the Connection Machine, arbitrarily long vectors must be mapped onto the fixed number of processor memories of the Connection Machine. This is implemented using a level of indirection. Each location of a *virtual vector memory* is a

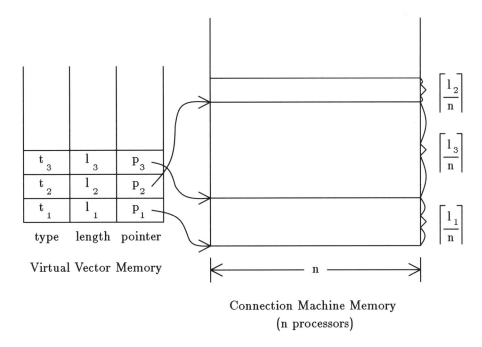

Figure 12.2: An illustration of how the vector memory is simulated on the Connection Machine. The *virtual vector memory* is stored on the front-end computer and contains pointers to slices of the actual Connection Machine memory.

structure which contains a pointer to a physical location in the Connection Machine memory where the vector is actually stored (see Figure 12.2). It also contains other information, including the length and the type of the vector. The virtual vector memory is stored on the front end computer.

Since the vectors can be longer than the number of processors in the Connection Machine, each vector might take up many slices of the Connection Machine memory. A vector of length m on an n processor machine, will require $\lceil m/n \rceil$ slices of memory. Since vectors in general are not a multiple of n long, the left over $n \times \lceil m/n \rceil - m$ elements are left unused. The elements within a vector are numbered so that contiguous indices are within the same processor. For a vector of length m, on a n processor machine, elements $0, .., (\lceil m/n \rceil - 1)$ are in processor 0, elements $\lceil m/n \rceil, .., (2 \lceil m/n \rceil - 1)$ are in processor 1, and so forth.

To implement the vector memory we need some sort of memory management, because it might be necessary to allocate space in the Connection Machine memory when we write a vector into the virtual vector memory. If the vector we write is the same length as the previous vector stored at that location in the virtual vector memory, then we can simply write over the old version. If, however, the vector is longer, the vector might require more slices of the Connection Machine memory and not fit in the position it was previously at. We therefore require some sort of memory management that allocates new space in the Connection Machine memory when writing into a location of the virtual vector memory, and that deallocates the space when another vector is overwritten. As with other memory management systems, this system might have problems with fragmentation of the memory, and might be required to occasionally relocate vectors. If vectors are allocated on a stack within the virtual vector memory, the allocation and deallocation is straightforward since we can keep an analogous stack in the Connection Machine memory and slices of memory can always be allocated and deleted from the top of the stack.

This general technique of mapping arbitrarily long vectors using a level of indirection can be used for a much broader class of machines than just the Connection Machine.

12.1.2   The Instructions

We now describe how the instructions of the scan vector model are implemented on the Connection Machine. The scalar instructions are simply executed on the front end and therefore need no explanations. All instructions with vector arguments take indices into the virtual vector memory rather than directly into the Connection Machine memory. When executed, each instruction calculates how many slices of memory each vector occupies and loops over these slices. We now describe the each class of instruction.

Elementwise Instructions

The elementwise vector instructions take as input some set of vectors each of the same length. Based on the length of the vectors and the size of the machine, they calculate how many slices of CM memory are taken by each vector. They then loop over each slice, loading the values into each processor from its local memory, executing the particular elementwise operation and storing the result back into their local memory. The elementwise instructions never require communication among processors.

Permutation Instructions

The permutation instructions are supported by the routing hardware of the Connection Machine. The router uses a packet-switched message routing scheme that directs messages along the hypercube wires to their destinations (see [53] for more details).

The router requires a processor address, and a location within each processor to deliver each value. Before executing the route, we must therefore translate the destination indices from the *index* argument of the permutation instruction into two parts: the processor address, and the slice number within that processor. This can be executed by dividing each index by the number of slices, using the result as the processor address, and using the remainder as the slice number within that processor.

It is important for the permutation instruction that each processor has independent addressing: different processors can access different locations simultaneously. This is because when a value arrives at the destination processor, the processor must place it in the correct slice. The values arriving at different processors might belong in different slices. The CM-2 has such independent addressing but the CM-1 does not. When there are many slices the permutation instruction is inefficient on the CM-1.

Another trick used to improve the performance of the permutation instruction is for each processor to randomly select the elements to be sent from its memory rather than to serially loop over them. This prevents the problem of having many elements in one slice going to a single processor and congesting the routing hardware.

Scan Instructions

The scan instructions are implemented on the Connection Machine using a mix of the binary tree and hypercube algorithms described in Chapter 13. The implementation uses the same hypercube wires as the router but does not use the routing hardware. The technique described in Section 3.7 is used when there are multiple memory slices.

Vector-Scalar Instructions

The `insert` and `extract` instructions are executed by translating the *index* argument of the instructions into a processor and slice number. This can be executed on the front end. The Connection Machine then selects the correct processor by broadcasting the processor address and having each processor compare itself to the address. Once a processor is selected, the value is read (`extract`) using the global-or wire, or written (`insert`) by broadcasting the value to the selected processor. Since the value will belong to a single slice, we need only do this for the appropriate slice.

The `distribute` instruction is implemented by allocating the appropriate number of slices on the front end and then broadcasting the value to be distributed to all the slice.

12.1.3 Optimizations

This section describes some optimizations that can improve the performance of the scan vector primitives on parallel machines. These are straightforward generalizations of optimizations considered by researchers involved with implementing compilers for APL [1, 85, 52, 30]. The optimizations discussed all involve viewing the vector instructions in a wider context and changing the execution of each instruction based on this wider context. Further generalization of this work is an interesting topic for future research.

The first optimization we consider is based on the *dragthrough* optimization suggested by Abrams [1]. Consider the expression, $D \leftarrow (A + B) \times (A - C)$, in which all the variables are vectors. The standard way to evaluate this in a vector model would be to add the two vectors A and B into a temporary vector, subtract the two vectors A and C into another temporary vector and then multiply the two temporary vectors. Let us now consider the case that the vectors are *long vectors* (have more elements than processors): let's say that the vectors are of length m and there are p processors. In this case, when looping over the slices, instead of completely executing the two subexpressions before multiplying them, we could execute the whole expression for each slice—the looping could be moved from inside each vector operation to outside the whole expression. This transformed routine would require 2 temporary slices of the Connection Machine memory instead of the $2 \lceil m/p \rceil$ required by the original routine. It might also be possible to optimize the transformed routine by keeping each slice of A in a local register for both the first and second subexpression.

We now consider a variation of the dragthrough optimization. Consider taking the outer-product of two vectors and then reducing along the second dimension. If the two original vectors are of length m_1 and m_2, the final result will be of length m_1. The intermediate result of the outer-product, however, contains $m_1 \times m_2$ elements. If this operation is simulated on p processors, and $p < m_1 \times m_2$, the required temporary memory can be reduced to $O(p)$ by generating p elements of the outer product at a time and reducing this part along the way. This particular case is an example of a broad range of cases in which very large intermediate results need not be generated if the code is viewed in a wider context. This optimization in its full generality is much more complicated to implement than the simple expression-dragthrough optimization.

As a final optimization, consider the `select-permute` primitive when the *default* vector, D, is much larger than the *data* vector. The `select-permute` primitive is defined so that instead of side effecting D, it makes a new copy with the inserted elements. To do this, the `select-permute` primitive might copy all the elements of D even though few of them have been changed. To avoid executing this potentially large copy, an optimizer might notice that the old vector D is never used again, so even though conceptually a new vector is being created, the implementation could just side effect D. Such an optimization is often used by compilers for functional languages. As with the other optimizations, this optimization requires that a compiler looks at the vector instructions in context.

Slices	Instruction			
	`p+`	`permute`	`+-scan`	`extract`
1	20	500	500	30
4	68	2100	620	30
16	260	8800	1100	30
64	1030	35000	3000	30

Table 12.1: Running times for a selection of primitives (one from each class). The times are for the CM-2 and are in microseconds. The times are all for 32-bit values.

12.1.4 Running Times

Table 12.1 tabulates the running times of some of the instructions of the scan vector model when executed on the Connection Machine (CM-2). The times are given for various different numbers of slices.

12.2 Simulating on P-RAM

In this section we discuss how the scan vector model can be simulated on a synchronous P-RAM. We show that a scan vector algorithms with a step complexity of s and an element complexity of e, can execute on a p processor EREW P-RAM with scan primitives with a time complexity $t = O(e/p + s)$. We first prove a more general theorem and then prove the specific case. The general theorem is a variation of Brent's scheduling principle [28] for the simulation of circuits on the P-RAM model.

Theorem 3 *If all the instructions of a V-RAM V for vectors of length l can be simulated on some P-RAM P with p processors with asymptotic complexity*

$$t = O\left(\lceil l/p \rceil\right) , \tag{12.1}$$

then any algorithm for V with an element complexity of e, and a step complexity of s, can be simulated on P with asymptotic complexity

$$t = O(e/p + s) . \tag{12.2}$$

Proof: Let us denote the length of the vectors used on step i of the algorithm as l_i. By definition,

$$e = \sum_{i=0}^{s-1} l_i . \tag{12.3}$$

The total time taken to simulate the algorithm on P is just the sum over the time of each step. Using equations 12.1 and 12.3, this is:

$$
\begin{aligned}
t &= O\left(\sum_{i=0}^{s-1}\left\lceil\frac{l_i}{p}\right\rceil\right) \\
&= O\left(\sum_{i=0}^{s-1}\left(1+\frac{l_i}{p}\right)\right) \\
&= O\left(s+\frac{1}{p}\sum_{i=0}^{s-1}l_i\right) \\
&= O\left(s+\frac{e}{p}\right)
\end{aligned}
\tag{12.4}
$$

□

We now show the specific case.

Theorem 4 *Any scan vector algorithm with an element complexity of e and a step complexity of s, can be simulated on a synchronous EREW P-RAM with scan primitives with asymptotic complexity*

$$ t = O(e/p + s) \,. \tag{12.5} $$

Proof: We only need to show that equation 12.1 is true for simulating all the instructions of the scan vector model on a synchronous EREW P-RAM with scan primitives. In Section 3.7 we already showed this for the elementwise, scan, and permutation instructions. The simulation involved assigning each processor to a block of elements and looping over the elements in the block. We are left with the scalar and vector-scalar instructions. To implement the scalar instructions we dedicate an additional P-RAM processor to act as the scalar processor. The `extract` and `insert` vector-scalar instruction only require that the dedicated scalar processor executes a read or a write into the vector. The `distribute` scalar-vector instruction can be implemented with a `copy` operation (see Section 3.4). We have therefore covered all the instructions. □

Chapter 13

Implementing the Scan Primitives

This chapter discusses many practical issues involved with implementing the scan primitives on parallel hardware. It defines a circuit, at the logic level, for implementing two primitive scan operations: a +-scan and a max-scan on unsigned integers. It shows that all the other scan operations used in this book can be implemented with these two primitive scan operations. The most interesting of these is the implementation of the floating-point +-scan. The chapter also illustrates how some of the other scan operations, such as the segmented scans, can be implemented directly rather than being simulated. A direct implementation of these scans is likely to execute in half the time as a version based on the two primitives.

13.1   Unsigned +-Scan and Max-Scan

This section introduces a practical circuit for implementing unsigned integer versions of the +-scan and max-scan operations. It starts by reviewing the standard tree implementation of the scan operation [80, 65, 41, 72], and then shows specifics of what hardware is needed at each unit of the tree to implement the two primitive scans, and argues that an actual implementation is very practical.

These two scan primitives can be used to implement all eight scan instructions of the scan vector model (the or-scan and and-scan on boolean vectors, and the +-scan, max-scan and min-scan on both integer and floating-point vectors). All but the floating-point +-scan involve simple bit manipulations. An unsigned min-scan can be implemented by inverting the source, executing a `max-scan`, and inverting the result. The signed versions of all the scans can be implemented by inverting the sign bit, executing the unsigned version, and inverting the sign bit of the result. The floating-point `max-scan` and `min-scan` can be implemented by flipping the exponent and significant if the sign bit is set, executing the signed version, and flipping the exponent and significand of the result back based on the sign bit. The `or-scan` and `and-scan` can be implemented with a 1-bit `max-scan` and `min-scan` respectively. The implementation of the floating-point `+-scan` is described in Section 13.3.

13.1.1   Tree Scan

Before describing details on how a circuit is implemented, we illustrate a general technique for implementing the scan operation on a balanced binary tree for any binary associative scan operator $\oplus$. The technique consists of two sweeps of the tree, an up sweep and a down sweep, and requires $2 \lg n$ steps. Figure 13.1 shows an example. The values to be scanned start at the leaves of the tree. On the up sweep, each unit executes $\oplus$ on its two children units and passes the sum to its parent. Each unit also keeps a copy of the value from the left child in its memory. On the down sweep, each unit passes to its left child the value from its parent and passes to its right child $\oplus$ applied to its parent and the value stored in the memory (this value originally came from the left child). After the down sweep, the values at the leaves are the results of a scan.

If the scan operator $\oplus$ can be executed with a single pass over the bits of its operand, such as integer addition and integer maximum, the tree algorithm can be bit pipelined. Bit pipelining involves passing the operands one bit at a time up the tree so that when the second level is working on bit n the first level works on bit $n + 1$. Such bit pipelining can greatly reduce the hardware necessary to implement the scan operations since only single bit logic is required at each unit.

As an example of how bit pipelining works, we consider a bit-pipelined version of `+-scan` for n, m bit integers. This bit-pipelined scan starts by passing the least significant bit of each value into the leaf units of the tree. Each unit now performs a single bit addition on its two input bits, stores the carry bit in a flag, propagates the sum bit to its parent in the next layer of units, and stores the bit from the left child in an m bit memory on the unit. On the second step, the scan passes the second bit of each value into the leaf units of the tree while it propagates the least significant bit of the sums on the first layer, to the second layer. In general, on the ith step, at the jth layer (counting from the leaves), the $(i - j)^{th}$ bit of the sum of a unit (counting from the least significant bit) gets propagated to its parent. After $m + \lg n$ steps, the up sweep is completed. Using a similar method, the down-sweep is also calculated in $m + \lg n$ steps. The total number of steps is therefore $2(m + \lg n)$.

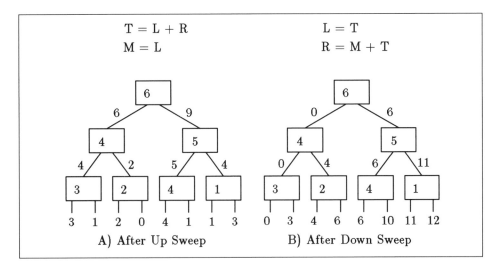

Figure 13.1: Parallel scan on a tree using the operator "+". The number in the block is the number being stored in the memory on the up sweep.

The down sweep can actually start as soon as the first bit of the up sweep reaches the top, reducing the number of steps to $m + 2 \lg n$.

13.1.2   Hardware Implementation of Tree Scan

We now discuss in more detail the hardware needed to implement the bit-pipelined tree scan for the two primitive scan operations $+-\text{scan}$ and $\text{max}-\text{scan}$. In Section 13.2 we consider what additional hardware is needed to implement some of the other scans directly, such as the segmented scans.

Figure 13.2 shows an implementation of a unit of the binary tree. Each unit consist of two identical state machines, a variable-length shift register and a one bit register. The control for a unit consists of a clock, a clear signal, and an operation specification, which specifies whether to execute a $+-\text{scan}$ or a $\text{max}-\text{scan}$. The control signals are identical on all units. The units are connected in a balanced binary tree, as shown in Figure 13.1, with two single bit unidirectional wires along every edge.

The *shift register* acts as a first in first out buffer (FIFO), with bits entered on one end and removed from the other. One bit is shifted on each clock signal. The length of the register depends on the depth of the unit in the tree. A unit at level i from the top needs a register of length $2i$ bits. The maximum length is therefore $2 \lg n$ bits. The length of the shift register can either be hardwired into each unit, in which case different levels of the

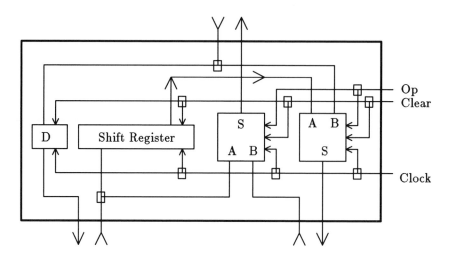

Figure 13.2:   Diagram of a unit needed to implement the tree algorithm. It consists of a shift register (which acts as a first in first out buffer), a one bit register (a D type flip-flop), and two identical sum state machines. These units are arranged in a tree as shown in Figure 13.1.

tree would require different units, or could be controlled by some logic, in which case all units could be identical, but the level number would need to be stored on each unit.

The *sum state machine* consists of three bits of state and a five input, three output combinational logic circuit. Figure 13.3 shows its basic layout and the required logic. The *Op* control specifies whether to execute a +-scan or a max-scan. Two bits of state are needed for the max-scan to keep track of whether A is greater, equal or lesser than B (if Q_1 is set, A is greater, if Q_2 is set, B is greater). The +-scan only uses one bit of state to store the carry flag (Q_1). The third bit of state is used to hold the output value (S) for one clock cycle.

To execute a scan on a tree of such units, we reset the state machines in all units with the *clear* signal and set the *Op* signal to execute either a +-scan or max-scan. We must tie the parent input of the root unit low (0). We then simply insert one bit of the operand at the leaves on each clock cycle. In a max-scan the bits are inserted starting at the most significant bit, and in a +-scan the bits are inserted starting at the least significant bit. After $2 \lg n$ steps, the result will start returning at the leaves one bit on each clock cycle. We do not even need to change anything when going from the up sweep to the down sweep: when the values reach the root, they are automatically reflected back down since the shift register at the root has length 0. The total hardware needed for scanning n values is $n - 1$

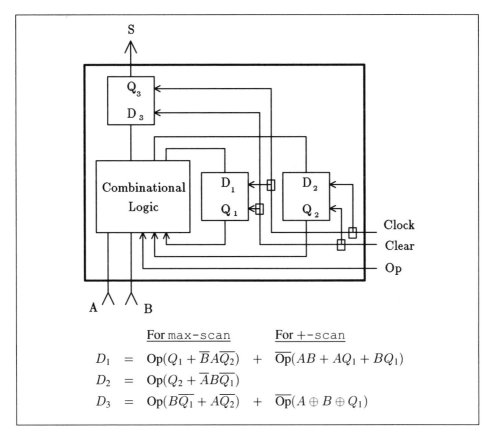

For max-scan   For +-scan

$$D_1 = \text{Op}(Q_1 + \overline{B}A\overline{Q_2}) + \overline{\text{Op}}(AB + AQ_1 + BQ_1)$$
$$D_2 = \text{Op}(Q_2 + \overline{A}B\overline{Q_1})$$
$$D_3 = \text{Op}(B\overline{Q_1} + A\overline{Q_2}) + \overline{\text{Op}}(A \oplus B \oplus Q_1)$$

Figure 13.3: Diagram of the sum state machine. It consists of three d-type flip-flops and some combinational logic. If the signal *Op* is true, the circuit executes a max-scan. If the signal *Op* is false, the circuit executes a +-scan. In the logic equations, the symbol ⊕ is an exclusive-or, and the symbol + is an inclusive-or. This state machine fits into a unit as shown in Figure 13.2.

shift registers and $2(n-1)$ sum state machines. The units are simple so it should be easy to place many on a chip.

Perhaps more importantly than the simplicity of each unit is the fact that the units are organized in a tree. The tree organization has two important practical properties. First, only two wires are needed to leave every branch of the tree. So, for example, if there are several processors per chip, only a pair of wires are needed to leave that chip, and if there are many processors on a board, only a pair of wires are needed to leave the board. Second, a tree circuit is much easier to synchronize than other structures such as grids, hypercubes or butterfly networks. This is because the same tree used for the scans can be used for clock distribution. Such a clock distribution gets rid of the clock skew problem[1] and makes it relatively easy to run the circuit extremely fast.

13.1.3   An Example System

We now consider an example system to show how the scan circuit might be applied in practice. We consider a 4096 processor parallel computer with 64 processors on each board and 64 boards per machine. To implement the scan primitives on such a machine, we could use a single chip on each board that has 64 inputs and 1 output and acts as 6 levels of the tree. Such a chip would require 126 sum state machines and 63 shift registers—such a chip is quite easy to build with today's technology. We could use one more of these chips to combine the pair of wires from each of the 64 boards.

If the clock period is 100 nanoseconds, a scan on a 32 bit field would require 5 microseconds. This time is considerably faster than the routing time of existing parallel computers such as the BBN Butterfly or the Thinking Machines Connection Machine. With a more aggressive clock such as the 10 nanoseconds clock being looked at by BBN for the Monarch[2] [6], this time would be reduced to .5 microseconds—twice as fast as the best case global access time expected on the Monarch.

In most existing and proposed tightly connected parallel computers [53, 86, 6, 102], the cost of the communication network is between 1/3 and 1/2 the cost of the computer. It is unlikely that the suggested scan network will be more than 1% of the cost of a computer.

---

[1]When there are many synchronous elements in a system, the small propagation time differences in different paths when distributing the clock signals can cause significant clock time differences at the elements.

[2]Because of the tree structure, it would actually be much easier to run a clock at 10 nanoseconds on a scan network than it is for the communication network of the Monarch.

13.2 Directly Implementing Other Scans

Although all the scans used in this book can be implemented with a small number of calls to the two primitive scans, in practice it might be beneficial to implement some of them directly; the direct implementation can save at least a factor of two in the execution time of the operations. In this section we look at the additional hardware needed to implement the backward scans and the segmented scans directly.

13.2.1 Backward and Segmented Scans

To implement the backward scans directly, each node only needs the capability of switching its left and right child. This capability requires four 1-bit multiplexers—one for each child input, and one for each child output. A 1-bit multiplexer consists of two *and* gates and an *or* gate. To simulate backward scans using only forward scans requires a permute, which might be expensive. Since the simulation might be expensive, backward scans are used frequently, and the hardware required to implement them is minimal, in a real system the backward scans should be implemented directly.

Implementing the segmented scans directly is conceptually slightly more involved but requires little additional hardware. The solution we suggest only involves changing the sum state machine on each unit by adding a few terms to the logic and a single bit of state. In this solution, the segment bit is appended as the first bit on the values to be scanned and therefore requires no extra wiring.

We first present a general technique for executing segmented scans and then show how this technique can be applied to our circuit. A segmented version of a scan for any binary associative operator $\oplus$ can be implemented using an unsegmented scan on a new operator $\oplus^s$ [101]. Each argument to this new operator is a pair of values—the value to be scanned and a segment flag. The new operator is associative but not commutative, and is defined in terms of the original operator as follows:

$$
\begin{aligned}
&\texttt{define } \oplus^s(\texttt{a, b})\{ \\
&\qquad \text{flag} \leftarrow \text{flag(a) or flag(b)}; \\
&\qquad \text{value} \leftarrow \textbf{if } \text{flag(b)} \\
&\qquad\qquad\qquad \textbf{then } \text{value(b)} \\
&\qquad\qquad\qquad \textbf{else } \text{value(a)} \oplus \text{value(b)};\}
\end{aligned}
$$

The segmented scan is therefore implemented by passing around segment-value pairs and using the modified operator to sum them.

To use the technique on our circuit, we can pass the segment-value pair by appending the segment bit to the front of the value. We also need to append an additional *header bit* to the front of the segment, value pair. The header bit is always set to 1 and is used to tell

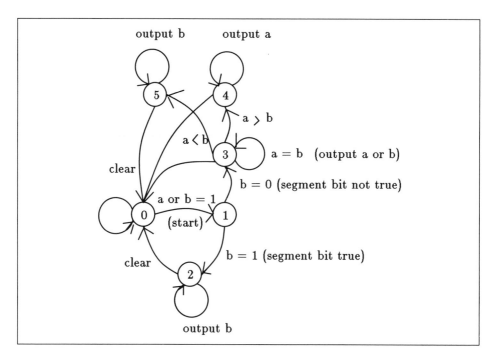

Figure 13.4:   The state diagram for a segmented max-scan. The state machine stays in state 0 until a 1 comes along on either input. This 1 is the *header bit* and is used to specify that the next bit is the *segment bit*. If the next bit of the right child (*b*) is 1, then the state machine goes into state 2 and henceforth outputs *b*. If the the bit is a 0, then it goes into state 3 and outputs the maximum of *a* or *b*. The states 3, 4 and 5 are identical to the states of the unsegmented version. The *clear* control signal brings the machine back to state 0.

the state machine that the next bit should be interpreted as a segment bit. As this header bit travels up the tree—one level on each step—it starts up all the state machines at that level when it reaches them.

Implementing the segmented versions of +, and max ($+^s$ and max^s) involves modifying the sum state machine. The new sum state machine requires an extra bit of state and the combinational logic needs to be slightly more complicated. Figure 13.4 shows the state diagram for the new *sum state machine*. Generating the logic equations from the state diagram is straightforward.

13.2.2   Multidimensional Grid Scans

The grid scans can be implemented directly also. This can significantly increase performance on algorithms based on dense matrices such as many discussed in Chapter 8. We are not going to discuss in detail how implemented but refer the reader to [4]. Because they require a more complex network, grid scans are inherently more expensive, and in general should not be expected to run as fast as one dimensional scans. They, however, should still run faster than general memory references.

13.3   Floating-Point +-Scan

In this section we discuss how a floating-point +-scan can be simulated with the two primitive scans. As mentioned at the beginning of the chapter, floating-point +-scan is the only one of the eight scan operations that involves more than trivial bit manipulations.

One problem with implementing a floating-point +-scan is that the floating-point + operator applied to fixed-precision floating-point numbers is not truly associative. For example, with single-precision IEEE floating-point numbers,

$$1.0e10 + (-1.0e10 + 1.0) = 0$$

whereas

$$(1.0e10 + -1.0e10) + 1.0 = 1.0 .$$

The goal for an implementation of floating-point +-scan on fixed-precision floating-point numbers is to return results which are as close as possible to the results that would be returned by using infinite-precision floating-point numbers.

In implementing a floating-point +-scan we are mostly concerned with the accuracy of the +-reduce built from the +-scan. This is because the floating-point +-scan is used almost exclusively to implement a +-reduce.[3] We will show that the technique we describe returns quite accurate results when used to implement a floating-point +-reduce. It returns a sum that is at most one bit off in the lowest bit of the significand from the results given by summing the values into an infinite-precision accumulator. This result is significantly better than the result given by serially summing a set of values into an accumulator which has the same precision as the numbers themselves.

The basic idea of the technique is to denormalize all numbers based on the maximum exponent, to use an unsigned +-scan on these denormalized values, and then renormalize the results. The following discussion assumes a signed magnitude representation of

---

[3]The only direct use of a floating-point +-scan I have come across is for block filtering [71].

floating-point numbers. We use the symbol e for the exponent of each number, and the symbol m for the significand.

1. Find the maximum exponent and distribute it to all the elements of the vector.

   This can be executed with a `max-distribute`. We will refer to the result as e_{max}.

2. For each element, denormalize the significand relative to e_{max}.

   This consists of exposing the hidden bit and shifting the bits of each significand right by $e_{max} - e$. If the vector is of length n, and the significand is d bits, we denormalize into a bit field of size $d + \lg n$ bits. This extra $\lg n$ is important. If

   $$(e_{max} - e) > \lg n,$$

   some bits are dropped.

3. Invert the negative numbers so that they are in signed integer representation.

4. Apply a signed `+-scan` to these integers.

5. Invert the negative numbers of the result so that all numbers are again in signed magnitude representation.

6. Renormalize each number, again relative to e_{max}.

To implement a floating-point `+-reduce` directly, an integer `+-reduce` can be used in step 4 instead of the integer `+-scan`.

Theorem 5 *The result of a floating-point* `+-reduce` *implemented as described is accurate to within one bit in the least-significant bit of the significand (relative to* e_{max}*).*

Proof: The inaccuracy of the total sum is at most the difference between the maximum and minimum possible sum of the lost bits—the bits that get shifted off the end when the numbers are denormalized. Since we are adding n values, and the padding region is of length $\lg n$, the sum of the lost bits cannot reach into the significand region (see Figure 13.5). This sum, therefore, cannot affect the significand relative to e_{max} by more than one bit. ☐

If there is a balance of negative and positive values, the leftmost nonzero bit might be within the left line. In this case, the loss of accuracy relative to the final exponent (rather than e_{max}) could be more than a bit. This problem with a balance of positive and negative numbers appears in almost all schemes for adding floating-point values (see the example at the beginning of the section).

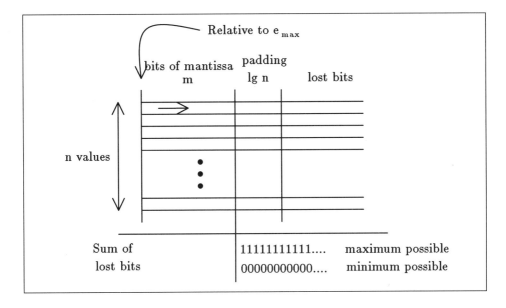

Figure 13.5: An illustration of the accuracy of a floating-point +-reduce. When we denormalize in step 2 each significand gets shifted to the right by the difference of the maximum exponent and their exponent. Numbers with an exponent more than $\lg n$ less than the maximum exponent, will have some of their bits pushed over into the *lost bits* region, which, in our algorithm, will be dropped. At the bottom, we show the maximum and minimum possible values of the sum of all the lost bits if we had kept them.

Chapter 14

Conclusion

This book introduced the *parallel vector models*. These models served both as algorithmic models on which to analyze the complexity of parallel algorithms and as a virtual machine model on which to compile high-level languages.[1] From the algorithmic side, the book showed how a broad set of algorithms—including sorting, graph, computational-geometry, and numerical algorithms—can be implemented and analyzed on parallel vector models. From the virtual machine side, the book showed how a high-level language, PARALATION LISP, can be compiled onto the instruction set of a parallel vector virtual machine. The book also showed how a parallel vector model can be implemented on a real machine, the Connection Machine, and how it can be simulated on another algorithmic model, the P-RAM model.

The parallel vector models obliterate the view of a parallel model as a set of independent communicating serial processors, and instead treat parallel operations as inseparable operations over collections of values. Treating operations as inseparable is similar to the way word operations are treated in the serial RAM model. The RAM model does not treat word operations, such as the additions of two words, in terms of a set of single-bit units and the logic operations among those units, but instead treats them as inseparable atomic operations. As the serial RAM model is a higher-level model than models based on manipulating bits, such as a Turing machine, the parallel vector models are higher-level models than parallel models based on a set of communicating serial processors, such as the P-RAM model. I claim that this higher level makes algorithms implemented on the parallel vector models easier to describe, program and analyze; on the other hand, understanding

---

[1] When trying to understand the motivation for having a model that naturally serves both purposes, keep in mind that part of reason for success of the serial RAM model as an algorithmic model was that it closely modeled the instruction sets of real machines and therefore the target code of real compilers.

parallel vector models involves a new mind-set—a mind-set that takes some effort to accept and only slips into place once the pieces are together.

The remainder of this conclusion contains a section listing the contributions of this book, a section on directions for future research, a section on implementation goals, and a section describing how the ideas in this book developed.

14.1 Contributions

The contributions of this book, by part, can be summarized as follows:

Models

- A formal definition of the *parallel vector models*, the complexity measures that accompany the models, and an illustration of the power of the models. The models were defined in Chapter 2 and their power was illustrated throughout the book.

- A careful analysis of the consequences of including a set of *scan* operations as "unit time" primitives in the P-RAM models. Section 3.1 summarized these consequences. Every algorithm in this book used the scan primitives is some way.

- The definition of segmented versions of all the instructions of a vector model, and an illustration of the broad applicability of these segmented instructions. The segmented versions of the instructions of the scan vector model were defined in Section 4.3 and the applicability was illustrated throughout the book.

Algorithms

- The definition of how graphs and trees can be mapped onto vectors so that they can be efficiently manipulated by the primitive vector operations. Also, the definition of a set of operations on these data structures (Chapter 5).

- The definition of many algorithms and algorithmic techniques. The most original algorithms included the halving-merge (Section 3.7.2), the minimum-spanning-tree (Section 7.1), and the binary-search (Section 6.1) algorithms.

Languages

- A careful comparison of the collection-oriented languages by placing them in a unified framework based on the collection types and the collection operations they supply (Chapter 9).

- The definition and proof of the *replicating theorem* and the formal presentation of the notions of replicating and flattening nested parallelism (Chapter 10). Also, the introduction of the *branch-packing* technique and of *contained* programs.

- The implementation of the PARALATION LISP compiler (Chapter 11). The interesting techniques used by the compiler included the simple implementation of nested parallelism with the *stepping-up* and *stepping-down* manipulations.

Architecture

- The implementation of the parallel vector models on the Connection Machine and the simulation on the P-RAM (Chapter 12).

- The definition of a logic circuit to implement both the unsegmented and segmented versions of the `+-scan` and `max-scan` operations on unsigned integers (Chapter 13).

- The implementation of the segmented versions of the scan primitives with a constant number of calls to the unsegmented versions (Section B.2.3).

- The implementation of the floating-point `+-scan` with the unsigned version of the `+-scan` and `max-scan` primitives (Section 13.3).

14.2 Directions for Future Research

This section outlines some directions for future research on topics related to this book.

Modifying the model to include locality: The assumption in the scan vector model that all `permute` operations on equal length vectors take equal time, as with the assumption in the serial RAM model that all memory references take equal time, has a problem in practice—the assumption ignores locality. In real machines, certain local communication patterns will always be faster than other non-local patterns. Aggarwal, Chandra and Snir have proposed models for taking account of locality in the serial RAM models [2] and suggested that the models could be extended to the P-RAM models. Ideas from these models might be transferred in the parallel vector models. Leiserson and Maggs have also proposed parallel models that take account of locality [69, 70]. These ideas might again be transferred to the parallel vector models.

Analyzing how wide serial control can be stretched: As mentioned in Section 2.2, almost all algorithms found in the literature can be mapped efficiently onto machines or models with serial control. But what about real world problems? What about compilers, text formatters and database applications? I believe that with the replicating theory in hand, many of these problems can be mapped naturally onto serial control. This, however, needs to be backed up with solid evidence. A careful study of a broad range of applications to see if they can be mapped onto serial control would be very useful.

Modifying the model to include parallel control: An interesting machine to consider is a machine with multiple control streams each of which controls a parallel vector machine. What would such a machine be useful for? Would it only allow a fixed number of control streams or could the number of control streams change dynamically? Could it allocate control streams like the elements of a vector in the parallel vector models? How would data from different control streams interact?

Analyzing various language features: Should a collection-oriented language be strongly typed? Should it include dynamic allocation? Should it be functional? Should it allow the user to access lower lever features such as the segmented scans? The fact that the languages manipulate whole collections might enhance different choices than for standard serial language. One important observation is that since the operations operate on large sets of data, the relative cost of dynamic type checking and memory allocation is lower than for serial languages—the checks and allocation only have to be applied once per collection instead of once per scalar.

Analyzing various parallel vector instructions: As discussed in Chapter 4, the parallel vector models permit a broad range of primitives. There are many interesting question regarding the selection of a set of primitives. How do various primitives affect the complexity of various algorithms? What is the complexity of simulating one set of primitives with another?

Modifying the model for the benefit of small changes to large data sets: In a parallel vector model, if a small number of changes are made distributed over a large data set, the cost (the element complexity) is proportional to the size of the large data set. Is this an accurate measure? Should the element complexity always be proportional to the longest vector when vectors of greatly different length are involved in a vector operation?

14.3   Implementation Goals

This section lists some future implementation goals. The purpose of these goals is both to give stronger support to the claims made in this book and to make available to the research community systems on which to write parallel algorithms and to have those algorithms run on a broad variety of machines.

To implement the scan vector instruction set on more machines: I am currently in the process of implementing it on the Cray X-MP and am looking at possibly implementing it on a iWarp [25]. To get a broad range of machines, the instruction set should also be implemented on some coarse grained parallel machines, such as the Encore Multimax and Alliant FX, and on some hypercube machines such as the Intel iPSC/2, and optimized versions of the instruction set should be implemented on various serial machines.

To collect more timing comparisons: It would be interesting to get more data on how the run-time of algorithms written in a high-level language and compiled through the scan vector model compare to algorithms optimized for particular machines. This should be tested over a broad range of algorithms and applications so that application specific deficiencies of the model might be identified.

To implement a complete Paralation-Lisp compiler: A complete and properly documented version of the PARALATION LISP compiler would be a very powerful tool that would allow researchers to quickly implement code to run on parallel machines.

To implement compilers for other languages: A compiler for SETL, for example, would be very interesting. An important issue that arises when implementing a compiler for languages such as SETL is how to extract parallelism that is not directly stated. For example, consider the PARALATION LISP and SETL definitions of quicksort shown in Figure 14.1. In the PARALATION LISP version, the parallel application of the two quicksorts is explicit in the `elwise`, whereas in the SETL version, a compiler would need to extract the two quicksorts and schedule them to be applied together.

Implementing a broader range of applications: Although this book describes many algorithms, it does not describe any full applications. Paul Resnick is currently implementing a simple text formatter using the scan vector instruction set. It would also be interesting to implement a compiler, some database applications, and other commonly used applications.

14.4 Development of Book Ideas

It is important to outline the history of the ideas in a dissertation so that the casual reader can understand the motivation, the admirer can understand the methodology, and the skeptic can understand where the research went astray. This section presents such an history of the ideas in this book (the book is a slightly modified version of my Ph.D. dissertation).

While employed at Thinking Machines during the summer of 1985, Abhiram Ranade and I implemented the *enumerate* instruction (see Section 4.2) as part of the original instruction set of the Connection Machine (CM-1). The instruction was seen as useful to

```
(defun quicksort (keys)
  (if (< (value-count keys) 2)
      keys
      (let* ((pivot (elt keys 1))
             (side (elwise (keys)
                     (if (< keys pivot) 0
                         (if (= keys pivot) 1 2))))
             (piles (collect keys :by (match (make-paralation 3)
                                             side))))
        (expand (elwise ((pile piles))
                  (quicksort pile))))))
```

Quicksort in PARALATION LISP

```
proc quicksort(keys),
  if #keys < 2
  then return keys
  else pivot := keys(1);
       lesser-pile := [keys: keys = t(i)| keys < pivot];
       equal-pile := [keys: keys = t(i)| keys = pivot];
       greater-pile := [keys: keys = t(i)| keys > pivot];
       return quicksort(lesser-pile) + equal-pile +
              quicksort(greater-pile);
  end;
end proc quicksort;
```

Quicksort in SETL

Figure 14.1: The code for quicksort in PARALATION LISP and in SETL.

implement the *cons* instruction, used to allocate elements to unused processors (see [31]).

While implementing the *enumerate* instruction, I realized that it would run faster than the *send* instruction, used to communicate among processors. I also realized that with small modifications of the code used for the *enumerate* instruction, I could implement a general +-scan and max-scan instruction; so in January of 1986 I did. On top of these two instructions I implemented the min-scan, or-scan, and and-scan, and also implemented the segmented versions and the floating point versions of the scans. These were implemented as described in Chapter 13 and Appendix B. I also implemented the split radix sort described in Section 3.4.1 which is currently the sort supplied by the CM-1 and CM-2 instruction set. With the support of Guy Steele, the scan instructions and the sort were added to the instruction set of the CM-1 before the first CM-1 was delivered during the summer of 1986.

During the summer of 1986, other people and I found a great number of uses for the scan instructions. Often the instructions lead to great performance benefits for applications. For example, we sped up a SPICE circuit simulator, a network learning algorithm [23], a rule based system [17, 18], and several numerical tasks such as a linear systems solver. During the year the idea of segments and segmented scans also became very popular among Connection Machine programmers and I implemented a set of utilities on top of *LISP [66] (the most commonly used Connection Machine language) for dealing with segments.

I then made my first attempt at abstracting the idea of a scan primitive away from the Connection Machine to see if applied to a broader class of machines. I realized that the scan primitive, under almost any practical assumptions, on any reasonable architecture, would always be cheaper to implement and run faster than a permutation primitive. In this first attempt on abstracting this observation, I basically took the P-RAM model and included on top of it a set of "unit-time" scan primitives [19, 20]. Based on this model I showed how the asymptotic running time of many P-RAM algorithms could be improved by a $O(\lg n)$ factor [22].

The CM software environment at this time supported so called "virtual processors". The idea of virtual processors was that the user could specify the number of processors they wanted, and if that many physical processors were not available, the software would simulate them by time slicing each physical processor. The problem with virtual processors was that the number of processors needed to be specified at *cold boot* time, and in many applications, the number of processors needed would change dynamically and frequently.

To resolve this problem, in January of 1987 I suggested what I now call *parallel vector models*. Jim Salem and Guy Steele also suggested changes to the environment to resolve the same problem. Cliff Laser took the various ideas, added more of his own and made a specification for a new model of "virtual processors", which has now been implemented. This specification was a compromise among the various ideas and is not exactly the parallel vector model described in this book, but for most practical purposes is the same. The main difference is that vectors of the same length are grouped into so called *virtual processor sets*. After suggesting the parallel vector models, I realized that the scan primitives would fit much better into a parallel vector model than into the P-RAM model. This was mainly because the scans imply a single source of control: all processors (elements) must be executing a scan operation at the same time.

Having spent a lot of time implementing algorithms and applications I had become quite interested in parallel languages—I wanted to reduce the time required to implement applications and algorithms on the Connection Machine. A language issue that particularly interested me, since it had turned up over and over again, was what I call nested parallelism. Up to this point, the notion of segments had been used to implemented nested parallelism on the Connection Machine. Maintaining segments, however, required a lot of work on the programmers part and often makes programs hard to debug. On the other hand, the two languages PARALATION LISP and CM-LISP both allowed the direct expression of nested parallelism, but, unfortunately, neither of their implementations took advantage of it: they would run each subcollection in parallel but serially loop through the subcollections. I wanted to merge the ideas of nested parallelism and segments.

During the summer of 1987 I implemented a compiler for a subset of PARALATION LISP which would map nested parallelism onto segments thus alleviating the programmer from having to deal with the segments themselves, but yet would take full advantage of the expression of nested parallel expressions. While implementing the compiler, I realized that if I organized things correctly I would only need to implement a single version of all the operators regardless if used in a nested call or not. This is where the replicating theorem originated.

Many of the ideas in this book were cleaned up over the next year while I was organizing and writing my dissertation. Since the dissertation, the following has been changed for this book: (1) I rewrote the introduction; (2) I added the section on containment in Chapter 10; and (3) I added the preface and the index. These changes were made during my first year at Carnegie Mellon.

Appendix A

Glossary

Access-Fixed Code: Code that uses on any but three of the scan vector instructions: the `cond-jump`, `move-scalar` and `move-vector` instructions.

Access-Restricted Code: Code that uses on the scan vector instructions that abides by some restrictions on the use of the `cond-jump`, `move-scalar` and `move-vector` instructions.

Backward Scan: A scan operation that starts at the last element of a vector and goes to the first.

Collection: A group of elements viewed as a whole.

Collection Oriented: When used to refer to an algorithmic model or a language, the term signifies that the model or language centers around collections of values, and a set of operations for manipulating the collections as a whole.

Contained Program: A program that satisfies certain rules needed to prove the step complexity bound in the replicating theorem.

Element Complexity: A time complexity measure for the parallel vector models. It is the sum, over the steps, of the lengths of the vectors manipulated in each step, and corresponds roughly to the serial complexity.

Element Space Complexity: A space complexity measure for the parallel vector models. It is the sum of the vector lengths over the locations used in the vector memory.

Elementwise: Signifies applying an operation independently to each of a collection of elements.

Enumerate: An operation that takes an vector of boolean flags and return the integer i to the ith true element.

Equal Time Assumption: For the parallel vector models, it is the assumption that all primitives take equal time on equal-length vectors.

Flat Collection: A collection whose elements are all scalars.

Flat Parallel Construct: A scalar operation applied in parallel over a set of elements or processors.

Flattening: When used to refer to a collection or to parallelism, the term signifies taking a nested collection or a nested parallel construct and turning into a flat collection or flat parallel construct.

Grid-Ordered Collection: A multi-dimensionally ordered collection: for a collection with n elements, each element is associated with a unique vector of d non-negative integers (the index along each dimension) such that the product of one more than the maximum integer in each position over the elements (the product of the range of each dimension) is n. Also called a dense array.

Homogeneous: When used to refer to a vector or collection, the term signifies that all the elements of the vector or collection are of the same type.

Linear-Ordered Collection: A one dimensionally ordered collection: for a collection with n elements, each element is associated with a unique integer between 0 and $n - 1$. Also called a vector.

Long Vector: When used to refer to mapping a vector onto a fixed set of processors, the term signifies a vector with more elements than there are processors.

Nested Collection: A collection whose elements are all themselves collections.

Nested Parallel Construct: A parallel operation applied in parallel over a set of elements— each application is itself parallel.

Pack: An operation that takes a vector of n elements and a vector of n flags, m of which are true ($m \leq n$). It returns a new vector with m elements such that elements in positions where a flag was false are removed, and the remaining elements maintain their order.

Parallel Random Access Machine (P-RAM): Defined at the end of the glossary.

Parallel Vector Model: Any of a class of algorithmic models based on a set of operations on vectors.

Prefix Computation: Another name for a scan operation.

Processor-Oriented: When used to refer to an algorithmic model or a language, the term signifies that the model or language centers around a collection of processors, a set of local operations on each processor, and a set of operations for communicating among the processors.

Processor-Step Complexity: In a model with a fixed number of processors, such as the P-RAM model, it is the number of steps multiplied by the number of processors.

Replicating: A technique for translating a parallel routine that executes an operation on a set of data, into another routine that executes the same operation over many sets of data in parallel.

Scan Operation: Another name for a prefix computation.

Scan Vector Model: A parallel vector model with three classes of primitive instructions— elementwise instructions, scan instructions, and permutation instructions.

Segment Descriptor: A structure used to describe the segmentation of a segmented vector.

Segmented Vector: A vector that is segmented into contiguous blocks.

Serially Linear Model: A model in which all the primitives are serially linear.

Serially Linear Primitive: A primitive of a parallel vector model that when applied to a vector of length n will take $O(n)$ time to simulate on a RAM model.

Serially Time Optimal: A parallel vector algorithm whose asymptotic element complexity is equal to the optimal serial algorithm.

Simple Vector: A vector of scalar values.

Step Complexity: The number of steps taken by an algorithm.

Vector: A linear-ordered collection.

Vector Memory: The part of a V-RAM used to store vectors. Also called the virtual vector memory.

Vector Model: A shortened name for parallel vector model.

Vector Random Access Machine (V-RAM): A machine architecture based on parallel vector models.

Vector Space Complexity: A space complexity measure for parallel vector models. It is the number of locations used in the vector memory.

Virtual Vector Memory: The apparent vector memory seen by a user of a V-RAM. This must be mapped onto a physical vector memory on a real machine.

History of the Scan Operations

A parallel circuit to execute a particular scan operation was suggested by Ofman in the early 60s [80] to be used to add binary numbers—the following routine executes addition on two binary numbers with their bits spread across two vectors A and B:

$$(A \otimes B) \otimes \texttt{seg-or-scan}(AB, \overline{A}\,\overline{B})$$

A general scan operator was suggested by Iverson in the mid 1960s for the language APL [61].[1] A parallel implementation of scans on a perfect shuffle network was suggested by Stone [109] to be used for polynomial evaluation—the following routine evaluates a polynomial with a vector of coefficients A and variable x at the head of another vector X:

$$A \times \texttt{x-scan}\,(\texttt{copy}(X))$$

Ladner and Fisher first showed an efficient general-purpose circuit for implementing the scan operations [65]. Wyllie first showed how the scan operation can be executed in parallel on a linked list [120] (this implementation is based on the P-RAM model). Brent and Kung, in the context of binary addition, first showed an efficient VLSI layout for a scan circuit [29]. Schwartz [101] and, independently, Mago [74] first suggested the segmented versions of the scans. More recent work on implementing scan operations in parallel include the work of Fich [41], which demonstrates a more efficient implementation of the scan operations, and of Lubachevsky and Greenberg [72], which demonstrates the implementation of the scan operation on asynchronous machines.

As concerns terminology, *scan* is the original name given to the operation by Iverson. Ladner and Fisher introduced the term *parallel prefix operation*. Schwartz used the term *all partial sums*. I find the original term, scan, more concise and flexible—it, for example, can be used as a verb, as in "the algorithm then scans the vector" or "after scanning twice....".

---

[1]The history of the scan operator in APL is actually quite complex. It did not appear in the original definition [59], but appears in some but not all subsequent definitions.

P-RAM Models

The Parallel-RAM (P-RAM) models [42, 101, 104, 48, 49], also known as shared-memory models, are probably the most used algorithmic models of parallel computation. As with the RAM model and the vector models, the P-RAM models are based on a machine architecture. The general machine architecture consists of a set of standard RAM (random access machine) processors connected to a shared memory. Each processor has its own instruction interpreter, and all processors can read and write to the shared memory. In the synchronous P-RAM models, it is assumed that all the processors are fed by a global clock.

There are several variations of the synchronous P-RAM models which differ in how they treat concurrent access to a single memory location. The exclusive-read exclusive-write (EREW) P-RAM model does not permit concurrent reads or writes to a single location in shared memory: it is an error to execute such an operation. The concurrent-read concurrent-write (CRCW) P-RAM models on the other hand do allow concurrent reads and writes. The CRCW P-RAM models can be further divided depending on the result when several values are written to the same location concurrently. Surveys of the variations can be found in [118, 51]. Probably the most powerful P-RAM model suggested in the literature is the *fetch-and-op* P-RAM model (see [50, 49, 93]).

Appendix B

Code

This appendix gives the code for many of the routines described in this book. It includes the code for (1) the operations defined in Section 4.2, (2) the translations between the different segment-descriptors described in Section 4.3, (3) the simulation of the segmented primitives with the unsegmented primitives, (4) the implementation of the pack and flag-merge needed for implementing the segmented conditionals discussed in Section 10.2, (5) the simulation of the scan instructions on the two scan primitives discussed in Chapter 13, and (6) various other routines described in this book.

The code is written in SV-LISP (see Section 11.2) and all the routines in this appendix have been tested. The only operations or forms used in this appendix which are not described in Section 11.2 or in the COMMON LISP manual are `append-bits, extract-bits` and `over-elements`. We briefly describe each of these.

The `append-bits` function takes two integer arguments and lexically appends the bit representation of one integer to the bit representation of the other. The result is therefore an integer with twice as many bits. In the implemented version, regular integers use 32 bits, and appended integers use 64 bits. The `extract-bits` function strips the high bits off of a long integer leaving only the low bits.

The `over-elements` form is used to specify that the code inside the form is to be applied over the elements of a vector. It takes two arguments—a list of bindings and a body. Each binding is a free variable followed by a vector. All the vectors must be of the same length. For example, the form:

```
(over-elements ((element-a vector-a)
                (element-b vector-b)
  (+ element-a element-b))
```

will elementwise add the elements of vector-a and vector-b.

B.1 Simple Operations

```
;; Converts a vector of boolean flags to ones and zeros.
(defop flag-to-number (flags)
  (over-elements ((f flags))
    (select-value f 1 0)))

;; Numbers the elements with their flag set to T.
(defop enumerate (flags)
  (plus-scan (flag-to-number flags)))

;; Given a length, returns an index vector of that length.
(defop index (length)
  (plus-scan (distribute 1 length)))

;; Sums the elements of a vector.
(defop plus-reduce (values)
  (+ (extract (plus-scan values) (1- (length values)))
     (extract values (1- (length values)))))

;; Finds the maximum element of a vector.
(defop max-reduce (values)
  (max (extract (max-scan values) (1- (length values)))
       (extract values (1- (length values)))))

;; Finds the minimum element of a vector.
(defop min-reduce (values)
  (min (extract (min-scan values) (1- (length values)))
       (extract values (1- (length values)))))

;; Counts the number of T flags in a vector.
(defop count (flags)
  (plus-reduce (flag-to-number flags)))

;; Given two vectors of pointers and two vectors of values,
;; merges the values into the positions specified by the pointers.
(defop join (v1 p1 v2 p2)
  (default-permute
    v1
    p1
    (default-permute
      v2
      p2
      (distribute nil (+ (length v1) (length v2))))))
```

```
;; Appends two vectors.
(defop append (v1 v2)
  (join v1 (index (length v1))
        v2 (over-elements ((i (index (length v2)))
                           (l (distribute (length v1) (length v2))))
              (+ i l)))))

;; Packs the values from positions where the flags are set to T.
(defop pack (values flags)
  (select-permute values
                  (enumerate flags)
                  flags
                  (distribute nil (count flags)))))

;; Splits the NIL values to the bottom of a vector and the T values
;; to the top.
(defop split (values flags)
  (let ((not-flags (over-elements ((f flags)) (not f))))
    (permute values
             (over-elements ((h (enumerate flags))
                             (l (enumerate not-flags))
                             (f flags)
                             (o (distribute (count not-flags)
                                            (length values))))
               (select-value f (+ h o) l)))))

;; Merges two vectors according to a set of flags.
(defop flag-merge (flags v1 v2)
  (let ((indices (index (length flags))))
    (join v2 (pack indices flags)
          v1 (pack indices (over-elements ((f flags)) (not f))))))

;; Fetches the values from the positions specified by the indices.
(defop i-permute (values indices)
  (let ((returnp (index (length indices)))
        (default (distribute nil (length values))))
    (select-permute
      values
      (default-permute returnp indices default)
      (default-permute (distribute t (length values)) indices default)
      indices)))

;; Returns the sum of a vector to all positions of a vector.
(defop plus-distribute (values)
  (distribute (plus-reduce values) (length values)))

;; Returns the maximum element to all positions of a vector.
(defop max-distribute (values)
```

```
    (distribute (max-reduce values) (length values)))

;; Returns the minimum element to all positions of a vector.
(defop min-distribute (values)
  (distribute (min-reduce values) (length values)))

;; Returns the index of the maximum element.
(defop max-index (values)
  (min-reduce
    (over-elements ((max (max-distribute values))
                    (v values)
                    (l (distribute (length values) (length values)))
                    (i (index (length values))))
      (select-value (= max v) i l))))
```

B.2   Segments

B.2.1   Useful Utilities

```
;; Returns a boolean vector of length LENGTH with a T in the first element.
(defop set-first-element (length)
  (insert (distribute nil length) t 0))

;; Returns a boolean vector of length LENGTH with a T in the last element.
(defop set-last-element (length)
  (insert (distribute nil length) t (1- length)))

;; Returns previous element of a vector; DEFAULT is placed in the
;; first element.
(defop previous (values default)
  (select-permute values
                  (over-elements ((i (index (length values))))
                    (+ i 1))
                  (over-elements ((f (set-last-element (length values))))
                    (not f))
                  (distribute default (length values))))

;; Returns next element of a vector; DEFAULT is placed in the
;; last element.
(defop next (values default)
  (select-permute values
                  (over-elements ((i (index (length values))))
                    (- i 1))
                  (over-elements ((f (set-first-element (length values))))
                    (not f))
```

```
                    (distribute default (length values))))

;; Returns a boolean vector set to T in positions where the value changes.
(defop boundary (values)
  (over-elements ((f (set-first-element (length values)))
                  (p (previous values 0))
                  (v values))
    (simple-or f (/= p v))))

;; Like enumerate but it includes the flag in the sum.
(defop i-enumerate (flags)
  (let ((number (flag-to-number flags)))
    (over-elements ((enum (plus-scan number))
                    (f number))
      (+ f enum))))

;; A backward version of enumerate: it starts at end.
(defop b-enumerate (select)
  (over-elements ((enumerate (enumerate select))
                  (flag (flag-to-number select))
                  (total (distribute (count select) (length select))))
    (- total (+ flag enumerate))))
```

B.2.2 Segment Descriptor Translations

```
(defop head-pointer-from-length (lengths)
  (plus-scan lengths))

(defc  head-pointer-from-head-flag (head-flags)
  (pack (index (length head-flags)) head-flags))

(defop length-from-head-pointer (head-pointers total-length)
  (over-elements ((next (next head-pointers total-length))
                  (this head-pointers))
    (- next this)))

(defop length-from-head-flag (head-flags)
  (length-from-head-pointer
    (head-pointer-from-head-flag head-flags)
    (length head-flags)))

(defop head-flag-from-head-pointer (head-pointers head-pointer-flags
                                                   total-length)
  (select-permute
    (distribute t (length head-pointers))
    head-pointers
    head-pointer-flags
```

```
      (distribute nil total-length)))

(defop head-flag-from-length (lengths)
  (head-flag-from-head-pointer
    (head-pointer-from-length lengths)
    (over-elements ((l lengths)) (> l 0))
    (plus-reduce lengths)))
```

B.2.3   Segmented Primitives

```
(defop s-max-scan (values segment-head-flags)
  (over-elements ((r (max-scan
                        (over-elements
                          ((block (i-enumerate segment-head-flags))
                           (value values))
                          (append-bits block value))))
                  (f segment-head-flags))
    (select-value f 0 (extract-bits r))))

(defop s-copy (values segment-head-flags)
  (over-elements ((r (max-scan
                        (over-elements ((i (index (length values)))
                                        (f segment-head-flags)
                                        (value values))
                          (append-bits (select-value f (+ i 1) 0) value))))
                  (f segment-head-flags)
                  (v values))
    (select-value f v (extract-bits r))))

(defop s-plus-scan (values segment-head-flags)
  (let ((total-sums (plus-scan values)))
    (over-elements ((total-sum total-sums)
                    (head-sum (s-copy total-sums segment-head-flags)))
      (- total-sum head-sum))))

(defop s-permute (values pointers segment-head-flags)
  (let* ((offset (s-copy (index (length values)) segment-head-flags))
         (real-pointers (over-elements ((p pointers)
                                        (o offset))
                          (+ p o))))
    (permute values real-pointers)))

(defop s-extract (values indices segment-head-pointers)
  (let ((real-indices (over-elements ((i indices)
                                      (p segment-head-pointers))
                        (+ i p))))
    (i-permute values real-indices)))
```

```
(defop s-insert (pvector values indices segment-head-pointers)
  (let ((real-indices (over-elements ((i indices)
                                       (p segment-head-pointers))
                        (+ i p))))
    (default-permute values real-indices pvector)))

(defop s-distribute (values lengths)
  (let* ((head-pointers (head-pointer-from-length lengths))
         (head-pointer-flags (over-elements ((l lengths)) (/= 0 l)))
         (total-length (plus-reduce lengths))
         (head-flags (head-flag-from-head-pointer head-pointers
                                                   head-pointer-flags
                                                   total-length))
         (default (distribute 0 total-length)))
    (s-copy (default-permute values head-pointers default) head-flags)))
```

B.2.4 Segmented Conditionals

```
(defop pack-segments (values flags lengths)
  (pack values (s-distribute flags lengths)))

(defop flag-merge-segments (flags v1 v2 lengths)
  (flag-merge (s-distribute flags lengths) v1 v2))
```

B.3 Other Routines

```
;; This routine fixes a near-merge as part of the halving-merge
;; routine.
(defop fix-near-merge (near-merge)
  (over-elements ((max-previous (max-scan near-merge))
                  (min-next (back-min-scan near-merge))
                  (self near-merge))
    (min min-next (max max-previous self))))

;; This routine implements the insert instructions based on
;; the other instructions
(defop insert (destination index value)
  (over-elements ((i (index (length destination)))
                  (d destination)
                  (v (distribute value))
                  (p (distribute index)))
    (select-value (= i p) v d)))
```

Appendix C

Paralation-Lisp Code

This appendix contains examples of PARALATION LISP code for many algorithms. Section C.1 defines a set of generally useful functions used by many of the other algorithms. Section C.2 defines the line drawing routine described in Section 3.6.1. Section C.3 defines a quad tree routine based on the algorithm described in Section 6.2. Section C.4 defines the quickhull convex-hull technique as described in Section 6.4. Section C.5 defines a quicksort routine as described in several places in this thesis. Section C.6 defines routines that determine the entropy and the conditional entropy of a sequence, as defined by Shannon [103]. Section C.7 defines a set of routines that implement Quinlan's ID3 learning algorithm [91]. This routine along with a *LISP version written by Donna Fritzsche has been used in practice over many sets of data [21].

C.1   Utilities

```
;; Gives each element of a field its rank in the sorted order
;; determined by the predicate pred.
(defun rank (field pred)
  (<- (index field)
      :by (match (index field)
                 (elwise ((elt (sort (elwise ((f field)
                                              (i (index field)))
                                         (cons f i))
                                pred :key #'first)))
                   (cdr elt)))))

;; Same as collapse but guarantees that the field will be collapsed
;; in such a way that the collapsed values of the field are in
;; sorted order.
```

```lisp
(defun scollapse (field pred &key (key #'identity) (test #'eql))
  (match (sort (<- field
                   :with #'arb
                   :by (collapse field :test test))
               pred
               :key key)
         field))

;; Same as (elt (sort (elwise (field) field) pred :key key) 0))
;; It returns the first element of the sorted field.
(defun limit (field pred &key (key #'identity))
  (flet ((op (a b) (if (funcall pred (funcall key a) (funcall key b))
                       a b)))
    (vref field :with #'op)))

;; Returns the index of the minimum element with respect to the
;; predicate pred.
(defun rank-limit (field pred)
  (cdr (limit (elwise ((f field)
                       (i (index field)))
                (cons f i))
              pred :key #'car)))

;; Returns the number of different values in a field.
(defun value-count (field &key (test #'eql))
  (vref (<- (elwise (field) 1)
            :with #'arb
            :by (collapse field :test test))
        :with #'+ :else 0))

;; Functions for testing the routines in this file.
(defvar *test-list* '())

(defmacro deftest (name &body keyword-pairs
                        &key string input output function)
  (declare (ignore keyword-pairs))
  `(defun ,(first (pushnew name *test-list*)) ()
     (let* ((input ,input)
            (output ,output)
            (string ,string)
            (function ,function)
            (result (funcall function input)))
       (when (not (equalp output result))
         (format t "~%~s test failed,~% Got:    ā ~% Expected: ā"
                 string result output)))))

(defun test-all ()
  (dolist (test *test-list*) (funcall test)))
```

C.2 Line Drawing

```
;; A simple line drawing routine

(defun point-location (endpoints fraction)
  (let ((e1 (first endpoints))
        (e2 (second endpoints)))
    (list (+ (first e1)
             (round (* fraction
                       (- (first e2)
                          (first e1)))))
          (+ (second e1)
             (round (* fraction
                       (- (second e2)
                          (second e1)))))))))

(defun line-length (endpoints)
  (let ((e1 (first endpoints))
        (e2 (second endpoints)))
    (1+ (max (abs (- (first e1) (first e2)))
             (abs (- (second e1) (second e2)))))))

;; Determines all the points on a line given the endpoints.
(defun line-draw (endpoints)
  (let ((line-length (line-length endpoints)))
    (elwise ((point (make-paralation line-length)))
      (point-location endpoints (/ point (float (1- line-length)))))))

;; Draws multiple lines given a field of endpoint pairs.
;; It also removes all duplicate points.
(defun multi-line-draw (endpoint-list)
  (let ((points (expand (elwise ((endpoint-pair endpoint-list))
                          (line-draw endpoint-pair)))))
    (<- points
        :with #'arb
        :by (collapse points :test #'equal))))

(deftest line-test
  :string "Line Drawing Routine"
  :input #1f(((0 0) (5 5)) ((4 3) (2 7)) ((4 4) (6 4)))
  :output #1F((0 0) (1 1) (2 2) (3 3) (4 4) (5 5)
              (4 3) (3 5) (2 6) (2 7) (5 4) (6 4))
  :function #'multi-line-draw)
```

C.3 Quad-Tree

```
;; a quad tree algorithm
```

```lisp
(defun quad-split (points)
  (if (> (length points) 1)
      (let* ((half-length (/ (length points) 2))
             (match (match (index points)
                           (elwise (points) (second points)))))
             (back-pointers (<- (index points) :by match)))
        (elwise ((pts (collect
                        (elwise ((point (<- (elwise (points)
                                                    (first points))
                                            :by match))
                                 (back-pointer back-pointers))
                          (list point (mod back-pointer half-length)))
                        :by
                        (scollapse (elwise ((back-pointer back-pointers))
                                     (truncate back-pointer half-length))
                          #'<))))
          (quad-split pts)))
      (first (vref points))))

(defun sort-init (points)
  (let* ((y-rank (rank (elwise (points) (second points)) #'<))
         (x-rank (rank (elwise (points) (first points)) #'<)))
    (<- (elwise ((i (index points)) (yp y-rank)) (list i yp))
        :by (match (index points) x-rank))))

(defun quad-tree (points)
  (quad-split (sort-init points)))

(deftest quad-tree-test
  :string "Quad Tree Algorithm"
  :input #1f((.32 .91) (.75 .53) (.63 .38) (.21 .49)
             (.56 .77) (.48 .09) (.24 .87) (.96 .02))
  :output #1F(#1F(#1F(3 5) #1F(6 0)) #1F(#1F(2 7) #1F(4 1)))
  :function #'quad-tree)
```

C.4 Convex Hull: Quickhull

```lisp
;; a convex hull algorithm (QuickHull)

(defun cross-product (o p1 p2)
  (- (* (- (first p1) (first o)) (- (second p2) (second o)))
     (* (- (second p1) (second o)) (- (first p2) (first o)))))

(defun line-side (e1 e2 point)
  (plusp (cross-product e1 e2 point)))

(defun triangle-area (p1 p2 p3)
```

```
    (abs (/ (cross-product p1 p2 p3) 2)))

(defun split-direction (p1 p2 ps point)
  (let ((l (line-side p1 ps point))
        (r (line-side ps p2 point))
        (e (equal ps point)))
    (cond (e 1) (l 0) (r 2) (t nil))))

(defun hull-split (points p1 p2 ps)
  (let* ((sfield (make-paralation 3))
         (match (match sfield (elwise (points)
                                (split-direction p1 p2 ps points)))))
    (expand
      (elwise ((new-points (collect points :by match))
               (new-p1 (elwise (sfield) (elt (list p1 ps ps) sfield)))
               (new-p2 (elwise (sfield) (elt (list ps ps p2) sfield))))
        (if (> (length new-points) 1)
            (hull-split new-points new-p1 new-p2
                        (limit new-points #'>
                               :key #'(lambda (new-points)
                                        (triangle-area new-points
                                                       new-p1
                                                       new-p2))))
            new-points)))))

:(defun convex-hull (points)
  (let ((min-x (limit points #'< :key #'first))
        (max-x (limit points #'> :key #'first)))
    (hull-split points min-x min-x max-x)))

(deftest convex-hull-test
  :string "Convex Hull Algorithm (Quickhull)"
  :input #1f((4 2) (6 5) (1 12) (3 8) (12 1) (6 15) (14 5)
             (11 17) (13 13) (17 14) (19 9))
  :output #1F((6 15) (11 17) (17 14) (19 9) (12 1) (4 2))
  :function #'convex-hull)
```

C.5 Quicksort

```
;; A quicksort routine

(defun qsort (data pred)
  (if (> (value-count data) 1)
      (let* ((pivot (elt data (random (length data))))
             (side (elwise (data) (if (funcall pred data pivot) 0 1)))
             (sets (collect data
```

```
                                        :by (match (make-paralation 2) side)))))
           (expand (elwise ((set sets))
                      (qsort set pred)))))
       data))

(deftest qsort-test
  :string "Quicksort Algorithm"
  :input #1F(97 68 16 70 55 3 11 47 75 53 1 21 16 15 78 13 72 38 88 24)
  :output #1F(1 3 11 13 15 16 16 21 24 38 47 53 55 68 70 72 75 78 88 97)
  :function #'(lambda (data) (qsort data #'<)))
```

C.6 Entropy

```
;; This function determines the entropy of the values of the INPUT field.
;; Mathematically this is H(I) = - \sum_i p(i) \lg p(i).
;; The sum is over all possible values and p(i) is the fraction of times
;; that the value i appears (the probability of i).

(defun entropy (input-string)
  (vref (elwise ((prob (<- (elwise ((is input-string))
                             (/ 1.0 (length input-string)))
                       :by (collapse input-string) :with #'+)))
          (* prob (- (log prob 2)))))
        :with #'+))

(deftest entropy-test
  :string "Shannon Entropy Routine"
  :input #1f(0 1 0 1 0 1 0 1 a b c d a b c d)
  :output 2.5
  :function #'entropy)

;; This function takes two fields from the same paralation:
;; an input and an output.
;; It determines the conditional entropy of the output based on the input.
;; Mathematically this is H_I(O) = - \sum_i \sum_o p(i, o) \lg p_i(o).
;;     p(i,o) is the fraction of positions in which the input i and the
;;            output o appear together.
;;     p_i(o) is the fraction of the positions where i is the input in which
;;            o is the output (conditional probability of o based on i).
;; This function calculates it in the form:
;; H_I(O) = - \sum_i p(i) \sum_o p_i(o) \lg p_i(o)
;;        = \sum_i p(i) H_i(O)   = (\sum_i l(i) H_i(O)) / l(I)

(defun conditional-entropy (input output)
  (let* ((input-sets (collect output :by (collapse input))))
    (/ (vref (elwise ((input-set input-sets))
```

```
              (* (length input-set) (entropy input-set)))
          :with #'+)
      (vref (elwise ((input-set input-sets)) (length input-set))
          :with #'+)))))

(deftest cond-entropy-test
  :string "Shannon Conditional Entropy Routine"
  :input #1f((0 a) (0 b) (0 a) (0 b) (1 c) (1 c) (1 c) (1 c))
  :output .5
  :function #'(lambda (in) (conditional-entropy
                              (elwise (in) (first in))
                              (elwise (in) (second in)))))
```

C.7 ID3: Quinlan's Learning Algorithm

```
;; This function removes the nth element of a sequence.

(defun remove-elt (sequence index)
  (remove-if #'(lambda (arg) t) sequence :start index :end (+ index 1)))

;; This function takes a field of sequences (INPUT), a field of values
;; (OUTPUT),
;; and the number of elements in the sequences (INPUT-LENGTH).
;; For each position J up to INPUT-LENGTH of the INPUT sequences, it
;; determines
;; the conditional entropy of OUTPUT based on that position of the INPUT.
;; It returns a field of length INPUT-LENGTH; each element is a
;; conditional entropy value.

(defun parameter-entropies (input output imask input-length)
  (elwise ((parameter-position (make-paralation input-length)))
    (if (elt imask parameter-position)
        (conditional-entropy (elwise (input)
                                (elt input parameter-position)) output)
        (entropy output))))

;; This structure is used for each node of the decision tree.
;;    Par-Value -- contains the input value of the node of the tree.
;;    Next-Par-Position -- contains which one of the input positions
;;        should be used for branching.
;;    Position-Entropies -- Contains the conditional entropies for
;;        each position.
;;        The minimum of these entropies is used to select
;;        Next-Par-Position.
;;    Output -- Is the default value for the node (the most common
;;        output value).
;;        If there is no child that corresponds to the given input value,
```

```
;;            then this value should be selected.
;;       Child field -- This is a field which contains all the children.
;;             There can be as many children as possible input values.

(defstruct (qt-node (:print-function ptree))
  par-value
  next-par-position
  position-entropies
  output
  child-field
  count)


;; These variables and the function assign a cost to creating each
;; node of the decision tree.
;; They are used so that a node will only branch out if more
;; information can be reduced than the cost of creating all the
;; children nodes.
;; Its effect is to prune the tree.
;; This cost is in number of bits.

(defvar *node-cost* 0)
(defvar *child-cost* 1.3)

(defun node-cost (children)
  (+ *node-cost* (* children *child-cost*)))


;; This is the routine that builds the decision tree.
;; It takes an INPUT and OUTPUT field that must both be from the same
;; paralation.
;; The INPUT must be a field of sequences; all sequences should be the
;; same length and INPUT-LENGTH is used to specify this length.
;; The INPUT sequences are used as the input parameter vectors--each element
;; contains the value of the parameter denoted by that position.
;; The parameter names are implicit in the positions.
;; The OUTPUT is a sequence of values - the values of the output parameter.
;; The FP-SEQUENCE argument can be used to specify a fixed sequence of
;; parameters to branch on -- one position per level of the tree.
;; This argument should be a list of length no greater than INPUT-LENGTH.
;; If less than the INPUT-LENGTH, then the function will stop building
;; the tree when it runs out of positions.
;; If an FP-SEQUENCE is specified, the entropy calculations are not
;; carried out.
;; The PAR-VALUE argument can be ignored (it is used for recursion).
;; This function returns a QT-NODE which is the root of a decsion tree.

(defun build-q-tree (input output imask input-length
                         &key (par-value :root) (fp-sequence nil))
  (let ((tree-node (make-qt-node)))
```

```
    (setf (qt-node-par-value tree-node) par-value)
    (setf (qt-node-output tree-node) (select-max output))
    (setf (qt-node-count tree-node) (length input))
    (when (and (plusp input-length) (< 1 (value-count output)))
       (let* ((par-entropies (when (not (car fp-sequence))
                                (parameter-entropies input output
                                              imask input-length)))
               (best-parameter-position (or (car fp-sequence)
                                         (rank-limit par-entropies #'<=)))
               (best-parameter (elwise (input)
                                  (elt input best-parameter-position)))
               (collapse (collapse best-parameter))
               (new-io-pairs (collect (elwise (input output)
                                         (list input output)) :by collapse))
               (input-chars (<- best-parameter :with #'arb :by collapse))
               (new-imask (copy-seq imask)))
          (setf (elt new-imask best-parameter-position) nil)
          (when (or fp-sequence
                    (> (* (length input)
                          (- (entropy output)
                             (vref par-entropies :with #'min)))
                       (node-cost (length input-chars))))
            (setf (qt-node-next-par-position tree-node)
                  best-parameter-position)
            (setf (qt-node-position-entropies tree-node) par-entropies)
            (setf (qt-node-child-field tree-node)
                  (elwise ((new-io-pair new-io-pairs)
                           (input-char input-chars))
                     (let ((new-input (elwise (new-io-pair)
                                         (first new-io-pair)))
                           (new-output (elwise (new-io-pair)
                                         (second new-io-pair))))
                       (build-q-tree new-input new-output
                             new-imask input-length
                             :par-value input-char
                             :fp-sequence (cdr fp-sequence)))))))))
   tree-node))

;; This routine takes a field of input parameter vectors and a tree
;; returned by BUILD-Q-TREE and returns a field of output values - the
;; best guess for each postion.
;; The INPUT must be a field of sequences (each sequence is a
;; parameter vector).
;; The input parameter positions must be in the same order as when
;; BUILD-Q-TREE was run.
;; The field of output values returned will be in the same paralation
;; as the INPUT field.
```

```
(defun find-outputs (input q-tree)
  (let ((par-position (qt-node-next-par-position q-tree))
        (child-field (qt-node-child-field q-tree))
        (default-output (qt-node-output q-tree)))
    (if (and child-field (plusp (length input)))
        (let* ((collapse (match (elwise (child-field)
                                    (qt-node-par-value child-field))
                                  (elwise (input)
                                    (elt input par-position))))
               (new-inputs (collect input :by collapse)))
          (field-merge
            (elwise (new-inputs child-field)
              (find-outputs new-inputs child-field))
            :by collapse :default (elwise (input) default-output)))
        (elwise (input) default-output))))
```

```
;; This function can be used as an interface to BUILD-Q-TREE.
;; It takes as input, a field of input-output pairs -- each pair is a cons.
;; The CAR of each cons must be a sequence of I-LENGTH and is used
;; as the input parameter vector.
;; The CDR is used as the output value.
;; FP-SEQUENCE can be used as described earlier.
```

```
(defun build-tree (io-field i-length &optional fp-sequence)
  (let ((input (elwise (io-field) (car io-field)))
        (output (elwise (io-field) (cdr io-field)))
        (imask (make-array i-length :initial-element t)))
    (build-q-tree input output imask i-length :fp-sequence fp-sequence)))
```

```
;; This function can be used to determine how well the decision tree
;; determines the correct output -- to test a decsion tree.
;; It takes as input, a field of input-output pairs in the same
;; format as BUILD-TREE.
;; It finds the predicted outputs using FIND-OUTPUTS and then compares
;; them with the given output.
;; The function returns the fraction that are correct.
```

```
(defun check-completion (io-field q-tree)
  (let ((input (elwise (io-field) (car io-field)))
        (output (elwise (io-field) (cdr io-field))))
    (/ (vref (elwise ((expected-output output)
                      (actual-output (find-outputs input q-tree)))
               (if (eql expected-output actual-output) 1 0))
             :with '+)
       (float (length input)))))
```

```
;; This function runs BUILD-TREE on (1 - TEST-FRACTION) of the io-field
;; and then runs check-completion on the remaning TEST-FRACTION part.
```

```
;; It rueturns the fraction that were correct, and the decision tree.

(defun check-generalization (io-field input-length test-fraction
                             &optional fixed-parameter-sequence)
  (let* ((generate-length (truncate (* (- 1 test-fraction)
                                       (length io-field))))
         (generate-set (subseq io-field 0 generate-length))
         (test-set (subseq io-field generate-length))
         (q-tree (build-tree generate-set input-length
                             fixed-parameter-sequence)))
    (list (check-completion test-set q-tree) q-tree)))
```

Bibliography

[1] P. Abrams. An APL machine. Technical Report SLAC 114, Stanford University, 1970.

[2] Alok Aggarwal, Ashok K. Chandra, and Marc Snir. Hierarchical memory with block transfer. In *Proceedings Symposium on Foundations of Computer Science*, pages 204–216, 1987.

[3] Alok Aggarwal, Bernard Chazelle, Leo Guibas, Colm Ò'Dùnlaing, and Chee Yap. Parallel computational geometry. In *Proceedings Symposium on Foundations of Computer Science*, pages 468–477, October 1985.

[4] Ajit Agrawal, Guy Blelloch, Robert Krawitz, and Cynthia Phillips. Four vector-matrix primitives. In *Proc. Symposium on Parallel Algorithms and Architectures*, pages 292–302, June 1989.

[5] M. Ajtai, J. Komlos, and E. Szemeredi. An $O(n \lg n)$ sorting network. In *Proceedings ACM Symposium on Theory of Computing*, pages 1–9, April 1983.

[6] D. C. Allen. The BBN multiprocessors: Butterfly and Monarch. In *Proceedings Princeton Conference on Supercomputers and Stellar Dynamics*, June 1986.

[7] Mikhail J. Atallah, Richard Cole, and Michael T. Goodrich. Cascading divide-and-conquer: A technique for designing parallel algorithms. In *Proceedings Symposium on Foundations of Computer Science*, pages 151–160, October 1987.

[8] Mikhail J. Atallah and Michael T. Goodrich. Efficient parallel solutions to some geometric problems. *Journal of Parallel and Distributed Computing*, 3(4):492–507, December 1986.

[9] Mikhail J. Atallah and Michael T. Goodrich. Efficient plane sweeping in parallel. In *Proceedings ACM Symposium on Theory of Computing*, pages 216–225, 1986.

[10] Baruch Awerbuch and Yossi Shiloach. New connectivity and MSF algorithms for Ultracomputer and PRAM. In *Proceedings ACM Symposium on Theory of Computing*, pages 175–179, 1985.

[11] Kenneth E. Batcher. Sorting networks and their applications. In *AFIPS Spring Joint Computer Conference*, pages 307–314, 1968.

[12] Kenneth E. Batcher. The flip network of STARAN. In *Proceedings International Conference on Parallel Processing*, pages 65–71, 1976.

[13] Jon L. Bentley. Multidimensional binary search trees used for associative searching. *Communications of the ACM*, 18:509–517, 1975.

[14] Jon L. Bentley and Michael I. Shamos. Divide-and-conquer in multidimensional space. In *Proceedings ACM Symposium on Theory of Computing*, pages 220–230, 1976.

[15] C. Berge and A. Ghouila-Houri. *Programming, Games, and Transportation Networks*. John Wiley, New York, 1965.

[16] H. J. Berliner. A chronology of computer chess and its literature. *Artificial Intelligence*, 10(2), 1978.

[17] Guy E. Blelloch. AFL-1: A programming language for massively concurrent computers. Technical Report 918, Artificial Intelligence Laboratory, Massachusetts Institute of Technology, November 1986.

[18] Guy E. Blelloch. CIS: A massively concurrent rule based system. In *Proceedings National Conference on Artificial Intelligence*, pages 735–741, August 1986.

[19] Guy E. Blelloch. Parallel prefix vs. concurrent memory access. Technical report, Thinking Machines Corporation, October 1986.

[20] Guy E. Blelloch. Scans as primitive parallel operations. In *Proceedings International Conference on Parallel Processing*, pages 355–362, August 1987.

[21] Guy E. Blelloch and Donna Fritzsche. A comparison of the parallel implementations of two learning algorithms. In *Proceedings of the AAAI Spring Symposium Series: Parallel Models of Intelligence*, pages 59–62, March 1988.

[22] Guy E. Blelloch and James J. Little. Parallel solutions to geometric problems on the scan model of computation. In *Proceedings International Conference on Parallel Processing*, pages Vol 3: 218–222, August 1988.

[23] Guy E. Blelloch and Charles R. Rosenberg. Network learning on the Connection Machine. In *Proceedings International Joint Conference on Artificial Intelligence*, pages 323–326, August 1987.

[24] Guy E. Blelloch and Gary W. Sabot. Compiling collection-oriented languages onto massively parallel computers. *Journal of Parallel and Distributed Computing*, 8(2), February 1990.

[25] S. Borkar, R. Cohn, G. Cox, S. Gleason, T. Gross, H. T. Kung, M. Lam, B. Moore, C. Peterson, J. Pieper, L. Rankin, P. S. Tseng, J. sutton, J. Urbanski, and J. Webb. iWarp: An integrated solution to high-speed parallel computing. In *Proceedings of Supercomputing '88, IEEE Computer Society and ACM SIGARCH*, November 1988.

[26] A Borodin. On relating time and space to size and depth. *SIAM Journal of Computing*, 6:733–744, 1977.

[27] O. Borŭvka. O jistém problén minimálím. *Práca Moravské Přírodovědecké Společnosti*, (3):37–58, 1926. (In Czech.).

[28] R. P. Brent. The parallel evaluation of general arithmetic expressions. *Journal of the Association for Computing Machinery*, 21(2):201–206, 1974.

[29] R. P. Brent and H. T. Kung. The chip complexity of binary arithmetic. In *Proceedings ACM Symposium on Theory of Computing*, pages 190–200, 1980.

[30] Timothy A. Budd. An APL compiler for a vector processor. *ACM Transactions on Programming Languages and Systems*, 6(3):297–313, July 1984.

[31] David Christman. Programming the Connection Machine. Master's thesis, Massachussets Institute of Technology, January 1984.

[32] C. Clos. A study of nonblocking switching networks. *Bell System Technical Journal*, 32:406–424, 1953.

[33] E. F. Codd. A relational model of data for large shared data banks. *Communications of the ACM*, 13(6), June 1970.

[34] Richard Cole. Parallel merge sort. In *Proceedings Symposium on Foundations of Computer Science*, pages 511–516, October 1986.

[35] Richard Cole and Uzi Vishkin. Approximate scheduling, exact scheduling, and applications to parallel algorithms. In *Proceedings Symposium on Foundations of Computer Science*, pages 478–491, 1986.

[36] Richard Cole and Uzi Vishkin. Faster optimal parallel prefix sums and list ranking. Technical Report Ultracomputer Note 117, New York University, February 1987.

[37] Stephen A. Cook. A taxonomy of problems with fast parallel algorithms. *Information and Control*, 64:2–22, 1985.

[38] Stephen A. Cook and H. James Hoover. A depth-universal circuit. *SIAM Journal of Computing*, 14(4):833–839, November 1985.

[39] C. J. Date. *Relational Database: Selected Writings*. Addison-Wesley, Reading, MA, 1986.

[40] C. C. Elgot and A. Robinson. Random access stored program machines. *Journal of the Association for Computing Machinery*, 11(4):365–399, 1964.

[41] Faith E. Fich. New bounds for parallel prefix circuits. In *Proceedings ACM Symposium on Theory of Computing*, pages 100–109, April 1983.

[42] Steven Fortune and James Wyllie. Parallelism in random access machines. In *Proceedings ACM Symposium on Theory of Computing*, pages 114–118, 1978.

[43] Jerome H. Friedman, Jon Louis Bentley, and Raphael Ari Finkel. An algorithm for finding best matches in logarithmic expected time. *ACM Transactions on Mathematical Software*, 3(3):209–226, 1977.

[44] F. Gavril. Merging with parallel processors. *Communications of the ACM*, 18(10):588–591, 1975.

[45] Hillel Gazit, Gary L. Miller, and Shang-Hua Teng. Optimal tree contraction in the EREW model. In Stuart K Tewsburg, Bradley W. Dickinson, and Stuart C Schwartz, editors, *Concurrent Computations*, pages 139–156. Plenum Publishing Corporation, 1988.

[46] Andrew V. Goldberg. Efficient graph algorithms for sequential and parallel computers. Technical Report 374, Laboratory for Computer Science, Massachusetts Institute of Technology, February 1987.

[47] Andrew V. Goldberg and Robert E. Tarjan. A new approach to the maximum flow problem. In *Proceedings ACM Symposium on Theory of Computing*, pages 136–146, April 1986.

[48] L. M. Goldschlager. A universal interconnection pattern for parallel computers. *Journal of the Association for Computing Machinery*, 29(3):1073–1086, 1982.

[49] Allan Gottlieb, R. Grishman, Clyde P. Kruskal, Kevin P. McAuliffe, Larry Rudolph, and Marc Snir. The NYU Ultracomputer—designing a MIMD, shared-memory parallel machine. *IEEE Transactions on Computers*, C-32:175–189, 1983.

[50] Allan Gottlieb, B. D. Lubachevsky, and Larry Rudolph. Basic techniques for the efficient coordination of very large numbers of cooperating sequential processors. *ACM Transactions on Programming Languages and Systems*, 5(2), April 1983.

[51] Vince Grolmusz and Prabhakar Ragde. Incomparability in parallel computation. In *Proceedings Symposium on Foundations of Computer Science*, pages 89–98, 1987.

[52] Leo J. Guibas and Douglas K. Wyatt. Compilation and delayed evaluation in APL. In *Conference Record of the 5th Annual ACM Symposium on Principles of Programming Languages*, pages 1–8, Tucson, Ariz, 1978.

[53] W. Daniel Hillis. *The Connection Machine*. MIT Press, Cambridge, MA, 1985.

[54] W. Daniel Hillis and Guy L. Steele Jr. Data parallel algorithms. *Communications of the ACM*, 29(12), December 1986.

[55] D. S. Hirschberg, A. K. Chandra, and D. V. Sarwate. Computing connected components on parallel computers. *Communications of the ACM*, 22(8):461–464, 1979.

[56] C. A. R. Hoare. Quicksort. *Computer J.*, 5(1):10–15, 1962.

[57] Paul Hudak and Eric Mohr. Graphinators and the duality of SIMD and MIMD. In *ACM Conference on Lisp and Functional Programming*, pages 224–234, July 1988.

[58] IBM. *APL2 Programming: Language Reference*, first edition, August 1984. Order Number SH20-9227-0.

[59] Kenneth E. Iverson. *A Programming Language*. Wiley, New York, 1962.

[60] Kenneth E. Iverson. A dictionary of APL. *APL Quote Quad*, 18(1):5–40, September 1987.

[61] Kenneth E. Iverson and Falkoff. APL 360 reference manual. The APL terminal system: Instructions for operation. IBM, November 1966.

[62] A. V. Karzanov. Determining the maximal flow in a network by the method of preflows. *Soviet Math. Dokl.*, (15):434–437, 1974.

[63] D.E. Knuth. *Sorting and Searching*. Addison-Wesley, Reading, MA, 1973.

[64] Clyde P. Kruskal, Larry Rudolph, and Marc Snir. The power of parallel prefix. In *Proceedings International Conference on Parallel Processing*, pages 180–185, August 1985.

[65] Richard E. Ladner and Michael J. Fischer. Parallel prefix computation. *Journal of the Association for Computing Machinery*, 27(4):831–838, October 1980.

[66] Clifford Lasser. The essential *Lisp manual. Technical report, Thinking Machines Corporation, Cambridge, MA, July 1986.

[67] Frank Thomson Leighton. Tight bounds on the complexity of parallel sorting. In *Proceedings ACM Symposium on Theory of Computing*, pages 71–80, May 1984.

[68] Charles E. Leiserson. Area-efficient layouts (for VLSI). In *Proceedings Symposium on Foundations of Computer Science*, 1980.

[69] Charles E. Leiserson and Bruce M. Maggs. Fat-Trees: Universal networks for hardware-efficient supercomputing. *IEEE Transactions on Computers*, c-34(10):892–901, October 1985.

[70] Charles E. Leiserson and Bruce M. Maggs. Communication-efficient parallel algorithms for distributed random-access machines. *Algorithmica*, 3:53–77, 1988.

[71] James J. Little, Guy E. Blelloch, and Todd Cass. Parallel algorithms for computer vision on the Connection Machine. In *Proceedings International Conference on Computer Vision*, June 1987.

[72] Boris D. Lubachevsky and Albert G. Greenberg. Simple, efficient asynchronous parallel prefix algorithms. In *Proceedings International Conference on Parallel Processing*, pages 66–69, August 1987.

[73] Michael Luby. A simple parallel algorithm for the maximal independent set problem. In *Proceedings ACM Symposium on Theory of Computing*, pages 1–10, May 1985.

[74] G. A. Mago. A network of computers to execute reduction languages. *International Journal of Computer and Information Sciences*, 1979.

[75] Gary L. Miller and John H. Reif. Parallel tree contraction and its application. In *Proceedings Symposium on Foundations of Computer Science*, pages 478–489, October 1985.

[76] Russ Miller and Quentin F. Stout. Efficient parallel convex hull algorithms. *IEEE Transactions on Computers*, 37(12):1605–1618, December 1988.

[77] Trenchard More. The nested rectangular array as a model of data. In *APL 79 Conference Proceedings*, pages 55–73. ACM, 1979.

[78] Trenchard More. Rectangularly arranged collections of collections. In *APL 82 Conference Proceedings*, pages 219–228. ACM, 1982.

[79] William M. Newman and Robert F. Sproull. *Principles of Interactive Computer Graphics*. McGraw-Hill, New York, 1979.

[80] Yu Ofman. On the algorithmic complexity of discrete functions. *Cybernetics and Control Theory, Sov. Phys Dokl.*, 7(7):589–591, January 1963.

[81] Stephen M. Omohundro. Efficient algorithms with neural network behavior. *Complex Systems*, 1, 1987.

[82] Mark H. Overmars and Jan Van Leeuwen. Maintenance of configurations in the plane. *Journal of Computer and System Sciences*, 23:166–204, 1981.

[83] C. H. Papadimitriou and K. Steiglitz. *Combinatorial Optimization: Algorithms and Complexity*. Prentice-Hall, Inc., Englewood Cliffs, NJ, 1982.

[84] M. C. Pease. Matrix inversion using parallel processing. *Journal of the Association for Computing Machinery*, 14(4):757–764, October 1967.

[85] Alan J. Perlis. Steps toward an APL compiler—updated. Technical Report 24, Computer Science Department, Yale University, March 1975.

[86] G. F. Pfister and V. A. Norton. 'Hot Spot' contention and combining in multistage interconnection networks. In *Proceedings International Conference on Parallel Processing*, pages 790–797, August 1985.

[87] Vaughan R. Pratt and Larry J Stockmeyer. A characterization of the power of vector machines. *Journal of Computer and System Sciences*, 12:198–221, 1976.

[88] Franco P. Preparata and Michael I. Shamos. *Computational Geometry—An Introduction*. Springer-Verlag, New York, 1985.

[89] Franco P. Preparata and Jean Vuillemin. The cube-connected cycles: A versatile network for parallel computing. *Communications of the ACM*, 24(5):300–309, May 1981.

[90] W. H. Press, B. P. Flannery, S. A. Teukolsky, and W. T. Vetterling. *Numerical Recipes*. Cambridge University Press, Cambridge, 1986.

[91] Ross Quinlan. Induction of decision trees. *Machine Learning*, 1:81–106, 1986.

[92] Abhiram G. Ranade. How to emulate shared memory. In *Proceedings Symposium on Foundations of Computer Science*, pages 185–194, 1987.

[93] Abhiram G. Ranade. *Fluent Parallel Computation*. PhD thesis, Yale University, Department of Computer Science, New Haven, CT, 1989.

[94] John H. Reif and Sandeeep Sen. Optimal randomized parallel algorithms for computational geometry. In *Proceedings International Conference on Parallel Processing*, pages 270–277, August 1987.

[95] Richard M. Russell. The CRAY-1 computer system. *Communications of the ACM*, 21(1):63–72, January 1978.

[96] Gary W. Sabot. *The Paralation Model: Architecture-Independent Parallel Programming*. The MIT Press, Cambridge, Massachusetts, 1988.

[97] James B. Salem. *Render: A data parallel approach to polygon rendering. Technical Report VZ88–2, Thinking Machines Corporation, January 1988.

[98] Carla Savage and Joseph Ja'Ja'. Fast, efficient parallel algorithms for some graph problems. *SIAM Journal of Computing*, 10(4):682–691, 1981.

[99] Fl. Schmidt and M.A. Jenkins. Array diagrams and the NIAL approach. In *APL 82 Conference Proceedings*, pages 315–319. ACM, 1982.

[100] J. T. Schwartz, R.B.K. Dewar, E. Dubinsky, and E. Schonberg. *Programming with Sets: An Introduction to SETL*. Springer-Verlag, New York, 1986.

[101] Jacob T. Schwartz. Ultracomputers. *ACM Transactions on Programming Languages and Systems*, 2(4):484–521, October 1980.

[102] Charles L. Seitz. The Cosmic Cube. *Communications of the ACM*, 28(1):22–33, January 1985.

[103] C. E. Shannon. A mathematical theory of communication. *Bell System Technical Journal*, 27:379–423, 623–656, July, October 1948.

[104] Y. Shiloach and U. Vishkin. Finding the maximum, merging and sorting in a parallel computation model. *Journal of Algorithms*, 2(1):88–102, 1981.

[105] Yossi Shiloach and Uzi Vishkin. An $O(\log n)$ parallel connectivity algorithm. *Journal of Algorithms*, 3:57–67, 1982.

[106] Marc Snir and Jon A. Solworth. The Ultraswitch—a VLSI network node for parallel processing. Technical Report Ultracomputer Note #39, New York University, January 1984.

[107] Guy L. Steele Jr. CM-Lisp. Technical report, Thinking Machines Corporation, 1986.

[108] Guy L. Steele Jr., Scott E. Fahlman, Richard P. Gabriel, David A. Moon, and Daniel L. Weinreb. *Common LISP: The Language*. Digital Press, Burlington, MA, 1984.

[109] Harold S. Stone. Parallel processsing with the perfect shuffle. *IEEE Transactions on Computers*, C-20(2):153–161, 1971.

[110] Quentin F. Stout. Sorting, merging, selecting and filtering on tree and pyramid machines. In *Proceedings International Conference on Parallel Processing*, pages 214–221, 1983.

[111] Robert E. Tarjan. *Data Structures and Network Algorithms*. Society for Industrial and Applied Mathematics, Philadelphia, Pennsylvania, 1983.

[112] Robert E. Tarjan and Uzi Vishkin. An efficient parallel biconnectivity algorithm. *SIAM Journal of Computing*, 4(14):862–874, 1985.

[113] Thinking Machines Corporation. Connection Machine parallel instruction set (PARIS), July 1986.

[114] Thinking Machines Corporation. Model CM-2 technical summary. Technical Report HA87-4, Thinking Machines Corporation, Cambridge, Massachusetts, April 1987.

[115] C. D. Thompson and H. T. Kung. Sorting on a mesh-connected parallel computer. *Communications of the ACM*, 20:263–271, 1977.

[116] A. M. Turing. On computable numbers, with an application to the entscheidungsproblem. *Proc. London Mathematical Soc. Ser. 2*, 42:230–265, 1936.

[117] Leslie G. Valiant. Universal circuits (preliminary report). In *Proceedings ACM Symposium on Theory of Computing*, pages 196–202, 1976.

[118] Uzi Vishkin. Synchronous parallel computation: A survey. Technical Report Ultracomputer Note #53, New York University, April 1983.

[119] Skef Wholey and Guy L. Steele Jr. Connection Machine Lisp: A dialect of Common Lisp for data parallel programming. In *Proc. Second International Conference on Supercomputing*, May 1987.

[120] James C. Wyllie. The complexity of parallel computations. Technical Report TR-79-387, Department of Computer Science, Cornell University, Ithaca, NY, August 1979.

Index

Artificial Intelligence

Patrick Henry Winston and J. Michael Brady, founding editors

J. Michael Brady, Daniel G. Bobrow, and Randall Davis, current editors

The MIT Press, with Peter Denning as general consulting editor, publishes computer science books in the following series:

ACM Doctoral Dissertation Award and Distinguished Dissertation Series

Artificial Intelligence
Patrick Winston, founding editor
J. Michael Brady, Daniel G. Bobrow, and Randall Davis, editors

Charles Babbage Institute Reprint Series for the History of Computing
Martin Campbell-Kelly, editor

Computer Systems
Herb Schwetman, editor

Explorations with Logo
E. Paul Goldenberg, editor

Foundations of Computing
Michael Garey and Albert Meyer, editors

History of Computing
I. Bernard Cohen and William Aspray, editors

Information Systems
Michael Lesk, editor

Logic Programming
Ehud Shapiro, editor; Koichi Furukawa, Jean-Louis Lassez, Fernando Pereira, and David H. D. Warren, associate editors

The MIT Press Electrical Engineering and Computer Science Series

Research Monographs in Parallel and Distributed Processing
Christopher Jesshope and David Klappholz, editors

Scientific and Engineering Computation
Janusz Kowalik, editor

Technical Communication
Ed Barrett, editor